TALES
that
TEACH

Don McCurry

Published by Ministries to Muslims

Unless otherwise noted, Scripture quotations are taken from the HOLY BIBLE: NEW INTERNATIONAL VERSION. Copyright © 1973, 1978, 1984 by International Bible Society. Used by permission of Zondervan Publishing House.

Cover and text design by Bill Thielker

Printed in the United States of America by Spire Resources, Inc.

ISBN Number: 978-0-9792877-0-1

INDEX

ACKNOWLEDGMENTS

First of all, it was the Lord who called me into His ministries, who enabled me to have all of the experiences that are reflected in these stories. In a sense He is the real author. Sometimes He led by dreams or special words. At other times He taught me through the people He sent me to serve. Whether He was disciplining me, encouraging me, pruning me, or enlightening me, He was always there, the Master Teacher and Friend. But He was much more than that as you will see when you begin to read these *Tales*.

This project would never have happened without the Administrative Board of Ministries to Muslims mandating it. Almost casually, they noted, "Don, you teach by telling stories. Why don't you write them down?" Nothing happened. Finally, they said, "Don, we want you to write one story a month for the next five years and include them in your month-end prayer letters." And that is how it began. It actually grew beyond the sixty stories mandated to the 101 that you will read in this volume.

Many thanks to each of you on the board: Dr. Gregory Roth, Dr. Tom Paterson, Capt. Bryce Herndon (American Airlines, Retired), Mr. Bryan Herde, and Mr. Gary Evans who, midway through these tales, retired from the board. And a very special thanks to Gary. For it was you who taught me so much about writing skills, transitions, weeding out irrelevances, focusing and keeping to one theme. Those skills helped me in the writing of the remaining stories.

Special thanks to my sharp-eyed, ever-patient Administrative Assistant, Mrs. Kate Bryant. Kate, you took up where Gary left off, plus all of the endless re-writings, reshuffling of the order and the final formatting of the text.

My gratitude to Dr. Gayle Herde, who went through the entire compilation and edited the stories to correct mistakes, smoothed out the flow of words and looked at them through the lens of sensitivity for our Muslim readers. Thanks also to Bryan Herde, who assisted with proofing and content issues; Mr. Bill Thielker for his creative design, page layout and production work for print readiness; and Mr. Andy Stimer for his efforts in distribution of this book. I am tremendously grateful for Callie and Tom Paterson's generous spirit. Their support made the printing of this book possible.

And finally, many, many thanks to my fellow-workers around the world who, in a sense, became my mentors as I learned powerful lessons from them along the way. Your names will surface in the tales with only one or two names that were disguised for the sake of protection.

INTRODUCTION

Tales That Teach was born out of a lifetime in the fields of the world. They began as a tribute to overseas nationals from whom I learned so much. It is true that in and behind every one of these brothers and sisters in the faith, and even those not in the faith, God was working. But humanly speaking, I felt compelled to tell the stories of the precious men and women who contributed so much to my life.

The *Tales*, written long after they happened, initially came in no fixed order. Later as the time came to compile them, it was thought best to arrange them chronologically. And as we did so, we realized that it would be helpful if there were a certain amount of biographical detail and dates to give an adequate background for them. Following are some of those details.

Essentially, the *Tales* begin with my conversion in the middle of my second year at the University of Maryland Medical School in Baltimore. This was in January, 1951.

After completing my second year and passing the Maryland State Board exams on that unit of work, I felt called to leave medical school and prepare for the ministry. Amazingly, my dean, after hearing my testimony, released me with his blessing and said that if I ever wanted to return and finish the remaining two years, the door was always open. As the Lord would have it, that never happened.

After three years of study at Pittsburgh-Xenia Theological Seminary, later named The Pittsburgh Theological Seminary, I accepted a call to pastor the First United Presbyterian Church of Colorado Springs, Colorado (now called "The Church on Boulder"). It was during that time that my wife Mary Jo and I experienced our call to missions.

After a year of preparation in the States, we arrived with the first four of our six children in Pakistan in November of 1957. We served with the United Presbyterian Church there for eighteen years, returning to the States in 1975.

It was at the recommendation of our mission's Personnel Development Interviewer that I enrolled in the School of World Missions at Fuller Theological Seminary, earning a Doctorate in Missiology. Upon the completion of the required residential courses, I was invited to stay on to teach on the subject of ministering to Muslims. From 1977 until 1985, that is what I did.

Simultaneously, having been appointed to design and direct the North American Lausanne Consultation on Muslim Evangelization, I was asked to found what became known as the Samuel Zwemer Institute of Muslim Studies, named after America's most famous missionary to the Muslim world. After directing this organization for seven years, I then founded Ministries to Muslims, which has enabled me to serve all over the world as a guest teacher, lecturer, mentor, and coach to workers in many countries.

In this book, the very earliest part has to do with our conversion and call, followed by eighteen years of work in Pakistan. More than half the *Tales* are from experiences in Pakistan.

Later, with the freedom that came with the founding of Ministries to Muslims, the Lord gave more experiences that were worthy of the telling in such countries as Norway, Turkey, India, Lebanon, Central Asia in general, then in Tajikistan, Kazakhstan, Uzbekistan, Kyrgyzstan, among Uighur refugees from China, Russia, Georgia, Armenia, Kashmir, Syria, Malaysia, Guinea, Burkina Faso, England, Egypt, Saudi Arabia, Cyprus, Brazil, Costa Rica, Guatemala and Spain. The final story is a USA-Pakistani one.

In the richness of the ministries the Lord has given, we have worked in several other countries besides the ones listed above, but, alas, it was all ministry with no memorable *Tales That Teach* from them.

As you read these *Tales*, may the Lord bless you, give you insights and encourage you in the greatest enterprise going this side of heaven—the missionary enterprise.

There is much left yet to do. May you find your place in this great work. In Matthew 24:14, we read that "This gospel [good news] of the Kingdom will be preached in the whole world as a witness to all nations [all ethnolinguistic groups of people] and then the end [of human suffering] will come."

Please join with us in completing our task and setting the stage for the return of the King, our Lord and Savior Jesus Christ.

HOW IT ALL BEGAN

Just before going into the U.S. Navy at the age of 17, those putting together our high school yearbook asked each hopeful graduate to make a statement about what he or she wanted to do or be after graduation. This would be after I got out of the Navy, of course.

This was a tough decision for someone who did not know himself very well, much less understand how the world works. Two alternatives occurred to me, both driven by pain:

1. Be a forest ranger. Get away from it all in God's wonderful outdoors.

2. Be a psychiatrist. Face your pain and maybe learn how to help others.

As the Lord would have it, after the Navy and after three years in an accelerated pre-medical program, I was accepted at the University of Maryland Medical School in Baltimore. Psychiatry was taught there from Day One.

All went well until the middle of my second year. One day a classmate asked our esteemed professor, Dr. Jacob Feinsinger, to define normalcy. Glibly, he stated, "Normalcy is the accepted behavior pattern in a given cultural milieu." My classmate persisted, "Suppose you mix some African Hottentots with some Boston socialites (our professor was a Bostonian), then what would normalcy be?" The professor said he supposed whatever turned out to be the normal behavior pattern. After two or three of these absurd matchups that always brought the same answer, another classmate observed, "Dr. Feinsinger, you don't really know, do you?"

And then the bombshell of a question: "Dr. Feinsinger, why are you here? What are you living for? What is the purpose of life?" I recognized that someone had articulated my question. We waited with bated breath for the answer. After an embarrassing silence, he finally said, "I don't know. I am still searching."

That was the end of the road for me. I had read enough philosophy to know that philosophers did not agree among themselves. I was fascinated with undergraduate psychology until the day my favorite professor committed suicide. Now I was seated at the feet of this world famous scholar of the human mind and he didn't know why he was alive. Bankrupt! End of the road!

At that point in time, Jim Read, my anatomy lab partner invited me to church. I declined by saying, "No thanks, Jim. I have been to them all and there is nothing there." He didn't accept that. He said, "You have not been to my church and you cannot say that." Caught in a logical trap, I grudgingly agreed to go—just one time—and said, "After that, don't bother me again."

That was when I heard the first really brilliant, convincing expositor of Scripture. The problem was he was in the fifth chapter of Mark which talks about Jesus casting demons out of a man. The demons entered two thousand pigs, which then run over the edge of the cliff, are drowned in the lake and the man is left in his right mind. I turned to Mary Jo and said, "Honey, I don't agree with fifty percent of what this man is saying, but he is the first preacher I have ever heard who has the guts to say what that book really teaches."[1]

Two nights later this man, Rev. Robert Smoot, was seated in my living room, making a follow-up call. I started on him with my usual "wipe out the minister" questions. He didn't wipe out. In fact, he loved my questions. He ate them up and always gave cogent, lucid answers. This whet my appetite to go back to church so I could ask more questions. And I always got good answers. Then I started reading the Bible so I could ask more questions.

This went on for two months. Then I came up against John 14:6, where Jesus said, "I am the way, the truth, and the life; no man comes to the Father, except through Me." I couldn't go on. Either Jesus was lying or He was insane or maybe, just maybe, this was true. In my foolishness, I tried every possible way to show this wasn't true. They all failed. Finally, it hit me. Jesus said the strange things He did simply because He could not lie—no matter how weird it sounded, He could not deny who He was.

I picked up the phone, called Rev. Smoot and told him what I now believed. He called Mary Jo and me to the office. He made sure that we understood that we, humanly speaking, were dead in our sins. He re-presented Jesus as the one who died on the cross for sins. He asked us if we truly believed that and asked if we also believed that Jesus was the Lord. He then asked us if we were turning away from our sinful habits and would we follow Jesus as Lord. When he was satisfied that we had truly repented and had received Christ into our hearts, he allowed us to join Chapelgate Lane United Presbyterian Church in Baltimore. That was in late January, 1951.

That was just the beginning of a period of rapid growth, increasing understanding, constantly making new discoveries, involvement in all kinds of Christian activities, including street preaching with older brothers like Milton

Fisher and Jay Adams, and increasing turmoil among my medical school classmates as I attempted to share my faith among them at every opportunity. Trouble was brewing and I didn't know it.

1 Most modern-day thinkers say science is the answer to abnormal behavior, not this "funky stuff" about casting out demons.

THE CRISIS
IN MEDICAL SCHOOL

Coming to Christ in the middle of my second year of medical school had surprising consequences. I went to medical school looking for answers to basic questions like, "Why am I here? What is the purpose of life? What am I supposed to be living for?"

Psychiatry has no answers to these questions. But Christ did. And when I finally received Him, He put a fire inside of me that was unquenchable.[1] I could not stop talking about Jesus whenever the opportunity presented itself. Some examples: When my friends asked me to join them in pitching coins to a line and the closest one takes it all, I said, "I don't think Jesus wants me to do this anymore." When beer was offered to me at the next party, I said, "I don't think Jesus wants me to drink this anymore." At home in our apartment, I smashed all the beer mugs with ladies in different stages of *déshabillé*, carved on the handles. My best friend, Jack, asked, "Why didn't you give them to me?" I replied, "If they are a stumbling block for me, they probably would be for you too." I even took on my professor in pharmacology lab, who asked Bob Levine, my classmate across the table, "Levine, are you a stoic or an epicurean?" I shot back, "Dr. Reimer, what's wrong with being a Christian?" His mouth fell open. He stared and then walked away. The whole room became deathly quiet.

One day, my friend, Jim Read,[2] said to me, "Don, cool it; the whole school is talking about you." Because of my great respect for Jim, I listened to him until that night. What I was doing in the book of Jeremiah as a young believer, I will never know. But I came across this verse: "Then I said, 'I will not make mention of Him, nor speak anymore in His name.' But His word was in my heart like a burning fire shut up in my bones; I was weary of holding it back, and I could not" (Jer. 20:9).

The next day, with my finger on this verse, I waited for Jim on the verandah of our med school. When he read it, he hung his head and said, "That is the call of God on your life." The fire did not go away.

One of my friends, Harry Weeks, had a two-year-old son who was destroying their apartment. Harry asked me what I thought he should do. I quoted Proverbs 22:15, "Folly is bound up in the heart of a child, but the rod of discipline will drive it far from him." Harry, who was of the school of permissiveness, looked hard at me, and said, "I would never send anyone to you for counsel."

Jack, my best friend, began telling my classmates, "I think Don has a brain tumor." They pointed out that I did not have those types of symptoms.

Meanwhile, my medical studies were being given second place to an intense studying of the Word of God. I also participated in all kinds of activities at the church. I was definitely entering a crisis of calling. Was I supposed to stay in medicine or leave and go into the ministry?

After a Youth for Christ meeting one Saturday night, I hung around to talk to my friends from the church. I told them I thought God was calling me to leave medical school and go into the ministry. The wonderful speaker, Deke

Ketcham, who had just been used to lead so many young people to the Lord, leaned across the circle and said, "Young man, the devil may want you to go to seminary." All the others chimed in and said something like, "God needs Christian doctors; you should stay in med school." I was dumbfounded. I expected them all to be ecstatic about my "call."

To make matters worse, my wife did not have this same sense of calling. At one point, she even said, "If you go to seminary, you will go alone; I will not go with you."[3]

After completing my second year and taking and passing the Maryland State Board exams on that two-year unit of work, I went to the Dean, Dr. Boyd Wylie, and told him that I thought God was calling me into the ministry and that I would be leaving medical school. He asked me to sit down and tell him what happened. I told him the whole story in great detail. His response thrilled my heart. He commented that in his twenty years at the University of Maryland Medical School, I was the first man he had ever seen come to grips with reality. Then he told me his story. He wanted to be a medical missionary, but his father died unexpectedly and left him in charge of his invalid mother. He never was able to go. And then he said to me, "Don, if God is calling you into the ministry, I send you with my blessing, and if you ever want to come back and complete your medical studies here, the door is always open." What a blessing.

When both sets of parents learned of our decision to leave medical school, all financial support ceased. This and all the opposition we faced was preparation for events that came much later.

The good news is, that in due time three married classmates, along with their wives, and two single classmates came to Christ and later all four of our parents came to a living faith in the Lord Jesus.

1 It still is to this present day.

2 The one who took me to his church.

3 Later on, God answered her "fleece" prayer in a remarkable way and God changed her mind.

THE CRISIS IN SEMINARY

At last—courses I truly enjoyed. Medical school classes were interesting; these classes in seminary were vibrantly alive. This is where I belonged. Medical school was *my* choice: I was Jonah, hiding in medical school. Seminary and the ministries to follow were God's choice.

Now I could study the Bible day and night and get credit for it. My grades reflected my new motivation. Greek and Hebrew were also a delight. After years of drought wandering in desert wastelands, I could drink and drink and still have more from the Book of Life, the Bible.

Extracurricular activities were of two kinds: the kind you got remuneration for and those you did without pay. Running recreational programs at the Northside Community Center was remunerative, as was the position of youth work in a local church.

Joining the team of men who did street-preaching in Northside Pittsburgh did not pay in money. But the lessons in courage, going against the grain, doing something rather than nothing, were very profitable. During the second year, I inherited the leadership of the team.

The third year, Billy Graham came to town. That changed a lot of priorities. A Navigator, Leroy Eims, came to do the follow-up work after the crusade. Cell groups were formed in our seminary and I became a leader of one of them. Along the way, Leroy began to disciple me personally. This was tough stuff. Chapter analysis of a book of the New Testament with special attention being paid to applying its lessons to my personal life. Scripture memory. Keeping track of my prayer life, my times of sharing the gospel with non-believers, and my finances. This was a new kind of accountability. Study was no longer about good grades, it was about growth in character and obedience to the Lord.

Then came the invitation to join the team of four men that would go into the fraternity houses at the University of Pittsburgh and Carnegie Tech. Again, a new kind of discipline in preparing my testimony for pagan university men. Learning courage again. Making appointments after each presentation. Seeing men come to Christ (forty in four months). Life was intensely alive—things were happening. Studies on the one hand and action on the other. I loved it and grew like a weed.

But there was another source of stimulation from an unexpected source. From time to time, missionaries, home on furlough, would come and address our student body or speak in our individual classes. These were always times of high excitement. A new kind of fire was kindled inside of me—a fire for missions. But along with it, confusion. How did one know if God was calling him to be a missionary?

My classmate, Dave Livingston, who became a missionary to Korea, posed this simple analogy. He said, "If ten men are carrying a heavy log, and nine are on one end and only one on the other, who needs the most help?" The answer seemed so obvious. But did "need" constitute a "call"? I was stuck on this question.

All of this came to a head one day in our class on missions. Our teacher, Dr. John Gerstner, opened his Bible to

Matthew 28:18-20, and read "The Great Commission" to us.[1] And then he said to our entire class, "Every one of you in this room is obligated to offer himself or herself for foreign mission work." I was stunned. "Is this true?" I asked myself.

Finally, I raised my hand. "Dr. Gerstner, I don't think that is true." Then I opened my Bible to Acts 13:1-5, a passage in which the Holy Spirit spoke to a group of five men who were fasting and praying, and said, "Set apart for Me Barnabas and Saul for the work to which I have called them." And I said to my esteemed professor, "See, that's how it works." Now it was his turn to be stunned.

Then Dr. Gerstner did something very unwise. He asked the class to vote on how many agreed with him and how many agreed with Mr. McCurry. The vote went something like this: Five percent of the class agreed with the professor, eighty-five percent agreed with me, and for whatever reason, ten percent refused to vote.

That settled it, right? If you didn't have that special kind of Holy Spirit call, then you were not called to be a missionary. Since I had no such "call," I was therefore destined to be a pastor.

As graduation time drew near, many opportunities presented themselves for accepting this or that call to one church or another. None of those cushy, local "calls" seemed to interest me. But the one from a broken-down church in Colorado Springs did. It had been on home mission support for thirty years, had asked three previous pastors to leave and had only twenty-five people in attendance when I arrived. I wanted to see what God could do in such a hopeless-looking situation. And that's another *Tale*.

1 "Go into all the world and make disciples of all nations…"

CRISIS IN THE PULPIT

The Church on Boulder Street, Colorado Springs, was a challenge. The three previous pastors had been asked to leave. The church would have collapsed without home mission support over the previous thirty years. The membership rolls had not been purged in anyone's memory and attendance was down to twenty-five people when I arrived. This was in June, 1954.

In very short order, things began to turn around. Navigators Jack Chisholm and Dottie McClintock, who had just moved to Colorado Springs, became Sunday school teachers. Bob Mitchell of Young Life began directing high schoolers to the church. Leaders of InterVarsity Christian Fellowship began to attend. With the large influx of young people, an effort was made to win their families, with some success. Church attendance began to grow. Volunteers began to help with the administrative side of the Church. The elders and deacons became effective and functioning bodies again.

As the congregation began to grow, I introduced midweek family potluck suppers to help the congregation come together as a family. I taught weekly lessons on stewardship to encourage the church to renounce home mission support and become financially independent—which it did.

All the while, the missionary fire that had begun in my heart in seminary was still burning very brightly. To help the congregation become mission-minded, I invited missionaries into my pulpit (with session approval) on six successive Sundays. As these furloughing missionaries from various countries of the world presented the needs on their fields, I began to pray. And that was when the "crisis" began.

Of all the ways to respond to these challenges, the minimum one was to pray. My wife, Mary Jo, and I began to pray something like this, "Lord, do you see all those talented young people out there in the congregation? Call some of them to become missionaries and to risk their lives at the ends of the earth for the sake of the Gospel and for Your glory."

The Lord responded in a most disturbing way. Even though we did not audibly hear His voice, He entered into a dialogue with us that went something like this. The Lord: "You hypocrites. You are asking Me to send these young people to risk their lives and you are not willing to go first—to be a role model for them—and to demonstrate your own obedience to My command."

My reply: "Lord, I am not a hypocrite. You know I am willing to do anything for You." Foolishly, I began to remind Him of the few brave things I had done for Him. His response? "That doesn't mean anything to Me." In desperation, I asked, "Lord, how does someone convince You they mean what they say?"

His answer? "I am the living God. I know how to open and close doors. Offer yourself to Me unconditionally, to go anywhere, to do whatever I say, and then you will know that you are not deceiving yourself anymore." And that was what we did. The repercussion in the congregation and among our families was not pleasant. But the very wise executive of our presbytery said, "Don, if you had not volunteered, you would not be effective in the hands of the Lord." Then he went through the list of the pastors in the presbytery and told me the story of each one and his commitment to missions.

We resolved this crisis of call by offering ourselves unconditionally to the Lord through our Mission Board in Philadelphia. In being interviewed by this committee, it turned out that some were critical of my term as pastor of the church. At the end of two hours of grilling, I was emotionally drained. On the train from Philadelphia to Washington that night to visit with my parents, all I could hear with the clickity-clack of the train wheels on the rails were these words, over and over again, "McCurry, you don't have what it takes, you don't have what it takes." I was despondent. I felt I had failed to qualify.

No one was more surprised than I the next morning when I received a telegram saying that we had been appointed to career mission service and that I should return to Philadelphia at once.

Upon my arrival back in Philadelphia, I met privately with Dr. Everett Grice, the head of our mission. I recounted to him how I felt the night before on that train ride to Washington. To my utter shock, that godly man leaped out of his chair, came over, stuck a finger in my chest, and said, "McCurry, don't you ever forget it! You don't have what it takes and the day you think you do, you are finished with the Lord. He resists the proud and gives grace to the humble."

This was in 1956. And so began a career that is still in process. More crises were to come. They will be shared as needed as we weave together lessons learned in these cameo studies which we have called *Tales That Teach*.

SOME BIRTHDAY PRESENTS ARE FOREVER

We were very poor. Our salary at the First United Presbyterian Church of Colorado Springs was $3,300 for the year! And we had four children! There was nothing left over for presents for either birthdays or anniversaries.

Since my birthday is June 3rd and our anniversary is June 5th, we decided to put both celebrations together in a dinner out on June 4th.

As I began to think about birthday presents and anniversary presents, the thought occurred to me that God might give me/us a present. What could it be? With my dear wife, Mary Jo's, consent, I asked God to let me share the knowledge of Him with someone who didn't know Him that very night at the restaurant.

It was a lovely drive to Cheyenne Mountain Lodge high up on the slope of the mountain overlooking the city. Once there, the view was spectacular. At a glance you could see all the lights from one end of the city to the other. The illumination on the two main intersecting streets formed a cross. How appropriate, I thought—the cross laid out in lights in the heart of Colorado Springs.

As the meal progressed we were perplexed. We were the only customers! Oh, well! We were in love. We had one another. The food was great. And the view was as good as it gets. We would enjoy what the Lord had provided.

About eight-thirty, the proprietor and his wife sat down to dinner at the far end of the restaurant. A few minutes later they were joined by a burly younger man who looked mightily disturbed.

We were about to begin our dessert when the noise of their arguing grew very loud. Finally, in a burst of anger the young man shouted, "If I have to, I will go down into the city and nighthawk!" We had no idea what "nighthawk" meant.[1]

Finally I couldn't stand it anymore. I walked over to their table and said, "I am a local pastor here in town. It is obvious you are in the middle of a big problem. Is there anything I can do to help you?"

The atmosphere changed dramatically. Everyone calmed down. They begged us to come and sit with them. While the proprietor brought two more chairs, his wife went and called Mary Jo and brought our dessert to their table.

This was the situation: Dick had just come in from Massachusetts. He had lost his job. His wife had multiple sclerosis. The Commonwealth of Massachusetts was about to take their three children away from them. Dick was out of his mind with rage. He had come to his mother and step-father, the proprietors, for help. They were broke.

I asked what it would take to save his family. This is what he said: "If you will write to the authorities in Massachusetts that you will be responsible for my family when they arrive, I will get a job, earn enough money to go back and get my family and bring them out here." We said we would do it.

We took Dick into our home and made a place for him in the basement. The youth group at our church adopted him. We all prayed mightily for him. One night in the evening service, he came forward weeping and accepted the Lord kneeling there at the platform. Those high school kids were ecstatic. God had heard their prayers and ours too.

Dick earned enough money to go back to Massachusetts and bring his family. While he was gone, I was asked to bring a devotional talk to the Christian Businessmen's Committee meeting. Afterwards, Bill Moore, who had only known the Lord for a year, asked me to go swimming with him at his home in Woodland Park. I told him that I was not free, that I was looking for an apartment for this man and his family. He asked, "What man? Why are you doing this? What is the story here?" I told him everything. He said, "I didn't know you were doing this." Then we parted.

Meanwhile, back at our home, Mary Jo was "having it out" with the Lord. We had no money. Our older three children needed shoes. Our son Stephen had just been born. In her having it out with God, she said, "Lord, if you approve of what we have been doing for Dick, then prove it to me by sending me $25 before noon today so that I can buy shoes for my children."

At ten minutes to twelve, Bill Moore showed up at our home with a large glass jar filled with money. Bill had been a chain smoker. Every time he had the urge for a cigarette, he reached into his pocket and put whatever change was there into this jar. He said to Mary Jo, "Don told me what you two are doing. I have been asking the Lord what to do with this money. Here, this is for you." And then he left.

I came in a few minutes later and found Mary Jo sitting on the kitchen floor, straddle-legged, bawling her head off, trying to count all this money spread out there in her skirt. It was a little over $52—more than twice what she asked for!

And Dick? He became an outstanding Christian.

When we left for Pakistan, he migrated back to his family homestead in North Carolina. Our first year in Pakistan, we received a letter from him with a newspaper clipping of him. He had won the award for being the model semi-tractor-trailer-rig driver for the year in his home state.

What a birthday present! And it will last for eternity.

---

1 Later, we found out it meant "armed robbery." I am glad I didn't know then.

THE PLACE OF DREAMS

In the dry, dead, anti-supernatural culture of the West, this kind of a *Tale* is most difficult to write, the reason being that this anti-supernaturalism, so prevalent in the secular world, has seeped into the churches, the Bible schools and seminaries of evangelicalism. And the graduates of these institutions who have responded to a missionary call spread this foundational pillar of secularism around the world!

To share a dream, a personal-experience dream, not the five-year "dream" of the planning committee of an organization, is to risk one's credibility—in the West. In fact, it is to put your whole ministry in jeopardy.

So I am a risk-taker. Before this chapter is over, I will have shared a live, personal-experience dream and relate its function in our lives and how, in a surprising way, it literally came true.

Having pilloried secular evangelicalism, let me go on to comment on those non-Western cultures where the supernatural, both good and evil, is readily acknowledged. In that *other world out there*, meaning the mission fields, dreams are highly valued. In fact, in my beloved sub-continent of India, Pakistan and Bangladesh, you can go to any book market in any city and buy books on the interpretation of dreams. Sigmund Freud, whose theories of psychoanalysis are now discredited, was a late-comer to this field!

What is the place of dreams in human lives? Do they really have a place? The answer, of course, is yes. At this point we are entering dangerous ground. Dreams can be meaningless or they can reflect emotional stresses and tensions in one's life. They can even produce solutions to teasing problems that are bubbling in one's subconscious. And they can be either the expression of demonic activity or a divine communication.

When one turns to the Bible, we can either start with dreams as they are first mentioned or we can go to a bold declaration of the Lord where He promises to give dreams. Let's start with this last idea.

In the words of Joel the prophet, given around 800 B.C., we read, "Afterward, I will pour out my Spirit on all people. Your sons and daughters will prophesy, your old men will dream dreams, and your young men will see visions" (Joel 2:28).

These words were quoted by Peter on the day of Pentecost to support the amazing phenomena attending the outpouring of the Holy Spirit, when people spoke in fifteen different languages—languages not learned, but languages that suited the international gathering in Jerusalem (Acts 2:2-17).

There it is: "Men will dream dreams." And from the early Scriptures of Genesis to the closing book of Revelation, God used dreams to speak to his servants. Just to mention a few of the more famous ones, note these men who had dreams: Jacob and Joseph in Genesis, Daniel in exile, Mary's husband, Joseph, Paul's vision of the man of Macedonia and finally John in the book of Revelation. All were spoken to by the Lord through dreams.

Does the Lord still speak to people through dreams

today? According to a survey of field workers, about forty percent of Muslims who have come to Christ have done so because of a dream they had.[1]

My own modest story starts in western Pennsylvania. Mary Jo and I, with our four young children (we had two more later), were on the eve of our departure for Pakistan. It was a time of apprehension and tormenting fears.

In the night, God gave me this dream: *I was standing in a dusty road in Asia. In the distance, a girl of about six, barefoot, olive-skinned, black hair, wearing a tattered dress was approaching me. As she got closer, I studied her face. It was the face of my own six-year-old daughter.* And then the Lord spoke: *Now the children of Asia are becoming your children.* What a comfort! The Lord is in this. It is going to be okay or He wouldn't have given that dream. *Let's go!*

During my first term on the field, while living in the city of Lyallpur (now called Faisalabad), I was involved in managing rural schools. We stopped at one to check on the progress of the children. And there she was: *a six-year-old in a tattered dress, no shoes, with bright and shining eyes and lovely black hair—a radiant lass, who was now one of my children.* A literal fulfillment of that pre-field dream back in Pennsylvania. "Old men will dream dreams and young men will see visions." Our Living God is a master communicator and this is one of His ways. To Him be glory forever and ever! Amen.

1 My unprovable theory is that they are the result of people praying for them.

WHAT? HAVE YOU BECOME A MUSLIM?

My introduction to culture clash was a shocker. Upon our arrival in Pakistan, we had been assigned a venerable old man by the name of Joseph Sain Dass as our teacher in the Urdu language. His name tells you two things. "Joseph," rather than the Urdu version "Yusuf" tells you right away that he has an *anglicized* name. "Sain Dass" tells you right away that his forebears were from a *Hindu* caste background. So my teacher was an anglicized descendant of Hindu converts to Christ.

By way of background information, Christians constitute about two percent of the population of Pakistan: one half is Roman Catholic, the other half is made up of a variety of Protestants. Virtually all are descendants of converts from Hindu sub-caste backgrounds. Naturally, they brought with them many of their customs and especially their language— laced with Hindu "loan" words.

The official language of Pakistan is Urdu. It was the language that grew out of a polyglot army under Muslim rulers. Its beginnings can be traced back to the 13th Century. The soldiers came from many linguistic backgrounds: Turkish ("Urdu" is a Turkish word), Persian, Arabic (the language of the earliest conquerors), Prakrit (a precursor of Punjabi) and Hindi (with its Sanskrit grammatical syntax).

Officially, the British ruled India from 1858 to 1947.

They called this polyglot language "Hindustani." This reflected their disdain of Muslims and their perception of India as a land predominantly Hindu.

At the time of the Partition of India in 1947, the British divided this vast land into Hindu India, and Muslim East and West Pakistan. After gaining independence, the two countries sought to distance themselves from one another culturally and linguistically. India chose to call its language "Hindi," reverting to its Hindu roots, and Pakistan reclaimed "Urdu" from the heritage of India's early Muslim rulers.

Our family arrived in Pakistan ten years after the trauma of this partitioning of old India. It was not a peaceful division. Seven million Muslims abandoned their home in India and migrated to the two wings of Pakistan, and five million Sikhs and Hindus did the same as they abandoned their homes in what was now Pakistan and migrated to India. They slaughtered one another as they filtered through each other's ranks. About one million died.

Naturally, these bitter and bloody transmigrations only heightened their hatred of one another. Language became one of the subsequent battlegrounds, with Hindi becoming more sanskritized (and more Hindu-ish) in India and Urdu becoming more arabicized (and Islamicized) in Pakistan.

And the Christians? They stayed put, whether in India or Pakistan. The problem was that in Urdu-speaking Pakistan, the Christian vocabulary of Urdu reflected their Hindu roots, especially in music.

This was the setting for our introduction to the learning of Urdu. Naturally, one of the first things you want to learn is how to greet one another. From our teacher, we learned to say "*Namaste*," and the other person was supposed to say in response "*Taslimat*."

Off to the city I went to practice my greetings with folks I met. But when I said "*Namaste*," all I got was cold, hostile stares. After two or three more rebuffs, I withdrew to a corner of a popular store, sat there on a stool and listened to people greet one another. What I heard was "*As-salam-alayikum*" (Peace be to you); and the response, "*Wa-alayikum salam*" (And peace be to you). I practiced this and it worked everywhere. I could hardly wait to greet Joseph the next day.

Nothing prepared me for the unexpected reaction of my teacher. He froze in his tracks and shouted, "What, have you become a Muslim?" In his mind, with his Hindu background, he perceived me as adopting the language of the hated Muslim oppressors. Of course I had not become a Muslim, even though I had used their lovely way of greeting one another.

This early experience was only a harbinger of many more serious, emotionally-charged issues that would surface as we, with one foot in the local church from a Hindu background sought to reach out with the gospel to the majority community of Muslims, ninety-seven percent of the population.

Joseph's outburst, so long ago, still echoes in my brain when I take steps to adjust to the culture and language of the Muslims I am trying to win. How far can we actually go in adjusting to local Islamic culture without becoming Muslim? This is the question that is rocking mission and church communities throughout the Muslim world today.

Joseph's question was valid then, although alarmist. Today we know we can go far beyond what he was willing to tolerate. Tragically, some have gone too far. May our God guide us as we earnestly seek the most effective ways to communicate the Good News of Jesus Christ to our Muslim friends.

OUR MOST LOYAL CRITIC

I admired Pastor Prabhu Dass for two reasons: He loved the Lord with all his heart and he loved me. I loved him too. I can still see him in my mind's eye. He was short of stature with rich brown skin (no melanin deficiencies here!). He had very thick glasses to compensate for his cataract operations: Cataracts are endemic to that part of the world. His head was adorned with this outrageously copious and plumed Punjabi turban. His dark coat covered his local *shalwar-qameez* outfit (a long, loose shirt hanging out over his very baggy cotton pants, typically five feet wide at the waist with a drawstring to tighten them). He was the chaplain at our Mission Hospital in the city of Sialkot, Pakistan, where we did our first year of Urdu language study.

It was Jesus who brought us together: he, a seasoned Punjabi pastor-chaplain, and I, a newly arrived, zealous fire-brand eager to win Pakistan to Christ. We recognized one another as kindred spirits from the beginning.

Prabhu Dass proclaimed the good news of Jesus every morning to the patients who had arrived at the hospital for treatment. I admired the fearless way he opened up the Word of God and lovingly explained the meaning of the Gospel to those needy Pakistani Muslims and Christians. Later I would occasionally accompany him on his "rounds" as he went through the male wards to pray with the patients.[1]

Afterwards we would go to his little office on the second floor for a cup of tea. I noticed every available shelf in his office was filled with Bibles and tracts ready for every need. This man cared and was prepared.

I remember listening to him talk about his call and how, after completing his training, he was appointed as a pastor in an extensive district with scores of villages. He had no car or motor scooter, so he spent hours every day on his bicycle in the fiery heat of Pakistan, enduring the simple fare of the poor. It was in that furnace on the scorching plains of the Punjab that God tested and refined his servant. Out of those testing fires came this special man who was chosen to be the chaplain at our famous Memorial Christian Hospital in Sialkot.

His modest house in Christian Town was not far from the fourteen-room bungalow we shared with senior missionaries there on the mission compound. From time to time, he would stop by and visit on his way to the hospital. I loved these times of fellowship. Our children, too, enjoyed this lovable and venerable Punjabi saint with his fascinating turban.

But our conversations were not always comfortable. The disparity in the standard of living between us missionaries and our Pakistani co-workers was downright embarrassing. And Prabhu would often speak to me about the incongruity. He was never rude, nor was he greedy. He was just a man in pain—the pain of the poor moving in and out of the orbit of the rich.

It's just that he could "see." And we, in some terrible way, were "blind." He could see that our standard of living was much higher than his. We ate richer food. We traveled in a car—an old rebuilt Chevrolet Carryall, to be sure, but nevertheless a great luxury then. He saw that our children were better dressed than his. He knew we could afford to send them off to boarding schools in the cool mountains, while his kids sweat their way through ill-equipped schools in the sweltering heat of those Punjabi plains.

I squirmed when he made his needs known. "Sahib,[2] the tires on my bike are completely worn out and I can't buy new ones because my children's school fees are due." Or, "Sahib, how much do you spend on gasoline each month for your car? You know I could buy a new bicycle with just six months of your gasoline money." And other such comments.

Prabhu was always polite, you understand. But he was also always in my face. I could not avoid him (remember, I loved him), nor his needs, nor the needs of his precious family.

Perhaps all of this could have been avoided if I hadn't preached a very moving sermon on Pentecost Sunday in the downtown church in Sialkot. Naturally, I used Acts 2 as the text for that day. It ends like this: "All the believers were together and had everything in common. Selling their possessions and goods, they gave to anyone as he had need (Acts 2:44-45)." And this is repeated later in Acts 4:32, "All the believers were one in heart and mind. No one claimed that any of his possessions was his own, but they shared everything they had." Oh! Oh! Oh! I was skewered by my own preaching!

I rationalized to myself: "By Pakistani standards he has an adequate salary and my salary is fitting for an American!" But this kind of thinking was of no avail. There he was, a very honest, righteous man of God, standing in front of me, unflinching in his poverty, hopelessly exposed in his needs, just standing there before this younger "brother" whose salary was no less than forty times greater than his.

This, of course, precipitated a crisis in our family. I

told them about the needs and comments of this precious Pakistani Christian brother. What were we to do? This problem was compounded by special gifts that had been sent by loving, supporting churches for us to use as we saw fit. We sat and discussed this dilemma with our children.

It was then as a family that we decided not to spend these gifts on ourselves, but to give them to Prabhu Dass for his family and their needs. At other times, we didn't wait for special gifts, we just gave out of what we had.

Many other missionaries did the same. Yes, we learned to share, all of us in one way or another. And these "investments" returned dividends many times over! One of Prabhu's sons rose to be the principal of the famous Murray Christian College there in Sialkot. All of his grandchildren are also believers and outstanding Christian servants: Today, one is a doctor and the others are teachers.

I thank God for Prabhu Dass. By his entrapping questions and shameless confessions of need, he made us face the inequities of this world. He never openly criticized us or condemned us. He was too polite for that. But you could tell that deep down inside he was critical of the lifestyle of the missionaries. His remarks kept us all honest and forced us to do something about these gross inequities. In the end, he proved to be both a beloved co-worker and our most loyal critic.

1 Male evangelists are not allowed to work with female patients in Muslim Pakistan—that is the work of the Bible Women.

2 How I hated that term. It was years before I earned the right to be called Brother Don.

THE MAN OF GOD HAS COME

The Punjab is the land of five rivers. To control flooding and increase land production, the British, during their reign in India, built connecting canals between these rivers. The only problem was that these canals acted like dams preventing the natural runoff of water during heavy rains. The monsoon rains were heavy that year. The inevitable result was widespread flooding. Mud houses tend to erode in raging floodwaters. Drinking water gets contaminated. Diseases set in. We had a disaster on our hands.

The available men of our mission were called to abandon all other work and plunge into the desperately needed relief work. Cars could only go so far. Bicycles could do okay as long as you could ride on the raised earthen mounds between the fields. But then there comes a point when you could see nothing but water between the devastated villages. What to do? Ah, horses. That's the solution. And so it was...

While putting together our threesome of borrowed horses, it never occurred to me to investigate their sexes. We ended up with a beautiful young filly and two large stallions of amorous intent. When the truth finally dawned, we discovered the only working relationship was to put the filly in front, the bigger stallion next and God's missionary "hero" riding ignominiously at the rear on the weaker stallion.

Horses and I never got along.

Have you ever observed, at close range, how one male horse goes about trying to bite his rival? At a distance of about three feet, I noted the violent flaring of the nostrils, the heavy breathing, the bulging eyes rapidly turning red, and the incredible pulling back of the upper and lower lips to reveal the most fearsome set of gnashing incisors and grinders I had ever seen. Memories of a photo of a man who turned up at our Taxila Mission Hospital with his lower jaw being completely bitten away by an angry camel flashed into my mind. My knees turned to jelly. I saw myself being dismembered and finally stomped to a pulp in the mud at the bottom of this horsey triangle love affair.

Somehow we managed. My companions, thinking me more accomplished than I was, decided to treat me to a ride on the spirited filly. She really was a beauty. I was enjoying our comfortable canter, when out of nowhere a group of pack horses, turned loose by their master to find their own way home, approached the rear of my filly. She panicked and began to gallop. I pulled back on the reins. She ran faster. Again I tried to rein her in. If anything, she increased her speed. Then it hit me. This horse had been trained in the ancient sport of "tent-pegging," a favorite equestrian skill in Pakistan. The more you pulled her head up, the faster she ran. This was so her rider, at a full gallop and carrying a spear, could lean way over under her head and attempt to uproot the tent pegs of his enemy's tent, causing it to collapse on him.

As soon as I realized this, I pulled her head down as hard as I could. Her front legs went out like two steel stakes plowing the ground to a near instantaneous stop. As I flew over her head, I remember saying to myself, "McCurry, hold on to these reins or you will never see this horse again." After three clumsy barrel rolls, I came up on my feet still holding the reins, but no horse. It took a while to catch the runaway filly and repair the broken bit and bridle. We decided to trade horses again.

At last I was on the powerful stallion. All was well until we neared a flooded village. My helper thoughtlessly rode his horse between the filly and mine. I found myself half-falling, half sliding down the back of my enraged stallion as he went up on his two hind feet, flailing the air with his two front legs, intending to demolish my partner's horse. After pulling him back to earth, I ran my hands up the reins and twisted the bit in his mouth until I had control of him. Together, in mutual disgrace, we walked to the nearest clump of trees and I tied him there. I had had it with horses. We waded toward the village. A passing farmer said all the people had left. We thought we had better check. A good thing we did.

There she was sitting on her rope bed, utterly delirious with malaria, nursing her tiny baby. Her husband had died a short time before. As soon as she saw me, she cried out, "The man of God has come." Against all my efforts to stop her, she, in her delirium, boiled up the only egg left in the village and from twigs prepared "tea." Over and over, I heard her saying, "The man of God has come." She had to honor the man of God.

Many times since then I have thought about those words of Rayshum Bibi, for that was her name, "The man of God has come." That was not how I perceived myself. I was a most unhappy, miserable, reluctant missionary, cursing horses and my fate on that day. I did not perceive myself as "a man of God." But she did. It has often made me think of how I perceive my coworkers and myself. Men of God? Women of God? A man of God?

Rayshum Bibi taught me how to honor God's servants. She didn't see the disgruntled, flawed man; she saw the anointing, the name of God on His servant. Ever since, whenever I am tempted to think less of a servant of God, there has been a check in my spirit. Rayshum Bibi taught me to see His servants as men and women of God and to honor them as such. She had it right. Jesus said, "He who receives you receives me" (Matthew 10:40).

I AM NOT YOUR FATHER: YOU ARE MINE

The question of paternalism has plagued missions from the beginning. What happened in Pakistan is no exception. Our mission work began there in 1858.

In due process, churches were founded, and when there were enough of them, presbyteries were formed. After the mass evangelistic movements with about half a million untouchables becoming Christians between 1890 and 1930, the work mushroomed. More presbyteries were formed. In due process, these were incorporated into a synod.

This synod was called "The Synod of the Punjab of the United Presbyterian Church of *North America*." Now you see the problem developing. Should we follow the Roman Catholic pattern of creating a structure that keeps our work united all over the world? Or do we entertain the thought of creating sister churches and denominations wherever our mission work flourishes overseas?

What did the Pakistani pastors and elders think about all of this? As you can imagine, two schools of thought emerged. One, influenced by the money coming from the States, wanted to stay tied to the mother church that birthed them. The other chafed at foreign control. This group was especially sensitive to the criticism of the non-Christian population (97%) that the church was an American church and all of the pastors and elders were *chumchas*. Perhaps the least offensive equivalent of this word in English would be *boot-lickers*.

By the time we arrived on the field, a polarization had begun to take place. The majority of the ordained missionaries wanted the Synod of the Punjab to stay under the General Assembly of the mother church in America. In opposition to them, some firebrand Pakistani Christian leaders wanted the Pakistani Church to become independent, free, and to be recognized in Pakistan and abroad as such.

As this crisis intensified, it was apparent to the missionaries that this was going to become an issue to be debated at an upcoming full meeting of the Synod.

In preparation for this, all of the men of the mission were called together in a closed session to try to reach a consensus on where we all stood. It was apparent that there was a division in the mission over this. The older missionaries, some of whom had been on the field since the days of the British Rule (called the Raj), wanted the Synod of the Punjab to stay tied organically to the mother church in the States. The younger missionaries, of whom I was one, were revolted by the paternalism that we saw everywhere and longed for the Pakistani Church to become a self-respecting, freestanding church (read: denomination) in Pakistan and in the world.

In the heat of some torrid debating, one of the older missionaries stood up and said, "This church is not ready for independence. We missionaries are the conscience of the church." This was more than I could stand. I stood up and said, "Sir, you have just blasphemed against the Holy Spirit." The older man sat down, stunned. And this was the end of the meeting. We could not reach a consensus.

The greatly anticipated Synod meeting took place. The firebrand Pakistani leaders waxed eloquent. They dwelt on the shame and indignities of being subservient to foreigners. Other Pakistani pastors devoted to the missionaries (in a good way) and fearful of the cutting off of the money that independence might mean, stoutly defended the ties of the Synod of the Punjab to the mother church in America.

Somewhere in the middle of this debate, I made my little speech on why I thought the Pakistan Church should become a sister church and no longer remain a daughter church. The reaction of the older fellow-missionaries was hard to take. The word "betrayal" was used. And the feeling of hostility was palpable.

But what was even more gut wrenching was when one of the oldest, white-haired Pakistani pastors, about 70 years old, stood up and said to me, a 30-year-old, with tears streaming down his face, "You are our father. You cannot abandon us like this."

It was my turn to be shocked. How could a man who had been walking with the Lord for at least fifty years or more, say to me, a young, foreign whippersnapper, "You are my father"?

I couldn't stand it. I stood and said, "Respected Elder, I am not your father; you are mine. You have been walking with the Lord for many decades longer than I. You know more about the Lord than I do. You are my elder. You are my teacher."

The godly man sat down like he had been shot. He never dreamed, perhaps had never been taught, that he could be my elder, my teacher.

When the vote was finally called for, those in favor of the Pakistan Church becoming free had the majority. At last the Pakistan church was independent and equal.

INSPECTOR AYOUB

Getting up at three o'clock in the morning was no fun. But it was a necessary part of the game. Our plan was to arrive just as school opened in a faraway desert village. Inspector Ayoub and I constituted a surprise inspection team of two.

This "tale that teaches" took place in the Thal Desert Development Project on the fringe of the Punjab in Pakistan where new canal water was being brought in to transform the desert into farmland. Homeless Christians had migrated into this newly formed village in the desert.

Eighty-five percent of the adults there could neither read nor write. Ayoub and I believed with a passion that their children should not be doomed to a life of illiteracy and serfdom. Ministering to them in rural primary schools was our way to save the children.

Typically, these schools were one-room affairs with a veranda attached and protected by a large enclosed play area surrounded by mud walls. They were usually located near one of our churches.

Establishing these schools, though, created new problems. How do you maintain accountability among the teachers when there is no supervision? Our answer was surprise inspections. Show up with no warning. Is the teacher on the job? Are the children coming to school on time? What is the quality of the teaching?

Before accepting his position as Inspector of Schools, Ayoub had been the Assistant Principal of a large Christian high school. Out of his deep concern for seeing that these children got an education, with its attending hope of a better life, he gave up the comfort and the high-profile recognition of a secure position to devote himself to the betterment of these otherwise "doomed to illiteracy" children. What an example of love and humility he was to me.

After several hours of hard driving, we arrived at our destination. This surprise visit in the village was a time of high excitement for the students and a time of genuine anxiety for the teacher. After the hubbub subsided, the serious work began. Ayoub kept the teacher's feet to the fire by asking to see his lesson plans and the record of progress of each student. He also examined the children. Through it all, he was a great motivator. When he had to, he "pulled the ears" of naughty little boys. He could also coax shy little girls to share what they had learned.

This particular trip happened at a time in my life when I was working hard at learning the language. In fact, you could say I was on "super-alert," imitating others, asking questions, doing whatever it took to improve my skills in Urdu. Naturally, if something sounded out of the ordinary, it caught my attention.

That is why what I heard that special morning startled me. Ayoub was examining a barefooted little girl in a tattered dress. With her eyes shining ever so brightly, she proudly recited her lesson to the Inspector. He was pleased. He said, "*shabash, baytay*" (well done, son!). He called that little girl "son!" He should have said "*baytee,*" the feminine form (girl). But no, it was "*baytay*" (boy).

Muslim culture in the Punjab did not so honor girls. For a Muslim mother to bring a girl into the world was an occasion of great sorrow. Only boys count! This could be traced back to Muhammad, the founder of Islam, who said women were inferior to men.

His ignorance was understandable: he had no access to a Bible in his day.[1] He had never read the words of God in Genesis 1:27, "So God created man in his own image, in the image of God He created him; male and female He created them."

The recent disaster of the Taliban rule in Afghanistan highlights the pernicious result of Muhammad's teaching. Girls' schools were closed. Female teachers were told to stay home. Single female doctors were forbidden to go outdoors. Widows also were forbidden to run the orphanages. Thousands of widows and orphans died. How stark is the contrast between the teaching of Muhammad and the teaching of Jesus on women.

Inspector Ayoub, of course, was a Christian. He knew Jesus rebuked His own disciples for forbidding children to come to Him. Jesus blessed children, male *and* female. In love, he even raised a young girl from the dead.

Ayoub was also well acquainted with the teaching of Paul. In Galatians 3:26-28, he wrote:

> You are all sons of God through faith in Christ Jesus, for all of you who were baptized into Christ have clothed yourselves with Christ. There is neither Jew nor Greek, slave nor free, *male nor female*, for you are all one in Christ Jesus (emphasis added).

Wherever the Gospel goes, there the quality of life for men and women begins to improve. Inspector Ayoub himself had been transformed by the Gospel. He was once one of those little village boys. God had valued him and developed him. He understood that our Lord Jesus could do the same for this precious little village schoolgirl.

What Ayoub did that day will live forever in my memory. I can still see him standing in front of that little bright-eyed, barefoot girl in the tattered dress and I can still hear him saying "*Shabash, baytay,*" "Well done, son." He saw her as God did: neither male nor female, but rather as a child of our heavenly Father. And in doing so, he helped me see things God's way. Thank you, Inspector Ayoub, friend and mentor.

---

1 Muhammad lived from 570-632 A.D.

TWO BLIND MEN, BUT ONE COULD SEE

As newly arrived missionaries in Pakistan, our first summer was spent trudging off to Language School in the lovely hill station of Murree. It was a breath-taking walk along the curving mountain road from Jhika Gali to the school.

Invariably, when we neared the center of town, we encountered this blind man. You couldn't help but notice him. There were no eyeballs in his sockets. Where the eyes were supposed to be, the skin had grown completely over the hollow area.

His very appearance was a challenge to my faith. Could Jesus heal this man? After all, in his own lifetime, Jesus healed a man born blind. Surely nothing was impossible with God. Jesus could do this.

So many times I wanted to stop and talk to this man. My heart was bursting with faith to believe the Lord could heal him—give him new eyes where none existed before. But I was mute. I had to learn the language first.

Other missionaries noticed him too. We learned that his name was Kalu Khan and that he was a Muslim. He lived in a hillside village nearby and came into town frequently.

One day a friend of mine who could speak the language talked to him about Jesus. "Even in the Muslim holy book, the Quran," my friend said, "it is written that Jesus could heal the blind." And so my friend asked if he could pray for him in Jesus' name.

Kalu Khan responded by cursing the missionary. He called the missionary a *kaffir*[1] and said he was going to hell because he believed Jesus was the Son of God.

When I heard this, I asked myself, "Where is this reaction coming from? Why did he think this way?" In truth, his response served as a quick introduction to Islam. Muhammad, the founder of Islam, pronounced a curse on everyone who believed Jesus was the Son of God (Quran 9:30).

Words from the Bible came to my mind, "Cursed is the man who leads the blind astray..." (Deuteronomy 27:18). Muhammad and his teaching had led blind Kalu Khan astray. My heart grieved.

Then there was Daniel Maseeh. He too was born blind. But he had the good fortune to be born in a Christian village.

Daniel was also blessed with a beautiful voice. From childhood on, he learned lots of psalms and hymns. Daniel had another gift, a heart for evangelism and teaching. But he found it hard to bend the familiar psalms and old time hymns to his purpose.

Eventually he discovered an indigenous form of Indian music called *kuwwali*. This grew out of a style of music that was common to the mystics, both Hindu and *Sufi* Muslim. In it you could express your devotion to God. The style was that of antiphonal singing. The lead singer, usually playing a harmonium, would sing out a line, and then the other singers would lead the audience in singing the line back in response. This was easily adapted as a way of teaching— story-telling through music.

When I first participated in one of Daniel's all-night *kuwwali* songfests, it was in a Christian village near Faisalabad.[2] In the agricultural year, there are seasons of inactivity—ideal times for a good Christian Punjabi sing-along. It was such a time.

We were seated on reed mats in a large, open courtyard. The village sounds were all around: buffalo, donkeys, camels, barking dogs, children playing—until Daniel began. His melodious voice filled the night air. He began with Adam and Eve, teaching in music. We, the audience, were learning to sing the epic stories of the Bible. It was a perfect communication technique for illiterates, semi-literates, children and me.

When he got to the miracles of Jesus, I choked up. Daniel sang, "And Jesus made the blind to see." The audience repeated, "And Jesus made the blind to see."

Daniel was blind, but he saw. His soul radiated the light of the indwelling Christ. He was totally healed inwardly. "The night of my sins was washed away. The light of Christ has come to stay," I sang with tears, aware of the great victory that I was witnessing. Daniel could see. He saw Jesus

How I hated what Islam had done to Kalu Khan. How I rejoiced in what Jesus had done for Daniel Maseeh. Two blind men, but one could see.

Lord Jesus, thank you for blind Daniel who helped me to see the greatness of your victory. And Lord,

Take away the veil from Muslim eyes;
Send Your truth to defeat their lies.
Lead their blind in Your own way;
Turn their darkness into day.

1 Ungrateful blasphemer.
2 Formerly named Lyallpur.

CHINIOT WITHOUT A SINGLE CHRISTIAN

The Punjab is the province known as the breadbasket of Pakistan. The word itself comes from two words, *punj*, meaning five and *ab*, meaning water or river. So we are talking about the land of the five rivers. Chiniot is on the eastern bank of the middle river, the Chenab.

This town was famous for its fish. Pakistani families by the carload would often come to Chiniot for the most delicious fish kabobs in the Punjab.

Once, traveling with a group of fellow missionaries to a retreat, we had just reached the outskirts of Chiniot, when one of the team said, "You know, there is not a single Christian in this town of twenty thousand people."

Abruptly, I pulled the car into the shade of a giant banyan tree and said, "Let's ask God to open a door for us to come here and do evangelism." In the sweltering heat of that crowded van we prayed for God to do just that. And then we drove on to Sargodha for our meeting. All too quickly, the incident was forgotten, along with the prayers that were prayed.

But God doesn't forget so easily. This concern was close to His heart. He began to go to work.

Six months later, a dozen pastors from Faisalabad District came to us missionaries and presented a challenge. "We want to hold an evangelistic campaign in Chiniot." Whoa! Suddenly I woke up. This is what we had prayed for.

Two pastors were sent on ahead to find accommodations for us. There was nothing suitable. So we got out our tents, loaded them onto a trailer and trusted God for a place to set them up on the edge of the city.

For the next three days, we moved through the city, distributed gospel portions and stopped at strategic street corners and preached. First we sang to attract the people. When the crowd had gathered, our best evangelist would preach. His name was Chaudhry Inayatullah Mujahid.

Chaudhry was a title of respect. *Inayatullah* meant "the blessing of God." *Mujahid* was from the Arabic word *jihad* (holy war) and meant "warrior," a holy warrior for God. So here we had "a respected blessing of God holy warrior," in other words, an evangelist.

What was so fascinating to me, as a very young inexperienced missionary, was Inayatullah's extraordinary ability to use the Quran and explain away the Muslim objections to Christian truth. He was quoting Arabic texts fluently and blowing away their objections and misunderstandings. And well he could, for he himself had been a former preacher of Islam of the Ahmadiya sect, the most effective group in propagating Islam. Was I glad he was on our side. It was awesome.

The problem for me was that Inayatullah's method of preaching did not match any of my pre-conceived ideas or previous training on how to do evangelism. So, as a young know-it-all, I said, "I don't think that is a very good approach. That's not for me."

Still, wonderful things happened on that trip. The head of the English department of the local Islamic college came to our tents at nighttime to ask more questions and to venture a comment on Islam. He said there is no love in Islam. He saw love in us—and wanted it.

Then the roadside shoe repair man, the *mochi* who heard all of our preaching just opposite his little set-up shop, believed on the spot.

Later, a student came from Chiniot into Faisalabad to find us so he could ask for a complete Bible and someone to study it with him. He too soon came to Christ.

Did I miss something? Was God trying to teach me something through this former Muslim preacher, now turned Christian evangelist? I thought so but I wasn't ready.

It was only later, much later, I regret to say, that I finally humbled myself before the Lord and asked Him to teach me how to work with Muslims. It was then that the extraordinary example of Chaudhry Inayatullah Mujahid came to mind.

Sweep away the misunderstandings by using the Quran; clear the rubble from the playing field so there can be a fair chance for our Muslim friends to actually hear the good news of our Lord Jesus Christ.

Chiniot on the banks of the Chenab River was a fishing town, the town where you go to get the best fish. I watched an expert fisherman catch men. But I was too proud to learn a new way—his way to fish.

That came later. Thank God for Chaudhry Inayatullah Mujahid who, in the end, finally taught me how to fish among Muslims: how to catch Muslims for Christ.

THE PIG
OF JESUS CHRIST

"Truth versus lies" is a battle that rages around us all the time. Behind it are two titanic personalities: Jesus Christ, who said, "I am the way, the truth and the life; no man comes to the Father, but through Me," and against Him, his sworn enemy, the Father of Lies, the Devil, the murderer, that great adversary, Satan.

Each is the head of a Kingdom: Jesus is the true King, who came to introduce the wonderful Kingdom of God. Satan is the usurper. He is called the Prince of this world. His Kingdom is one of unrelieved gloom. He can masquerade as an angel of light; but it is all a disguise.

Jesus' servants abide in Him; therefore, they abide in Truth. Satan also has his servants. They masquerade as servants of righteousness (2 Corinthians 11:15). But they shut the kingdom of heaven in men's faces (Matthew 23:13).

How do we do battle against those who masquerade as righteous people, but are really in the enemy camp?

Abdul Haqq[1] came to Christ out of Islam as a young man. Immediately, he had to struggle mightily against the attacks of his Muslim relatives, neighbors and eventually the greatest of the Muslim scholars of his day. He saw the issue between Christianity and Islam as a battle of Truth versus lies.

To prepare himself for this conflict, Abdul Haqq

learned Arabic and how to recite passages from the Quran by memory. But far more importantly, he became exceedingly well-versed in the Scriptures. He knew that, in the end, all attacks were on God and His Word. By diligent study and constant engagement with Muslims, he learned how to answer all Muslim efforts to destroy our faith in Jesus Christ as the Son of God and all efforts to discredit the Bible.

In time, Abdul Haqq grew to be the greatest of all the Christian debaters against Muslims in India and Pakistan. Coming against him was a constant stream of Muslim debaters who erroneously thought Allah was on their side and that they would be invincible. A very famous debater who called himself "The Lion of Islam" illustrates the conceit of these foolish Muslims.

In an effort to further amplify the message of the truth of Jesus Christ, Abdul Haqq began calling himself "The Pig of Jesus Christ." To orthodox Muslims, the pig is the most unclean of all animals. According to their law, you cannot eat it; you cannot even touch it, dead or alive. It represents the vilest of all the scum of the earth.

Because truth really was on his side, Abdul Haqq consistently won his debates with Muslim opponents. And it was especially galling to them to see their "Lions of Islam" defeated fair and square in public debate by "The Pig of Jesus Christ."

When he was in his seventies, Abdul Haqq was a guest in my home during a great Christian convention in Faisalabad,[2] Pakistan. As a young missionary, I was astonished to see the most esteemed *Muslim* scholars in our city pay homage to this man.

Dignified, white bearded *ulema*[3] came to my home, bowed down before him and touched their foreheads to his knee. In that culture, this was a sign of highest respect. It even indicated that you acknowledged this person as your guru (religious teacher). Over the course of several days, Abdul Haqq and I had many conversations about "Muslim work."

However, I will never forget that moment when this venerated, Christian man said to me, "Don, if I had to live my life over again, I never would have participated in all those debates; I would simply have preached Jesus Christ." The profound effect of that confession, coming from such an eminent person, has stuck with me to this present day.

As a result of this growing conviction, Abdul Haqq shifted his emphasis from debating to preaching the message of Christ. He became one of the most effective preachers of the simple message of Jesus Christ on the Indian subcontinent.

Even though his track record in debating with Muslims would easily qualify him for "The Hall of Fame" in his field, in the end, he came right back to where another brilliant scholar found himself under similar circumstances. The Apostle Paul wrote, "I resolved to know nothing while I was with you except Jesus Christ and Him crucified" (1 Corinthians 2:2).

"The Pig of Jesus Christ" laid aside his debating name and became a simple but highly effective preacher of the Lord Jesus Christ. What a lesson for a young missionary. Simply preach Jesus Christ.

1 His name literally means "Servant of Truth."
2 Formerly named Lyallpur.
3 Muslim scholars

MR. MOODY'S DINNER

The invitation was sent by hand. Mr. Moody's servant was standing there in the shade of the veranda, waiting for an answer. I talked with Mary Jo and the children. Yes, we could come. In fact, we were excited about the opportunity.

Mr. Moody was the most prestigious foreigner living in Faisalabad, a city of four hundred thousand people, in the heart of the Punjab. Everyone knew him. He was the manager of The Chartered Bank. But time was running out for him and his family. The colonial era had come to an end. Jobs like Mr. Moody's would be taken over by Pakistanis trained to fill them. The Moodys would soon be returning home to England to take up a new life among their own kind of people again.

The Moodys had been our neighbors from the time that we had moved from Sialkot to Faisalabad to begin our very first mission assignment after a year of intensive language learning. Like them, we had chosen to live in People's Colony, a new housing development populated with middle class Pakistani Muslim families. Our goal was to establish friendships among the Muslim people. No more mission compounds for us. We wanted to live in the midst of Muslim families.

As it turned out, the house we rented was just across the street from the Moody's. They had one son and so our children played with Ian during the vacation times. Of course, we banked at Mr. Moody's bank.

Even though we were both Westerners and spoke a common language (more or less), our paths seldom crossed except for business and things pertaining to our children. We had never eaten with them before, nor had they ever come to our home: our work was focused on reaching the Punjabi Muslim people.

So this invitation was unique. We felt honored to be invited to their home. And this would be a change of menu for us who normally ate Punjabi food. The Moodys' cook had been trained to prepare food the English way. And their waiter had been trained to serve in proper English style. We wondered what the food would be like and hoped our manners would be acceptable in this cultured home.

Before describing the meal, you need to know that Pakistani Muslims have certain taboos they observe about food and drink. For them, drinking wine in this life is forbidden, although in their version of paradise, they can drink unlimited quantities of wine and never get a headache! And the other "no-no" is eating any kind of pig meat.

In our family, we decided at the beginning of our career that we would observe these taboos as long as we worked among Muslims. Paul's teaching in his letter to the Romans molded our decision. In his day, the issue was meat offered to idols and the drinking that characterized their orgies. So although the issues were different, the principles are the same. Here is what Paul wrote:

> Do not destroy the work of God for the sake of food. All food is clean, but it is wrong for a man to eat anything that causes someone else[1] to stumble. It is better not to eat meat or drink wine or to do anything else

that will cause your brother[2] to fall[3] (Rom. 14:20, 21).

After a brief time of socializing with the Moodys in the sitting room, we were ushered into the dining room. Uh-oh. Wine glasses on the table with wine in them! And then the food was brought out. Pork! What should we do? Although we were free to do as we pleased, there were other considerations.

There, plastered against the window in the door between the kitchen and the dining room were two faces—Muslim faces—the cook and the server waiting to see what the new missionary family was going to do with the wine and the pork. Should we exercise our freedom and join the Moodys in their normal fare or abstain out of consideration for the people to whom God had sent us?

I said to Mr. Moody, "You know we are Christian missionaries. We have been sent here to work among the Muslims. And you know as well as I do that they are not allowed to drink wine or eat pork. Your Muslim servants are watching at the window in the door. What I do will make or break my reputation among the Muslims of this community. I hope you understand, we cannot drink this wine or eat this pork." His face saddened, but he said, "I understand." So we drank fruit juice instead of wine and extra veggies in place of ham.

A few days later, our Christian gardener said to Mary Jo, "Mem Sahiba,[4] all the people in the neighborhood are saying that you are a godly family. You don't drink wine and you don't eat pig meat." I wish that was all it took to qualify for godliness! Nevertheless, that is how the Muslim neighbors perceived us. Our reputation was made. Doors began to open. From that moment on we noticed that the neighbors became friendlier. Among them, Colonel Ramzan and his wife, Rashida, became good friends. We participated in a variety of social activities together, even picnics. During these times we had many opportunities to talk about the Lord.

Whoever would have thought that Mr. Moody's "pork and wine" dinner invitation would indirectly open for us the door of opportunity to share the Gospel among our Muslim neighbors there in People's Colony?

1 E.g., a Muslim.
2 Or a Muslim friend.
3 To fall away from listening to and accepting the Gospel.
4 "Respected Lady"

THE FOX IN THE CHICKEN COOP

Islam, like Christianity, has been cursed with innumerable sects. One that is worthy of mention is the Ahmadiyya sect. It was founded by a man named Mirza Ghulam Ahmad around 1889 in the town of Qadian, India.

The setting for the rise of this heresy was in British India. Muslims chafed under British rule, which began in 1857 and ended in 1947. Islam teaches its members that they are not to live under foreign rule—ever. They are to live only under the rule of Allah and his laws.

Shortly after the British takeover of India, a split developed in the Muslim community. Those who had been educated in British type schools and had come to terms with Western culture decided to accommodate to their rule and proceeded to alter Islam to fit the circumstances.

In reaction to this compromise, two other movements were born. The first was the founding of Deoband Seminary in 1858, which sought to bring Muslims back to orthodox Islam and resisted the British at every opportunity, eventually leading to the creation of Pakistan.

The second reaction was far more sophisticated. Mirza Ghulam Ahmad saw himself as a reforming prophet. His major reforms were: 1) the interpretation of *jihad* to mean peaceful preaching to make converts, not military war; 2) the law that called for the killing of a Muslim who turned to another faith was to be abolished; and 3) Islam was compatible with modern-day science.

Mirza Ghulam Ahmad also reacted to two more nettlesome problems: poorly educated *mullahs* were unable to answer Christian missionaries who questioned the Muslim faith and, similarly, the same *mullahs* were unable to stand up to the philosophical arguments of the Hindu *pundits*.

Ahmad intended to put a stop to all of this. In the case of the Christians, he "finished off Jesus" by teaching that He only appeared to die on the cross, was put in a tomb, revived from His swoon and migrated to Kashmir. He preached until He was 120 years old, then died and was buried in Kashmir.

Furthermore, in 1889, Ahmad claimed to be the returned Messiah of the Christians, and the returned *Mahdi* of the Muslims. To rebut the Hindu scholars, in 1893 he claimed to be the *Avatar*[1] of the Hindu God Krishna.

Ahmad and his followers were well acquainted with the problem passages in the Bible and became experts in debates with Christians, causing no end of troubles to Christians who neither knew the Bible very well, nor, much less, how to answer Muslim attacks on it.

After the founding of Pakistan in 1947, the Ahmadis moved their headquarters from Qadian, India, to Rabwah, Pakistan. That was when they fell under our sphere of activity.

Who would have thought of marching into their headquarters in Rabwah and taking them on? Not me. But my friend, Barkat A. Khan could not be deterred. He invited me to go with him. He went prepared. He had researched the Quran to show that their Muhammad could not be a prophet. And it was child's play to show from the Bible how he could not be the returned Messiah. I tagged along to learn from this valuable mentor.

When the Ahmadi leaders sensed my early inadequacy in Urdu, they suggested I visit their missionaries in training, the ones who spoke English. They were from England, Germany, Holland, Canada, Australia and the U.S. Their intent was to practice their deadly attacks on Christianity, using me as the guinea pig. What fun!

During the exchanges, one unsuspecting young man said something like, "Of course, you were born a Christian." That was the opening I was waiting for. I told him, "Not so," that I became a Christian when I was a 24-year-old student in medical school. Then I proceeded to give all the details of my testimony.

They were astonished. They had never heard anything like it. They were shaken and they did not know how to answer. Some wanted to hear more, but Barkat appeared and said it was time to go. I promised to come back. When I did, the authorities would not let me anywhere near their trainees. Once was enough for letting this Christian fox into their Muslim chicken coop.

Lessons learned? Barkat taught me boldness. Go into their nests. And I saw the power of giving one's testimony to the living Christ.

1 Reincarnation.

THIS MAN HAS
A DEMON

Pakistan is not only on the other side of the world, geographically, but, even more importantly, its cultural and religious life stand in direct contrast to our Western worldview.

In this tale, I would like to highlight one of those cultural differences: the problem of abnormal behavior. In the West, we have boundaries: we categorize that person as insane. We have labels for different forms of insanity: schizophrenia, manic-depressive, paranoia, etc.

Before attending seminary, I had studied to be a medical doctor. I learned that we can diagnose every illness and attempt a scientific solution to any problem. Abnormal behavior, therefore, is considered a medical problem. During my two years in medical school, I was trained in these areas. Nothing prepared me for what I saw in Pakistan.

It was unnerving to see the neglect of those mentally ill. Among the poor, it was a common sight to see a man or woman in a disheveled state, with unkempt hair, unwashed, wandering about the streets, muttering strange things.

The most unforgettable of all was a scene at the city bus depot in Faisalabad. A man, stark naked, covered with filth, with long matted hair, walked about, shouting and talking to himself. People avoided him at all costs. Occasionally, someone would leave food for him. But no one really knew what to do. We Westerners labeled him as deranged. The local Pakistanis attributed his behavior to *jinn*.[1] All of this is by way of comment for the tale that follows. But before I can tell it, there is another important piece of information you need to know.

During my pastorate in Colorado Springs, Colorado, before going to Pakistan, I was trained by Lorne Sanny, then the vice-president of the Navigators. I learned how to train counselors and arrange for the follow-up of those who responded to the invitation during an evangelistic crusade. When Dr. T. W. Wilson, a Billy Graham associate evangelist, came to Colorado Springs, I was the one who trained the counselors and arranged for the follow-up of those who came forward.

I never dreamed that these skills would be put to use so soon after arriving in Pakistan. A dear friend, Ian North, was in charge of arrangements for the Dr. Akbar Haqq "Life in Christ" gospel team crusades which came to Pakistan. Ian requested our mission to release me to do the counselor training for these crusades in Lahore, Rawalpindi and Faisalabad. After much controversy, due to my limited language skills at that point in time, the mission granted permission.

Everything proceeded smoothly in Lahore and Rawalpindi. It was in my hometown of Faisalabad that we got a shock. Right in the middle of Dr. Haqq's first message, a young man came screaming down the aisle and then collapsed at the foot of the platform. Not knowing what to do, I picked him up, carried him into a counseling tent and called for a doctor.[2] The doctor could find nothing wrong with him. Nor could he explain why the young man remained unconscious.

Dr. Haqq proceeded unperturbed, finished his message, saw many respond to his invitation, and then gave a short after-speech to those who came forward. In the mean-time, we had carried the unconscious young man into the mission house just a few yards away, in order not to distract those who came for counseling.

When Dr. Haqq was free, he came into the mission house, saw the unconscious young man stretched out on a couch and said, "Don, come on over here. This man has a demon and we are going to cast the demon out."

In the seminary I had attended in the States, I re-ceived no instruction in this area. In fact, it was more or less implied that these things didn't really exist: in Jesus' day this was the only way to explain mental illness. But here was Dr. Haqq, a Ph.D. in psychology from the University of Min-nesota, who believed this man had a demon. What was I to do?

I joined Dr. Haqq. In a stern voice he commanded the demons to come out. The young man became semi-con-scious and began to speak with strange voices. One by one, Dr. Haqq commanded each demon to identify himself. Then in Jesus' name he commanded each one to leave. Finally, there were no demons left. The man came into his right mind. We carefully explained the Gospel to him and he duly repented and professed Christ as his Lord and Savior.

As a medically trained person, still being a little skep-tical, I took his case history and even verified it with his friends. What he said was true: he had gone down the road of alcohol, immorality, drugs and, finally, dabbled in the oc-cult. He had fallen prey to demons.

Dr. Haqq, born in Sialkot, not far from Faisalabad, grew up in this Indo-Pak, non-Western, non-secular culture. Bible truths in the area of spiritual warfare were self-evident. They could not be explained away by secular humanists because—well, because they are true.

Thank you, Dr. Haqq, for helping me to recover a Biblical worldview, for helping me see that the Bible and Jesus got it right. You opened my eyes to the other spirit world and to the power and authority of Jesus to operate in it.

---

1 A Quranic category of wicked spirit who causes much evil.
2 Remember, I am a Westerner where everything is a *medical* problem.

ARE YOU TRYING TO CONVERT ME?

Mary Jo and I had finished our first year of language study and were well into our second. We were waiting in Sialkot for our fifth child, our daughter, Ruth, to be born. After that event, and making sure mom and daughter were okay, we would take up our first assignment in the city of Lyallpur.

We had been living in a huge mission compound for a year and a half. That was enough to tell us we never wanted to live like that again. We asked our colleagues, already working in Lyallpur, Joe and Marjory Altar, to begin searching for a modest-sized house for us in People's Colony. The neighbors would all be Muslims, of course. After all, they were the people we needed to reach with the good news of Jesus Christ.

In due course, the day came for us to meet our new landlord there in Faisalabad, Colonel Mahmud Ramzan. He turned out to be one of the friendliest Muslims I have ever known. Well-educated, he spoke excellent English. Surprisingly, his wife did too. She was what you might call a liberated Muslim woman. She wore a colorful head covering, called a *doputta*, but made no effort to veil her face.

A great friendship grew out of this landlord-renter relationship. We often met socially and had tea together. On those occasions, we chatted about everything under the sun. Naturally, they were curious about our work. We had no qualms in talking to them about the rural schools we built and managed for Christian boys and girls and about the work going on among the illiterate Christians living in the rural areas.

Part of my assignment was to work among the university and college students in the city. I chose badminton as my way to break into those circles. With Colonel Ramzan's permission, we built a playing court in our backyard. By God's grace, I became good enough to beat about half of the best players in town. And that put me into the circles where I wanted to be. I was called upon to play and even to referee.

There were always tea parties after the games. From there it was only a short step to be invited to the poetical symposiums. Later I was asked to become a judge in their English debates. More and more doors were opening to me. Through these contacts, the Lord gave me grace and favor to introduce Moody Science films into the university and two colleges in town. These films were distinctly Christian.

Yes, Colonel Ramzan wanted to know all about these developments too. We were quite open about everything we did. On one occasion, he and his wife invited us to accompany them on a delightful outing to the famous *Hiran Minaar* (Deer Tower), which a great Mogul emperor had built in memory of his favorite deer. It was a wonderful picnic spot by a stunningly beautiful man-made lake with a causeway leading to an enchanting, airy gazebo in its midst.

From time to time, religious subjects did come up: things they believed as Muslims; things we believed as Christians. But they were always handled delicately and politely on both sides. After all, we were their renters and we did not want to step over a line of impropriety and cause undue offense.

In the meantime, from other sources we were gradually learning what Islam really was all about. Let me share some of their ways of thinking about Christians and about themselves as Muslims.

Islam teaches that *Allah*[1] revealed the final form of religion to Muhammad. Implied in this is that Jews and Christians had failed in their times to live the way God had ordained. Muhammad was sent to bring all mankind back to the true religion of Abraham. Islam was sent to replace the failed religions of Judaism and Christianity.

Because Muhammad taught that the unpardonable sin was to associate anyone else with *Allah*,[2] Muslims understand that anyone who believes this way is going to hell. Therefore, for a Muslim to convert to Christ is to choose hell and for a Christian to try to win a Muslim to Christ is perceived as an effort to send the Muslim to hell!

Now you can see why Islam teaches that Christians (and Jews) are to be subdued and not allowed to proselytize Muslims. In other words, these two religions are to be contained and, if possible, every effort should be made to convert Jews and Christians to Islam—to save them!

The above is necessary background information for what happened later at the famous Sialkot Convention, an annual event, first started in 1904 by a Presbyterian missionary named John Hyde ("Praying Hyde").

Out of curiosity, Colonel Ramzan accepted our invitation to attend this convention. Between three and five thousand people might attend, including many Muslims He was amazed to see this, especially the Muslims who attended.

Following one of the fervent evangelistic messages, Colonel Ramzan sought me out and began to ask a lot of direct questions. Things were now out in the open. Finally he asked, "You are not trying to convert me, are you?"

Risking all, I replied: "Colonel Ramzan, I do not exist for any other reason than to hold forth to you the Word of Life, whereby you may be saved from your sins through the atoning death of Jesus Christ on the cross."

Dear Reader, there is no way to avoid the Colonel's question. How and when it comes is always fascinating, but in the end, every servant of Christ will have to give an answer, "For Christ's love compels us..." (2 Cor. 5:14).

1 Their word for God.
2 Christians do this by calling Jesus the Son of God and also by saying that God is a trinity of Father, Son and Spirit.

LORD, TEACH ME

The problem with asking the Lord to teach you something is that He thinks you mean it. In His own way and in His time, He then teaches you. These lessons usually come with pain. This one happened in our wonderful mission hospital in Taxila, Pakistan.

Curiously, the story starts in another of our great hospitals in Sialkot. I was laying flat on my back with a bad case of hepatitis. It was near the end of our first four and a half year term in Pakistan. There was lots of time to think. What had I learned? What had I done? What did I have to show for this first term in Pakistan?

I thought about our primary goal, as I understood it then. Pakistan was a land that was about 97% Muslim. Leaving aside all the ministries in and to the existing church, how well had I done in terms of seeing Muslims come to Christ? A big fat zero! Nominal Christians born again and discipled? Some. Muslims? None!

As I lay there in that hospital bed, I writhed with a different kind of pain. I had failed to see a single Muslim come to Christ through my ministry. I talked to God about it, "O Lord, would you give me a second chance? Would you teach me how to work with Muslims?" He took me seriously. He began to teach me. In fact, He is still teaching me. Most of the lessons are painful.

Let me share one of them that has to do with attitude. Because of my modest ability in the Urdu language and my love for the Word of God and the gift of being able to teach it, I was invited to give a week of devotional talks to the staff of our Christian hospital in Taxila. The expositions were based on the book of Ephesians. Things went well until the last day. We had reached chapter 6, verse 12: "For our struggle is not against flesh and blood, but against the rulers, against the authorities, against the powers of this dark world and against the spiritual forces of evil in the heavenly realms."

I made the mistake of saying to my Pakistani audience, "You know the first day I set foot on Pakistani soil, I felt satanic oppression in this country." As soon as the words were out of my mouth, I lost my audience. I might as well have sat down right then and there. No one was listening after that, just murmuring among themselves.

When I finally finished, the senior superintendent of Nurses, Sister Makhzan, charged up to me and said, "Mister McCurry, you have no right to speak that way to us. We think you have come from the most satanic country on the face of the earth!"

Then she began: "We don't know of any country so depraved that it abandons its youth to come and die on our doorsteps at the end of the hippie drug trail, like America. We don't know of any country with a higher per capita crime rate than America. It is safer for your wife to walk the streets of Pakistan at midnight than it is for our men to walk in your cities at noontime. We don't know of any more hypocritical country that preaches democracy and yet has failed to solve its race problem. We don't know of any country with a higher standard of living and yet still has twenty percent of its people living below the poverty level. We don't know of any country so evil that it exports films of violence and pornog-

raphy, like America. We think you come from the most satanic country on the face of the earth."

I was stunned. Then angered. I *wanted* to say, "Nyaa,
nyaa, nyaa, if we're so evil, why does everyone want to come
to America?" But I didn't. Slowly a sense of burning shame
overcame me. I realized what I had done. In my blindness, I
had swept all the elements of the demonic in American society under the rug of my mind and could only see the evil in a
Muslim society.

My blunder was a classic illustration of what anthro-
pologists call "ethnocentrism." In the Bible, it is called
"pride." And even worse, it is gross hypocrisy. Quite unconsciously, I had ignored the sin of my own people while pointing the finger at the sins of Pakistani people. I had forgotten
that the Bible says, "All have sinned and fall short of the glory
of God" (Rom. 3:23).

I had asked God to teach me. He used the stinging
words of this courageous Pakistani sister: "You come from the
most satanic country on the face of the earth." That may or
may not be true. Does it matter? The Scripture says: "The
whole world is under the control of the evil one" (1 Jn. 5:19).
I had to get rid of my own ethnocentrism and spiritual pride,
whether working with Pakistani Christians or Muslims.

It was painful to acknowledge this. But it led to a
sense of brokenness and contrition—even a Godly sorrow—
for all of us are participants in the "fall." It led to a sense of
humility in preaching and teaching. We do not preach ourselves. We do not preach our country. We preach Christ crucified. That message indicts us all. But it is also the basis for
the saving of us all. Thank you, Miss Makhzan, for leveling
with me. Thank you, Heavenly Father, for using her to teach
me.

SONGS OF ZION

What is it like living in the most ideological Islamic country in the whole world? Pakistan has no other reason to exist as a nation except for Islam. You see, it was carved out of British India in 1947 as a place specifically for Muslims.

The answer to the opening question above is two-fold. The common people are normally friendly. In one-on-one situations, they are hospitable and exhibit all the virtues of good people anywhere. You can live among them as a friend. And we did so for almost twenty years.

Ah, but there is another kind of Pakistani, the ideologue. This person takes Islam seriously. And he or she bears the burden for Muslim issues all over the world. It's as though Pakistan is the "Muslim rights watch" country of the world.

This makes things tough for Christians. Even though we are to be tolerated as a protected minority, as the "People of the Book," we become the whipping boy for Muslim anger over all the bad things that happen to Muslims, whether they are in Sudan, Nigeria, Indonesia, Malaysia, Afghanistan, Chechnya or Kosovo.

By far the most sensitive of all of these issues is the Palestinian one. A former president of Pakistan, Muhammad Ayoub Khan, said, "The creation of the State of Israel is the greatest crime ever committed against humanity." Zionism, therefore, is seen as the fountain and perpetrator of the world's most wicked atrocities. Some Pakistanis feel they must deal with this great injustice, that is, taking Muslim land and giving it to Jews. Let me illustrate.

On a certain occasion, I struck up an acquaintance with an intelligence officer who knew I taught in the Gujranwala Theological Seminary. He asked, "What do you teach?" I listed the subjects I taught, including "Hebrew." This electrified him. He then tried every way under the sun to get me to teach him Hebrew. When I asked what his reason was, he unabashedly said, "To go to Palestine and fight the Zionists!"

This is all background material for what comes later in this tale. To get to that, I need to mention that almost every summer in Pakistan, I was involved in some kind of youth camp work up in the glorious mountains of that land. This particular summer I was functioning as the acting head of Campus Crusade for Christ. The Pakistani leader had resigned. As the Senior Board Advisor, I was asked to "carry" Crusade until they could train another leader at their base in the Philippines.

In preparing for the summer camps, one of the things I had done was to establish connections with the Campus Crusade leader in Iran. Mary Jo and I had visited him in Tehran on our way back to Pakistan from our recent furlough. During our visit, he showed us training materials he had developed on the formation of cell groups.

So back in Pakistan, when I invited him to come and teach in our camp, I sent a telegram asking him to be sure to bring his material on forming cell groups. I was young and naïve then. My "innocent" telegram caught the eyes of the secret police.

From that time on, I had a shadow that followed me everywhere. He always kept his distance. After a few days it began to bother me. I would stop to see if he would pass by. No. He stopped, too. I would take a circular route. So would he.

One day, I just couldn't stand it anymore. I stopped. He stopped. He was sitting on the railing of a little bridge near our house in Sunnybank. I went up to him and asked, "Can I help you in any way? Do you have any questions you would like to ask me? Look, my house is very near. Why don't you come and have a cup of tea with us?" He accepted! His name was Shauqat.

Mary Jo prepared tea. We talked about my telegram and what it was all about. Things went very well—until he looked at my bookcase there by his chair. Standing out like a sore thumb was a book with a black cover and gold print. It said in beautiful Urdu calligraphy, *Siun kay Geet*, "Songs of Zion." He saw it. Uh-oh. Trouble.

"Oh, you're a Zionist," he said. I broke out in a cold sweat. "No! I'm not. 'Zion' is a word that has many meanings," I blurted out. Instinctively, I reached for Webster's Collegiate Dictionary, not knowing what I would find. There it was. Meaning number five: "'Zion' refers to heaven." We then talked about heavenly things and end times with Jesus coming back.[1] He received my witness. He was satisfied with my explanations. I was not a political danger to Pakistan, just an overly spiritual Christian.

Many times I have thought about this episode. It all started with an innocent telegram. Because religion and politics are one and the same in Islam, "cell groups" had political implications for the Pakistan government. It led to surveillance and an interview with an intelligence officer in my own home.

There in our sitting room, *Songs of Zion* became an issue. "Zion" is another politically loaded word for Muslims. I thank God Shauqat raised the issue of Zionism. That in turn led to a wonderful discussion on deep spiritual, not political, truths: heaven, how we get there and the return of Jesus.

Much good came out of this encounter for both Shauqat and me. It taught me how careful we must be in our choice of words in politically sensitive Pakistan. *Songs of Zion* may carry precious meaning for the Christian, but why risk the danger of using those words in the super-charged atmosphere of Pakistan?[2] Thank you, Shauqat, for teaching me to be careful with words. Thank you, Father, for the opportunity to witness.

---

1 Something Muslims believe because it is mentioned in the Quran.
2 All surveillance stopped after that interview.

IN POETRY AND SONG

From somewhere in the room, a musically well-trained Pakistani voice was singing a beautiful Indian *raga*. I followed the voice. There behind the desk, seated on a small Persian rug, was my esteemed professor, Dr. Daud Rahbar, a Cambridge University graduate and a renowned scholar and author. Beside him there on the floor was an electric strumming instrument, tuned to sound like an Indian *sitar*, strumming away. He was sitting cross-legged in front of a pair of *tabla*, the "male and female" Indian drums. His head was cocked upwards as if listening to some heavenly strain. Out of his mouth was flowing this mesmerizing Indian music.

Seeing my look of shocked surprise, he chuckled and said in his whimsical way, "The fool you see seated here on the floor playing the *tabla* is more real than the stuffed shirt you see trying to teach you from behind the podium."

This was only one of the many delightful experiences along the way as I worked on a Master's degree in Urdu Literature under this gifted teacher. He led me through a study of the great Persian masters: Firdawsi, Amir Khusrao, Hafiz, Sheikh Saadi and Omar Khayyam. Then we plunged into Urdu poetry. We studied the poems of Vali, Mir, Dard, Sauda, Insha, Ghalib, Atish, Zauq, Momin, Anis and Dagh. These names may mean nothing to you, but for me they opened up the vast riches of the cultural heritage of the Muslims of Pakistan and India.

Studying with Dr. Rahbar had come about because of what I had experienced during my first term as a missionary in Pakistan. For four and a half years I had wrestled with Muslim theologians over the main theological issues that divide Islam from Christianity. I knew I needed to gain a knowledge and appreciation for many other aspects of Pakistani life and culture.

Therefore, as we returned to the States on furlough, I had asked God to arrange for me to study with a Pakistani Muslim convert Ph.D. in the area of Urdu Literature. There was only one: Dr. Daud Rahbar of the Kennedy School of Missions at the Hartford Seminary Foundation. God answered my prayer and allowed me to study with him.

Studying Urdu literature under his supervision turned out to be one of the most pleasurable and profitable periods of my missionary career. Later, it enabled me to move comfortably among the poets and prose writers of Pakistan, some of whom became my friends.

Among all the valuable insights that he shared, there was one that stood out from all the others. I don't know if Dr. Rahbar understood what a bombshell of an idea this was for a missionary. This is what he said, "Don, you can say anything you want to a Muslim in poetry or music and he will receive it; but if you preach it in prose, he will probably try to kill you."

After returning to Pakistan, I put it to the test. I had been chosen to be Summer Pastor for the mission community in Murree. After gaining the promise of support from musically talented missionaries, I went to the mayor of the city and asked permission to stage an International Music Festival. He allowed us to take over an abandoned roller skating rink. We presented a program of folkloric and religious music from thirteen countries. Embedded in the middle of this two-and-a-quarter-hour program was the best Pakistani Christian singing ensemble in the country. Their message was thoroughly biblical and pointed to Jesus Christ as Lord and Savior. The audience really heard the Gospel.

When the curtain closed, every Muslim in the audience was on his or her feet, heartily applauding. The mayor made a little speech. He said, "This is the greatest social event that has ever been staged here in Murree. We hope you who are guests in our country will come back and do this every year." I couldn't believe what had happened. Our Muslim friends had swallowed the whole Gospel in music.

Dr. Rahbar knew what most missionaries never learn. Muhammad, the founder of Islam, had forbidden the use of music in the mosque. He had associated music with prostitutes and dancing girls. As a result, Muslims are starved for music.

By experience, Dr. Rahbar had learned that music and poetry were open doorways to the Muslim heart. This is a lesson for which I am eternally grateful. I have taught it to generations of missionary candidates. In ministering to Muslims, poetry and music are our most powerful communication tools. Thank God for the gifts of poetry and music.

LET'S GO TO A MOSQUE TODAY

The suggestion hit me like a thunderbolt. What? Go to a mosque? Don't Muslims kill Christians who try to enter their mosques?

I stared at this Pakistani brother who had just spoken these words. What was I to do? I was supposed to be the brave missionary hero, the creative one who thought up all these daring incursions into Islam. And here was this simple, loving, courageous first-grade schoolteacher proposing we go to a mosque.

I resigned myself to my fate. I could not be out-couraged or out-loved by my Pakistani friend. I said, "Okay." But before setting out, I excused myself, took my wife into our bedroom, shut the door and said, "Honey, I may never see you again. Master Barkat A. Khan is asking me to go to a mosque with him today. How can I say no? Call our friends together. Get them to pray for us. And I hope I see you again."

As we were walking down the dusty bazaar road to the picturesque mosque there on the bank of the Jhelum River, I thought about this unusual man. He was only a first-grade school teacher, poor, with lots of children, godly and totally sold out to the Lord. He had taught himself Arabic, the religious language of the Muslims. He developed tracts based on Arabic texts of the Quran and then explained them in the light of the real Word of God. He gave all of his free time to evangelizing Muslims.

Outside the mosque, we took off our shoes since Muslims always take off their shoes and go through ritual washings of feet, hands and face before entering. Up front, we saw a thin line of Muslim *maulvis* (learned men) praying. We sat on the reed mats at the back of the prayer chamber and prayed for them while they prayed their obligatory memorized prayers in Arabic.[1]

When they had finished praying, we went forward to introduce ourselves. Seeing me, their first question was, "Are you Muslims?" I replied that we were those who had submitted ourselves to God,[2] but that we followed the way of *Isa* (the Quranic name for Jesus). They asked, "Why are you here? There is a Christian church in town."[3] We replied that we had a question.

Our question was, "How do you know God in Islam?" They were stunned. You see, they were orthodox Sunni[4] Muslims. They replied, "No one can know Allah. He is high and transcendent, far away, unknowable. He is not like us. No one can know Allah."

We asked, "Would you like to know how we know God?" When they said yes, we each gave our personal testimony. Afterwards, we asked, "Have you ever heard anything like that before?" They said, "No." Then we asked, "Have you ever read the Bible?" They said they had never even seen a Bible.

We pulled out Bibles from our shoulder bags and opened them to the first chapter of the Gospel of John, which talks about Jesus being the Word of God. And that is one of Jesus' names in the Quran, *kalamatullah*, a Word from God. They eagerly began to read for themselves.

At that point, we felt our mission was accomplished. We had put the Word of God into their hands and we left them reading it for themselves. After asking permission to leave (you never leave without asking permission in Punjabi culture), we walked out the door. Looking back, we saw these Muslim scholars reading the real Word of God for the first time in their lives.

Down through the years, from time to time, I have entered mosques to sit with Muslims, opened their Qurans to the Jesus passages, gotten them thinking new questions and left the real Word of God, the Bible, with them. My teacher, Master Barkat A. Khan, a simple, devout first-grade schoolteacher, showed me the way. His example of loving boldness lives with me to this day. He taught me to love Muslims and not be afraid.

1 Their mother tongue was Punjabi; their acquired national language was Urdu.
   For prayers to be valid, they had to be prayed in Arabic.
2 "Muslim" means "one who has submitted."
3 Only 250 Christians lived in this city of 43,000 Muslims.
4 Sunnis follow the example [*Sunnah*] of Muhammad.

TREASURE MY COMMANDMENTS

Tales That Teach was initially begun as a way to honor men and women in the host country where the Lord sent us to work. For us, this was Pakistan. So often, it was the nationals who were our best mentors. In some cases, what we learned from them meant we had to unlearn bad habits, attitudes and ways of thinking that we brought with us.

This tale has to do with how we treat the Bible. Even though we believe that all of it was written by men under the inspiration of the Holy Spirit, in the end, it is *physically* just a printed book, right? We could handle it as any other book, put it on a shelf, lay it on the floor or anyplace else. It wasn't what you did with the printed book that mattered; it was what you did about what was in the book. That's what we were taught.

It would not be uncommon to see Bibles with writing in the margins, underlining, and even various notes and peoples' addresses written inside the covers for convenience's sake. I have even seen Bibles with mutilated pages and the covers torn off and piled haphazardly in some corner of a room for youth meetings.[1]

Whether I learned the action that I am about to tell you from someone else or invented it myself, I cannot recall. But this is what happened. In a youth meeting in America, while illustrating the theme of an old time hymn, "Standing on the Promises," I actually put my Bible on the floor and stood on it. There was no shocked outcry, but rather a sense of amusement at the zeal of this youth leader trying to dramatize a point.

All of the above constitutes the baggage that your missionary takes with him to the mission field, for us, the Muslim country of Pakistan. There, in due course, I was appointed the Youth Secretary for our denomination of 250 churches.

Having learned very little of the local culture, in a youth meeting at our church in Sargodha, I reenacted the standing-on-the-Bible scenario. The explosion of protests, the disruption of the meeting, young men rushing forward to remove me from standing on the Bible and then carefully dusting off the Bible, left a lasting, burningly embarrassing memory in my mind.

One would have thought that with that wake-up call I would have begun to take note of cultural clues. But I was a slow learner and, worse, a little resentful of having my value system challenged by people of another culture.

The clues were all there. Visiting in Muslim homes, I observed that they handled their Quran with great respect, always wrapping it in protective cloth, placing it on the highest shelf in the room and even washing their hands before using it. This respect carried over even when they were traveling. The Quran would be put in the highest place in the bus or train and nothing would ever be put on top of it.

Christians, on the other hand, were divided over this issue. There were those who treated the Bible with the same respect Muslims showed for the Quran. On the other hand, there were those who were influenced by the casual attitudes of the missionaries.

Being a begrudging learner, I finally got around to wrapping my Bible in a clean cloth and carrying it in a shoulder bag. The bicycle posed a problem. In those days, bikes traditionally had a luggage rack behind the seat and a basket up front on the handle bars. My habit was to put my shoulder bag on the luggage rack behind my seat.

This came to a dramatic halt one day as I was pedaling down the main street of Jhelum on my way to preach and teach in a nearby village church. I had not gone very far when out from one of the shops, a tall, dignified, white-haired, white-bearded Muslim *maulvi* came out into the middle of the street and stopped me. Without a word, he untied my book bag from the luggage rack behind my seat and respectfully put it in the basket at the front of my bike. Then he spoke, "Don't you ever do that again!" In his eyes, I had dishonored the Word of God by placing it behind me and beneath my bottom.

Wow! This from a Muslim who respected the Word of God more than I did! And I might add that he, in all sincerity, revered and obeyed the teaching of his book, the Quran, with a loyalty that put me to shame. He literally treasured God's commands, both in real-life obedience and in reverence for the book, the Quran, which was for him the Word of God.

That rebuke was life-changing. In Proverbs 7:1, we read, "Treasure my commandments" (ESV). We can do this in two ways: obedience to the teaching, but also in the way we handle the Bible, the book that contains the inspired, written Word.

1 These are all unthinkable sacrileges in the Muslim world.

STARS SHINING IN THE NIGHT

The Pakistani night air was bitter cold. The stars shone bright and clear. Acrid smoke from burning dung cakes lingered in the air. Supper was over. Punjabi mothers were tucking their sleepy children into bed.

We had cycled to the edge of the city where the Christians lived. Propping our bikes against the adobe wall, we knocked on Ghulam Masih's rickety door. He was expecting us. Several of his Christian neighbors had also crowded into his small courtyard. Ghulam's wife, Taj Bibi, boiled up *desi chai* (tea) in a cheap aluminum pan and stirred in the milk and sugar. We drank gratefully from the clay bowls and ate the plain cookies embedded with caraway seeds. This was the standard hospitality of the poor.

Because the sleeping children occupied the single room that constituted their "house," we sat on reed mats in the courtyard. A kerosene-fueled petromax lamp was lit. The amount of heat it emitted was pitifully small in the pervasive and growing cold. We wrapped our large shawls more snugly around our heads and shoulders.

The conversation of the poor is exceedingly simple, their chitchat so painfully limited. There seemed to be no interest at all in the outside world. The neighbors' ubiquitous transistor radios belted out the latest film songs. Not much else.

It drove me nuts. During such visits I often thought about the chasm that separated us. We were highly educated American missionaries. They were illiterate Punjabi Christians. It seemed that each year of our study just pushed us up one level "higher" from where they were. On that particular night, I even asked myself, "What am I doing here?"

Then the worship began. Out came the harmonium whose accordion-like bellows one rhythmically squeezed with the left hand while playing the keyboard with the right. The tabla-player began to drum out the rhythm. These friends may have been illiterate and poor, but they were loaded with talent. How they could sing!

"*Mubarak ha vo admi...*" "Blessed is the man..." They sang all of Psalm 1 about the blessings of those who cherish God's Word versus the judgment on the evildoers. Next, "*Mubarak ha vo jiski khata bukhshi gai...*" (Ps. 32), "Blessed is the one whose sins are forgiven..." Then "*Ay ahle Zameen! Sub Khudavand kay hazoor may khushi ka nara maro...*" (Ps. 100), "O people of the earth! All of you make a shout of joy in the presence of the Lord..."

As they sang, you could tell they were "into it," heart and soul. We were caught up in the Spirit too. As God began to move on my heart, He brought a certain Scripture passage to mind:

God chose the foolish things of the world to shame the wise; God chose the weak things of the world to shame the strong. He chose the lowly things of this world and the despised things—and the things that are not—to nullify the things that are, so that no one may boast before Him" (I Cor. 1:27-29).

We were seated among the "foolish," the "weak," the "lowly" and the "despised." But they were the chosen of God!

Where was my education now? With regard to God, it was totally nullified! God would not allow anyone to boast in His presence. That fabulous education counted for nothing. The "wise" and the "strong" were put to shame.

Then the Bible study began. Ever so much care was taken to make sure each word was clearly understood. The memory work followed. The same glow that was on their faces as they worshipped the Lord returned with the mastery of their work. The Word of God was now living in their hearts and ready on their tongues. God's Spirit could now use His sword, whether against temptation, or for building up his saints, or witnessing to the lost.

As I saw the transforming power of God at work in these people who were "nothing," He formed a new question in my mind—in the mind of this person who was supposed to be "something." "Don, can you think of any place else you would rather be tonight?"

That starry winter night my bones ached from the hours of sitting on the cold ground. My leg muscles were beyond feeling, too stiff to move. I turned the question over in my mind, "Where would I rather be tonight?" I couldn't think of any place else in the whole world where I would rather be. "No, Lord. This is where I want to be tonight."

I was seated among the redeemed at the very cutting edge of the Kingdom. These were God's "stars shining in the universe" (Phil. 2:15). These were the "stars" that God showed Abraham long ago (Gen. 15:5). I looked again at the sparkling night sky and then at the radiant faces all about me. The heavenly stars were only a metaphor. These precious people were God's real stars, stars shining in the night, shining there in that darkened world of Pakistan.

YOU WILL HAVE TO KILL ME FIRST

The "all clear" had sounded. The noise of enemy planes had long since faded away. Pakistan was at war with India. The tension had been building for months. Finally it began.

It was about Kashmir. In 1947 the Indian Hindu ruler of Kashmir decided all by himself that he wanted to cede Kashmir to India. The problem was that Kashmir was 60% Muslim. And the Muslims wanted either to be free or join with Pakistan. Three wars had already been fought over this controversial "Switzerland" of the Indian subcontinent.

The events below happened during the second of these wars. They occurred in the picturesque bazaar of Jhika Gali, a bus-stop village stretching across the saddle of land connecting two seven-thousand-foot mountain ranges.

Less than a mile away was the missionary children's school. Up on the hill overlooking the bazaar were several missionary bungalows. This is where we came during our vacations to get relief from the intolerable heat (110° F) of the plains. It was also where families were reunited as the children came out of boarding school and lived at home with their parents.

From the very beginning of Pakistan's history, missionaries had been trading in this ramshackle cluster of tea houses, vegetable stands, fruit stalls, dry goods displays, hardware supplies, eateries, candy stores and a barber shop. Everyone knew one another by name.

My favorite was Misri Khan, the vegetable seller. I always loved to see the variety of vegetables that came in off the small terraced plots of land nearby. Misri Khan often invited me to sit and talk with him. You could always count on him to order delicious mixed tea boiled up with milk and sugar. We talked about everything under the sun. It was a good way to practice my Urdu and Punjabi.

Our family used to pray for him and others working there in those life-sustaining shops. Eventually I got my nerve up to share with him my own testimony, my own experiences of coming to know God in Christ. He listened with great respect. He even took Gospel portions on those occasions when I offered them.

Sometimes we were short of money. He didn't mind. He said, "Pay me when you can." He said, "We know you people. You are a good people. You are an honest people. You help us when we are sick, too."[1] There was tremendous trust between these shopkeepers and the mission community.

Coming back to Pakistan after a long furlough necessitated by visa problems, Misri Khan saw me walking in from Murree, the main town two miles away. He rushed into the street, embraced me with great gusto, danced me around the middle of the road and then swept me into one of the teahouses. He wanted to know about every member of my family. Naturally, I had to know all about his family, too. What a warm and affectionate reunion.

The night of the air raid, a rumor had spread in the villages where we were not so well known that missionaries had opened their doors and signaled the Indian airplanes as to where the strategic road to Kashmir was. We heard the commotion in the bazaar. Angry voices. Blazing torches. Even the glint of foreboding weapons. This was a very stirred-up, angry mob. They had come to burn the missionary houses and kill the missionaries.

It was Misri Khan who stopped them. He barred the way with his own body. He said, "These friends would never do what you think they did. This rumor is not true." Still there were outbursts of angry voices. It looked like they would carry out their furious intent. Finally, Misri Khan, raising his voice above the noise of the crowd, shouted, "You will have to kill me first." This stunned everyone into silence. He again vouched with his life for the missionaries. Because of his stature in the bazaar, his words carried the day. Slowly the mob dispersed. The hubbub subsided. The crisis was over.

Misri Khan was a Muslim. I've never gotten over it. He, a Muslim, was ready to give his life for me, for us, the Christians. I had to examine my own heart many times and ask myself, "Am I ready to give my life for my Muslim friends? Would I give my life for Misri Khan?" I had no choice. Yes, I would. Misri Khan, my Muslim friend, taught me the meaning of courage and of loving one's friends, even to the point of death.

Jesus said, "Greater love has no has no one than this, that he lay down his life for his friends." (John 15:13)

1 Tuberculosis was endemic in their smoke-filled mud houses clinging to those
  steep hillsides.

I DARED TO CALL HIM FATHER

Begum Bilqis Sheikh had been a powerful woman in President Muhammad Ayoub Khan's regime. Because the president's wife was uneducated, Bilqis, the wife of General K.M. Sheikh, the Minister of Interior, was called upon to act as the official government hostess.

Bilqis was not a religious woman. She mixed socially in diplomatic circles with all kinds, but especially Westerners. From them she picked up their ways, one of which was alcohol. It was her undoing. As aging took its toll and her husband's attention was focused on younger, more attractive women, alcohol took over. General Sheikh eventually divorced Bilqis and married a beautiful young wife.

Bilqis was devastated. Her alcoholism grew worse. Her family, being of considerable means, shipped her off to London for a "cure." When she came back to Pakistan, she turned to religion—to Islam.

But the Quran did not make sense. To her it was an incoherent jumble of ecstatic utterances by a seventh-century Arab would-be "prophet." In desperation, she began to cry out to Allah, her unknowable God.

Then something happened. She had a powerful night vision. In it she saw a man dressed in animal skins standing at a fork in the road, pointing down one direction. She sat bolt upright in bed and found herself saying over and over again, "John the Baptist." That was all.

Still puzzled by the vision, early the next morning, she went over to the home of some missionaries who were renting one of her cottages. Her first words were, "Synnove, who was John the Baptist?" Much to her surprise, the first words out of Synnove's mouth were, "John the Baptist was the prophet who said, 'After me is coming one greater than me who will baptize you with the Holy Spirit.'"

Synnove invited her in for morning tea, of course. After hearing her tell about her dream, Synnove gave her the *J.B. Phillips New Testament.*

After her baptism, the predictable family ruckus, and privately sharing her testimony with her old friend, President Ayoub Khan, she decided to reside in Murree where I happened to be the summer pastor. She invited me to come every morning to teach.

Her New Testament was well worn. There was hardly a line that had not been underlined in one color or another. She devoured it day and night. In truth, I was not her teacher, she was mine.

How can I forget those mornings when the Word of God would pierce her heart? She would fall to her knees completely oblivious of me and cry out to God either in words of praise and adoration or pleadings for forgiveness. She went straight into the presence of God, carrying me right along with her.

Gradually, I learned all of her story. I learned of the visions and the dreams, all of which subsequently came true, and the step-by-step account of how she came to the Lord. One story in particular, which happened before her conversion, had a powerful effect on me because of its profound significance for Muslim work.

Her grandson, whom she had legally adopted, was dying in a Christian hospital. Bilqis was hysterical. The Christian doctor said, "Begum Sheikh, why don't you pray?" To which Bilqis replied, "Good God, I haven't prayed since I was a little girl. I don't know how to pray anymore. What should I say?" His reply, "Just call him 'Father,' and talk to Him." To a Muslim, that was a shocking idea. Call God "Father"? But she did pour out her heart to God—as Father. He heard her cry. Little six-year-old Mahmud was healed. The healing, as great as it was, could not compare with the greatness of discovering that God was her Father.

You have to know Islam and the life of Muhammad to appreciate the significance of this. Muhammad's father died before he was born. He was fatherless. He chose Ishmael as his hero, not Isaac. Ishmael, too, after his expulsion from the family of Abraham, was fatherless. Curiously, and perhaps connected to the two above facts, you discover that in all of Islam, God is never known as or called Father. For a Muslim to call God Father is like a bombshell bursting in the midst of their fatherless theology.

When Bilqis finally wrote her autobiography, she entitled it *I Dared to Call Him Father*. This book in many translations has spread with tremendous impact throughout the Muslim world. Through her "Muslim eyes," I learned of the amazing value and powerful impact that teaching God as our loving Father has on our "fatherless" Muslim friends.

THE RAINBOW OVER WAH

The ruined gardens on the fringe of the small town of Wah in northern Pakistan still evidenced some of its former glory. Rows of stately poplars lined the deteriorated walkways. Lost beneath the underbrush, we found the remains of ancient pools and water canals long since dried up. The glory of previous regimes lay mute and barely visible under those tangled webs of brambles and bushes.

What a contrast to the cottage nearby, the cottage of the "flower lady" whose touch made everything come alive and burst into radiant glory in her well-tended garden with its fountain and pool. Here in this gorgeous setting lived a woman whose life, once ruined, now pulsated with the glorious life of her new-found Christ. Her garden seemed to reflect that.

Begum (an honorific title) Bilqis Sheikh had once been the official hostess for President Ayub Khan of Pakistan. After her tragic divorce and subsequent depression, successfully treated in London, she returned to her family cottage in this lovely setting and tried to find God.

Unfortunately, she looked in the wrong place. Nothing came of her reading the Quran. But something did come of the prayers of missionaries who had lived in that cottage before her and of the other missionaries who were living in one of her nearby rental houses. In answer to those prayers,

God gave her visions, first of John the Baptist, then of Jesus.

The story of her conversion and many subsequent adventures have been beautifully told in her autobiography entitled *I Dared To Call Him Father*. It is an event not recorded in that book that engages us now.

Leaders of our college group had heard of this famous woman who had become a Christian. They wanted to meet her, to hear her story firsthand. Bilqis, being a gracious woman, readily agreed. A small delegation of Christian college student leaders and I visited her in her home, which she had named "Peniel," meaning "Face of God," for it was here that she met Him.

On the mantle over the fireplace was a large portrait of Jesus as imagined by a famous artist. The furniture was all in white and so was Bilqis. Now that she belonged to Jesus, she chose the color of purity for both her home decor and her personal attire.

A servant lady brought out pastries and tea but Bilqis served us all with her own hands. After a few pleasantries, Bilqis then told her story. The young men were riveted by the dramatic account of how the living God brought this famous Muslim lady to Himself. But Bilqis was not content to stop with her testimony. God had put a powerful, prophetic spirit in her.

She was well aware of the sorry, spiritual condition in the local churches: the scandals, the quarreling factions, the disgraceful behavior and, worst of all, the sense of hostility that Christians had toward Muslims. She burned with holy indignation over every wrong. After all, she now belonged to the visible Church of Christ in Pakistan and she was being mocked by her Muslim family and neighbors for associating with such unworthy and reprehensible people.

From the constant reading of her well-worn Bible, she knew what the Church was supposed to be—a bride without spot or blemish, totally blameless. It was supposed to be a shining light in the midst of the darkness of that land. And it was not.

Bilqis could not hold back the fiery indignation that she felt because of the failures of the churches. Her torrent of exhortation and rebuke took us all by surprise. She laid on us the burden of reviving and purifying the churches to make them churches that would radiate the presence of Christ, churches that would be pure where Muslims could come and feel the love of God. She wanted all Christians to be righteous people filled with holy boldness, people who would walk with God and truly love their Muslim neighbors—her people.

In the end, it was her closing prayer and tears that caused all of our hearts to melt. No one left that room unchallenged and unchanged!

After we had expressed our thanks and asked permission to leave, we exited into a misty rain that was abating and there in the sky appeared a brilliant rainbow. It was as though God was refreshing our faces with the mist and dazzling our eyes with His smile, this rainbow over Wah, confirming the burning words of exhortation that poured forth from this woman who wept so unashamedly for the salvation of the Muslims of Pakistan.

GO TO FORMAN COLLEGE

These words came like fire, "Go to Forman College."
It was 2:00 in the morning. I had been dead asleep. It was the
night of our first day of vacation in Kabul, Afghanistan.
These were not words I heard, nor did I see them written.
But somewhere deep in my spirit, these words burned with
such fierce intensity that I sat bolt upright in bed.

Where were these words coming from? My subconscious? It couldn't be. Never in my wildest imagination had
I ever even dreamed of such a thing. Years before when the
question came up of becoming the chaplain at our own Gordon College in Rawalpindi, I deferred to my good friend and
former classmate from seminary days, Bob Noble. Forman
Christian College in Lahore had never even been part of our
mission. No one had ever crossed the line from our mission
to the work of another. It was unthinkable.

Prior to this short vacation trip, I had just completed
a very strenuous summer of nine weeks as summer pastor to
the mission community, running summer camps for college
kids and privately tutoring Begum Bilqis Sheikh, a recently
converted ex-Muslim lady from a high family of Pakistan.

The theme of those summer messages was the Holy
Spirit. Forty years before, our mission had gone through a crisis over the Holy Spirit. Fourteen of our 140 missionaries had
come into some unusual experiences of the Holy Spirit. One

married lady went so far as to say that unless you spoke in tongues, you were not saved. The mission disciplined her and forbade her to teach that. As a result, the other thirteen resigned from the mission.

After this crisis, a pall settled over our mission and the 250 churches related to it. For the next 40 years, no one in the churches can remember anyone giving any teaching on the Holy Spirit. It was just a taboo subject. To a lesser extent, this was also true in our mission.

Can you imagine the devastation this caused to the churches? The church became carnal and gave way to power struggles and fighting over property and money. They had cut themselves off from the Holy Spirit, the empowerer of the church, the One who gives gifts and manifests the fruit of Christ's presence. The damage was incalculable.

And so it was that I taught on the Holy Spirit for those nine weeks. Many missionaries came to the Saturday night prayer meetings. Some even came every morning to the church to pray with me. A fresh sense of power came into the worship services. It was a memorable summer.

But now back to my problem. How do you know whether that was the Lord speaking or not? On the way back to our work in Jhelum, we stopped to visit our dear friends, the Dave Mitchells in Wah. These were the ones with whom we could unburden our hearts anytime. After recounting this experience of a "word in the night," Synnove went to the bookshelf and pulled down Dr. Raymond Edman's book, *Out of My Life*. He was the president of Wheaton College.

There was his story. God had spoken to him in a similar way about his call to Wheaton College. There were more similar stories, including the one of Carl Henry, the cofounder of *Christianity Today*. So what had happened to me was not all that unusual.

Still, I wanted confirmation that these words were from the Lord. I'm afraid I was where Gideon was when the Lord spoke to him (Judges 6:36-40). I set out three "fleeces" before the Lord. First, that the Synod of the church would release me to go. Secondly, the man I would be temporarily replacing would be happy to see me come. And finally, that the head of our mission would give approval. It took exactly a year for all three to happen.

The cause of all this was the prayer of the Spirit-filled Pakistani principal of Forman Christian College, Dr. Julian Sinclair. He had heard of my summer ministry in Murree and had prayed and asked God for me for the college. His asking coincided with the date of that experience in Kabul.

As if to confirm that this was from Him, within the first hour of opening up my office on the campus of that college, God used me to lead a very worldly, nominal "Christian" president of the Student Christian Movement to Himself.

And that was the beginning of the brightest period of our missionary lives in Pakistan: sharing Christ with Muslim faculty members; Mary Jo leading the wife of one of them to Christ;[1] seeing Pakistani university students come to Christ; heading up the special program for Saudi Arabian students. There was an incredible trip to Saudi Arabia itself, sharing Christ every day with my Saudi students and finally with high government officials.

It all began with the prayer of one Spirit-filled Pakistani college principal. The fact that it changed the course of my life is incidental. He became my mentor in prayer. He taught me the power of Spirit-led prayer.

1 The husband came to Christ fourteen years later!

CARING FOR GOD'S OWN

Every missionary dreads that knock on the door. The man standing there represents an insoluble problem. He has come from a Muslim family. Now he is being drawn to Jesus. What should be cause for inexpressible joy turns out to be an incredible heartache.

Islam is a total way of life. It is an all-encompassing civilization. The fabric of society is so tightly woven that it is virtually impossible to get out. And if you do succeed, you are really out, *all the way out*, with no place to go. No more family. You may lose your wife and children, your job. Unutterable loneliness.

Think about it: there he is—standing at your door. You have come to this country for this very reason. You want to see people come to Jesus. And there he is. He's all yours. But without a family support system. Without a job. Without a friend. Maybe his life is threatened, too. You are his only hope.

What do you do? Take him in? Hide him? Send him to another missionary friend in another city where he will be safer? Give him a new name? Educate him? Help him to emigrate to another country to start life over? These are the questions that haunt every missionary to Muslims.

In countries where the Church already exists, this

should not be a problem—certainly not the missionary's problem. Let the Church take him in. Let the Church be the Church, the fellowship of believers. Let them bear the weight of the problem. Let them find him a new life, a new wife, a new job. Let them support him, shield him, protect him, hide him, if need be.

But the Church is not what it should be. There are ethnic realities to deal with. In a multi-ethnic society, the local church will not be from a Muslim background. The Christians have already suffered much at the hands of a persecuting Muslim majority. Resentment runs deep. Besides, there are language differences and lifestyle differences. There is an invisible sign out front, "Muslim-background people not welcome."

This is what makes Aslam Khan's story so remarkable. He was from a well-to-do family living in a village near Gujarat, Pakistan. He was provided with a personal servant while growing up. His father had an important government job. Aslam's future was very bright. His family married him to a lovely woman from another well-to-do, equal-status Muslim family. Everything was going his way.

The Bible changed all that. It started out as innocent curiosity: "What is this book of the Christians? Why are all my Muslim relatives so afraid of it? Why did my father say that if I read that book I would become a hated Christian? Did he know there was some strange power in that book?" Aslam's fascination with the Bible proved irresistible. He came to believe. All on his own he sought baptism.

There was an uproar in the family. His father beat him. He fled from his home. Proud, too proud to beg, he became a servant to a foreigner. The foreigner himself was soon transferred to another part of Pakistan. Aslam's life was so devoted to the Lord that the foreigner took note and soon himself became a believer. In the church in that part of the country, Aslam was welcome.

Aslam sent a message to his wife. She joined him while still a Muslim. Soon she, too, after reading the Bible, became a believer. Now he had a home and a job. All was well, except for one thing. God put it into his heart to be an evangelist to his own people, the Muslims. He could not stop talking about Jesus to the majority population. Christian leaders took note of this gifted man.

Eventually, he won a scholarship to a Presbyterian seminary. After graduation and being installed as a pastor in a church, he discovered that he still could not keep quiet. He had to go to the Muslims to tell them about Jesus. The church-at-large recognized the evangelistic gift of this out-standing man. A new organization had been formed in La-hore called St. Andrew's Brotherhood. It was designed to care for converts from Islam. It was supported by churches and individuals. Aslam was invited to be the head of it.

I was attracted to Aslam while still a young mission-ary. When I was later assigned to work in Lahore, it was in-evitable that we should become good friends. Gradually I became involved in this brotherhood caring for converts. This was an alternative solution to the missionary dilemma described above.

Aslam's compassion never ceased to amaze me. He would hunt day and night for frightened and fleeing Muslim-background believers. He would take them in. These new believers had a place of refuge: a place to be discipled, a place to be loved and accepted, a place from which to launch out in a new career when they were ready.

But it was his prayer life that impressed me even more. I have never known a man of such power in prayer. The range of his passion was so great. He would storm the very gates of heaven with his demands on our heavenly Father. But it was his tears, I think, that were more effective. This man wept for these new believers and for the lost. To pray with him was to allow your own heart to be broken for Muslims.

Thank God Aslam Khan did not run away. He stayed and was faithful until death in caring for God's own. May I, may *we*, be so faithful in caring for God's own.

ONE'S FOR HERESY, THE OTHER FOR HYPOCRISY

The ways of God in designing a life are beyond the power of human imagination. And so it was with the Pakistani Muslim young man in this tale. To preserve his anonymity, I have given him the name Kesh, the name of the place where his most famous ancestor was born.

Kesh grew up in a middle-class Muslim family in central Pakistan. His father was the chief of police in their town. His mother was the most beautiful woman I have ever met. There was a mountain near their town called *Jabal Isa* (Jesus Mountain). The only church in town was a small Roman Catholic one. There was also a Christian clinic run by an English lady doctor. All of these played a part in the early life of this brilliant young man.

Kesh's father was an alcoholic. In fits of drunken rage, he would invariably beat his wife. The Quran, incidentally, teaches that a man may beat his wife if he even suspects her of disobedience or infidelity. Kesh grew to hate his father and the religion that justified this kind of abusive treatment of his mother. His alienation with Islam was total.

The English lady doctor who lived nearby befriended Kesh and began to teach him English. In due time, he became quite fluent. While she was teaching him, she often spoke to him of the things of the Lord.

The emotional turmoil of living in his dysfunctional family made Kesh ripe for a change of religion. The Lord helped this process along by giving Kesh visions of the cross on the top of "Jesus Mountain." Kesh interpreted these repeated visions to mean that God was telling him he was to become a Christian.

The only version of Christianity that Kesh had seen up to that time was that of the Roman Catholic Church. He began his study of Christianity with the local priest. Having shown himself precocious in his studies, he was chosen to be sent to Rome for a five-year training program to become a Roman Catholic priest. For reasons that were never explained to him, the Bishop of Rawalpindi decided at the last moment to cancel Kesh's appointment to Rome.

Kesh was shattered. In bitter despair he decided to take his own life. Friends intervened to save him. Soon after this, evangelical friends in Rawalpindi befriended Kesh. Eventually, they sent him to a Protestant haven for Muslim-background Christians in Lahore, an establishment called "St. Andrew's Brotherhood," of which I was a part.

It was here that Kesh met Rev. Aslam Khan, who was a Muslim-background believer in Christ. Aslam was a tenderhearted pastor who ran this home for those whom Islam had rejected and threatened. He was one of the most loving evangelists among Muslims I have ever known. But, alas, Aslam was not a discipler. It was at this point that Aslam asked me to work with Kesh in grounding him in the Christian faith.

When I first met Kesh, he struck me as being a wounded tiger. Obviously he was not yet healed from this terrible rejection and the shame of his own attempted suicide. All of this contributed to a bitter and mocking spirit that surfaced in him.

Every night, when we tried to study together, it turned into a nightmarish struggle. He criticized whatever he could think of about the church and then the Bible. At the end of these grueling wrestling matches, I found myself drenched in sweat and utterly exhausted. Week after week we wrestled. I was at my wit's end. How do you deal with a guy like this?

This was about to change. At our next meeting, Kesh began to mock the apparent contradictions between the books of Galatians and James in the New Testament. That is when I lost it. I broke all the rules of how to do loving, tender, sensitive discipling. In total exasperation, I shouted at him, "Kesh, you are so stupid that, in spite of all your brilliance, you couldn't even figure out that Galatians was written to guard against heresy and James was written to guard against hypocrisy. Of course they look different! They were written for totally different purposes, you idiot!"

Kesh was thunderstruck at my explosion! To my amazement, in the providence of God, this was the turning point of his life! He saw the integrity of the Scriptures for the first time. From then on, our meetings became beautiful and fruitful times of studying the Word of God together.

In retrospect, I have often thought about that fateful night. It took this thundering statement that Galatians was written to guard against heresy and James to guard against hypocrisy to break this man's scoffing and critical spirit. Once his confidence in the Word of God was restored, his walk with the Lord took off.

Two lessons were brought home to me by this experience. The first is that Roman Catholics have a problem with the concept of "faith alone," which is so ardently taught by Protestants. Secondly, it often takes years for a former Muslim who has been brought up to believe that salvation is by works alone to understand that salvation is by faith alone!

Kesh had two strikes against him as he struggled with this issue, first as a Roman Catholic and secondly because of his Muslim background.

In the end, he saw the sufficiency of Christ's death and shed blood as the sole basis of his salvation. But even more, he came into a full understanding of his union with Christ in the resurrected life, his new life in the Spirit. Yes, there were ups and downs in his life, as in all of our lives, but he has proven to be a faithful servant of the Lord. Today he has a worldwide ministry.

I wonder how many of us have had our own confidence in the Word of God questioned by these apparent contradictions between passages or even whole books of the Bible? Thank God for the Holy Spirit who that night gave that brilliant flash of insight. Galatians guards against heresy, James against hypocrisy.

THE BEGGAR ON JARDANWALA ROAD

Beggary in Pakistan, over the years, had grown into a profession. It was not uncommon to see a raggedy-clad mother with an emaciated baby in her arms approach us for alms. What was more surprising was to see another "mother," a half hour later, carrying the *same infant*, also asking for alms. They took turns.

One of the perversities growing out of Islam has to do with the required duty of giving alms. Every Muslim is supposed to give one-fortieth of his income to the poor. Beggars thus approach people with the appeal, "By giving to me, you are accruing merit for Judgment Day." This institutionalizes beggary.

On the Jardanwala Road between Lahore and Lyallpur,[1] there was a very unusual beggar. As an infant, his mother had deliberately broken both of his arms and had set them in a way to make him look grotesque. When he got older, he hung out at gasoline stations all up and down that road. I had seen him many times and occasionally gave him something when stopping for gas.

I had been handling the counseling and follow-up for Dr. Akbar Haqq's evangelistic crusade in Lahore. One Sunday morning, after sorting out the decision cards from the Saturday night meeting and mailing each one to the nearest pastor in his or her neighborhood, I went to my room to pray.

While praying, the Lord gave me a vision of this beggar on the Jardanwala Road.

This vision recurred repeatedly every time I tried to pray. I talked to God about it. "God, are You trying to tell me I am to go out on the Jardanwala Road and find this man and bring him into the next meeting?"

Soon my talking turned to arguing, "But God, I just put on these clean white clothes this morning, and if I drive out there on the dustiest road in the country—and You know my car leaks like a sieve—I will ruin my clothes." And God replied, "Who gave you those clothes?" Then I argued about the high cost of gasoline and that I didn't have much money. And God replied, "Who gave you that car? Who supplies your money? When did I ever fail you?"

In desperation, I went to my friend, Ian North, the administrator of Dr. Haqq's team. I told him of the vision and poured out my complaints. I asked for his advice. He said, "Don, God is speaking to you. You will have to go find that beggar." Since I highly esteemed Ian, and inwardly I knew my arguing was in vain, I reluctantly agreed. We prayed together and off I went.

It was the *Eid* holiday. *Eid* follows *Ramadan*, the thirty days of fasting that Muslims do once a year. Everyone was on the road going home for the big feast. When I got to the Ravi River, the bridge was gone. Army engineers had made a makeshift "bridge" of long narrow, flat-bottomed boats put side by side with long, heavy planks placed crossways across the tops of these boats. I had to wait my turn to drive my car across this rickety and dangerous bridge.

While waiting, a young man approached me and asked for a ride. He said, "Sir, I have been waiting here for hours to get a bus. But you can see all the buses are full. Even all the space on the roof is taken and all the bars on the windows are filled with people holding on. I can't even find a place to hang on the outside. Please, sir, I want to go home to my family for *Eid*." I took him in and learned his name was Javaid.

Lying there beside me on the seat was my open Urdu Bible. I would read it whenever there was a stop in the traffic. He picked it up. I said, "Javaid, why don't you read it aloud and then we both can enjoy it." To my surprise, he read it with great feeling and understanding. I asked, "Are you a Christian?" He said, "No, I'm a Muslim."

As we drove along, I would slow down, turn to another passage and ask him to read. My goal was to give him a clear understanding of the Gospel. This went on mile after mile. All the while, my eyes were looking for the beggar alongside the road. Finally, just a few miles short of Lyallpur, Javaid said, "Hey, this is my village. When are you coming back from Lyallpur? Maybe I could ride back with you." I said, "I'm not going to Lyallpur." He asked, "Where are you going?" I told him this was as far as I was going. He was incredulous.

Then I told Javaid about my vision of that morning. He exclaimed, "I know that beggar," and he told me his name. I said, "Well I have been looking for him for all these miles and I haven't seen him." Then, I said, "Javaid, I believe God got me out here on this road today through this vision so that I could 'walk' you through the Scriptures and show you all about God's love for you through Jesus Christ."

Javaid couldn't believe his ears. "You mean you would go to all this trouble just for me?" I said, "Yep." He was ecstatic. He said, "Please, Mr. Don, let me buy you something to eat here at this roadside hotel." We sat there on rope beds, dust swirling all around us as the traffic roared by, and celebrated together his discovery of the Gospel.

As I turned my car around and drove out of that village, for the first time in my life, I heard these words from the Lord, "Well done, good and faithful servant." And then I thought, this is just like the Apostle Paul's vision of the man of Macedonia. He went there, never found that man, but he found Lydia and some women at the riverside prayer meeting. This modern-day event started on the banks of another river, the Ravi, there outside Lahore. And salvation came to a surprised young man.

1 Faisalabad today.

VIVE LA FRANCE

Death came ever so near. Deliverance came from such an unexpected quarter. The setting for this tale was in Lahore, Pakistan. It happened on the most famous street in the city, Mall Road.

To understand the passion and fury in this story, we need to go back to two historical events. The first was the birth of Pakistan on August 14, 1947. Pakistan only exists because Muslims of India did not want to live under Hindu domination.[1]

These immigrants paid a horrendous price for their homeland. Seven million Muslims walked out on everything they had into newly founded Pakistan. They were slaughtered by the hundreds of thousands as they walked through Hindu and Sikh territories to get to their "Holy Land.[2]"

After paying such a high price in blood and possessions, Pakistani Muslims are extremely sensitive to any event in the world that touches a Muslim. War in the Sudan, riots in Nigeria, the conversion of Muslims to Christ in Indonesia, or the jailing of a Muslim in the United States, are all immediately reported in the press. The language is always emotionally charged. Protest marches usually follow.

The second historical event that factors into this story is the founding of the modern state of Israel, May 15, 1948, just nine months after the creation of Pakistan. The spontaneous protest throughout the Muslim world led to war. Muslims perceive the creation of Israel as the most dastardly act the West has ever committed against Islam.

The roots of all this hatred go back to the time of Muhammad's rule in Medina, Arabia, from 622 to 632 A.D. Muhammad tried to convince the three Jewish tribes living there to believe in him as a prophet. He failed. They mocked him, called him a false prophet and consorted with his enemies. Muhammad's hatred of Jews was sealed with his own dastardly acts. He stripped the first two tribes of all their possessions and drove them away as penniless refugees. The third tribe did not fare as well. He killed every single Jewish man and sent all the women and children into slavery. His subsequent bitter pronouncements against Jews in the Quran have forever pitted Muslims against Jews.

The United States as the prime mover in the United Nations for carving the state of Israel, out of Muslim Palestine marks her as an enemy of Islam. Every weapon ever sold, every dollar of aid ever given to Israel is perceived as a dagger in a Muslim heart stamped "made in America."

Small wonder, then, that during the 1973 Yom Kippur war, gangs of Pakistanis and their Palestinian friends roved the streets of Lahore—looking for Americans. As I was driving home on the Mall Road, a dangerous mob of angry young men surged out of a side street to stop all traffic and look for Americans. I was taken by surprise and rendered helpless.

"Are you an American?" they demanded. I said, "Yes." Immediately my car and I were engulfed in a circle of frenzied, wild-eyed, shrieking fanatics. They began rocking my car to turn it over with me in it. Later on, they used homemade gasoline bombs that they carried in their pockets to burn down the United States Information Service building. They could just as easily have been used on me until…

A tall Jordanian stuck his head in my car window, looked at me, then at the dashboard of my Volkswagen Microbus. On it were these ridiculous decals in pidgin German: for the light switch there was *Das Glimmerblinken*; for the ignition, *Der Puttersparken*; for the windshield wipers, *Der Drizzleflippen*. He looked at me again and laughed and said, "You're not American, you're French." And turning to the crazed mob, he said: "This man is not American, he's French." Then shouting, "Vive la France, vive la France," he turned the mob away. What a wry sense of humor the Lord has. Knowing full well my aversion to things French, he saved me with those words, "Vive la France." Never again will I scorn France or things French.

Once again, as if to forever win my gratitude and the commitment of my life to the service of Muslims, God saved my life at the hands of a Muslim. Later, as I thought about this great mercy, a line from one of Frances Ridley Havergal's wonderful hymns came to mind: "I gave, I gave my life for thee, what hast thou given for me?"

Originally those words referred to Jesus dying on the cross. But then I thought of that Jordanian Muslim who stood there between me and certain death. What would I do for him and those he represents? The words of Hugh Sherlock's hymn say it better than I ever could:

> In the streets of every city where the bruised and lonely dwell,
> We shall show the Savior's pity, we shall of His mercy tell.
> In all lands and with all races, we shall serve and seek to bring
> All the world to render praises, Christ, to Thee, Redeemer, King.

.

1 The Quran mandates that all Muslims should live only under Muslim rule.
2 Pakistan means "Land of the Pure."

ALLAHU AKBAR

So many times, Muslims themselves have been used of God to challenge my commitment. I would like to relate one brief but unforgettable incident. To do so I need to give some historical background.

Pakistan among all the nations of the world is unique. It is the only country carved out of another country on the basis of Islam, the religion of Muslims. It has no other reason to exist.

India, by contrast is a democracy: multi-ethnic, many religions, hundreds of languages. Not so, Pakistan. Muslims, although they too speak several different languages, have been taught not to live under any other rule except Islamic Law.

In 1947, when Britain gave freedom to India, millions of Muslims wanted to have a separate country. It was a costly decision. Seven million Muslims left everything in newly independent India to live in either East or West Pakistan. Five million Hindus and Sikhs left their homes in newly created Pakistan to find their new homes in India. As these enemy groups filtered through one another to their "new" homes, fighting broke out. A million were slaughtered. Kashmir was the scene of some of the fighting.

Under the British, Kashmir had a Hindu ruler, even

though 60% of its people were Muslims. At the time of partition, the Hindu Maharaja unilaterally ceded Kashmir to India. Pakistan sent in "holy warriors" to wrest it away. India sent in its army. By the time the United Nations imposed a cease-fire, India held two-thirds of Kashmir and Pakistan held one third. Since partition, India and Pakistan have fought three wars over this disputed territory. The situation I am about to describe was on the eve of the third one.

This was all happening when the Christians still controlled their own colleges. I was teaching English at Forman Christian College[1] in Lahore. Most of the students were Muslim. In fact, I was right in the middle of a lecture with a class of seniors. Unknown to me, one of my students had smuggled a transistor radio into class. He sat in the back corner of the room. Keeping one side of his face turned away from me, he was using an earplug to monitor the news.

Just a word of explanation here: Islam divides the world into two camps, the *Dar-ul-Islam* (House of Islam) and the *Dar-ul-Harb* (House of War). Muslims claim that they are only allowed to fight defensive wars. Of course, we know that's not true. Just look at their conquest of the Middle East in the seventh century, their invasion of Spain in the eighth, their centuries-long war against the Greeks in what is present-day Turkey,[2] the seventeenth-century attack on Europe, to say nothing of their wars to the east.

The truth is that when Muslims think they have the advantage, they will attack. In the case of Kashmir, they could feel fully justified in declaring war on India. And so we watched and waited. The roads were clogged with military convoys moving to the border. The Air Force was fully aroused. Since we lived near the border, we were buffeted daily with the unnerving noise of sonic booms.

The principal of our college warned us on this particular day that war was about to be declared. He told us to try and keep our restless students in our classrooms. The tension and sense of expectation were so high that it was virtually impossible to teach.

And then it happened. War had officially been declared over all radio and TV stations. Right in the middle of my teaching, the student with the radio leaped to his feet. In a very loud voice he shouted, "*Allahu akbar*" (God is greater!). In an instant, all of my students were on their feet, shouting "*Allahu akbar*." Next, they burst through the verandah doors and were out in the open field joining their other two thousand fellow students and shouting "*Allahu akbar*."

By now Indian fighter-bombers were directly overhead making their runs on Pakistani border targets. Anti-aircraft shells were starting to fall on our campus. Out in the open field, my students were shaking their fists defiantly at the Indian pilots and shouting the Muslim war cry, "God is greater!"

I stood there on the verandah of my empty classroom watching this scene in utter amazement. These students, in their zeal for God,[3] a zeal fired not by love but by a passion to impose Islam on the world, were openly risking their lives by exposing themselves to enemy aircraft.

The thought came to mind: If Christians were even half as zealous for God as these Muslim students, we would have won the world to Christ hundreds of years ago. How odd that it was my Muslim students who brought the memory of God's Word, "Zeal for your house consumes me"—words Jesus quoted from Psalm 69:9.

Could I honestly say, "*Allahu akbar*," that God is greater than all else in my life? Could I live so openly and fearlessly for God? The answer has to be a "yes."

Unlike those Muslim students, our passion is not for

war in the name of God; our passion is love. Our weapons are the Word of God, the Sword of the Spirit, and prayer, all wrapped together in us—the living sacrifices—who believe God really is the greatest reason for living and even dying. We can say, with a blameless heart before the Lord, "*Allahu akbar*," God is greater than all else. I will live for Him.

1 Forman was awarded university status in 2004.

2 Which the Muslims won.

3 Of Whom they had no real knowledge.

HUNGERING FOR GOD

There is nothing as exhilarating as a shopping trip through the Anarkali Bazaar in downtown Lahore, the capital of the Punjab province of Pakistan.

Glitzy shops for blocks on end, gaudy colors, raucous hawkers, the hustle and bustle of endless humanity clogging this one long, narrow street. To make it even more challenging, bikes and motor scooters are looking for daylight as they careen their way through the endless parade of street vendors and pedestrians.

You name it, they've got it. It starts with the Bible House at one end and terminates with the Urdu book bazaar at the other. And in between—sweet shops, tea stalls, fashion shoes, ladies' *shalwar* and *qameez*, lingerie, tailor shops for men, office supplies, perfumeries, jewelry, bangles, cosmetics, clocks, watches, radios, TV sets, miniature hardware stores, toy shops, and endless pushcarts with everything under the sun on them. What a cacophony of noise fills the air over the heads of these surging waves of people. It's an absolutely delicious experience.

One memorable day in Anarkali, I was startled to hear someone calling my name: "Mr. Dawn![1] Mr. Dawn![1]" The voice was that of a young man selling audiotapes from his pushcart.

He said, "You don't know me. My brother is one of your students at Forman Christian College. He pointed you out to me one day and said that you were his professor of English."

After our exchange of pleasantries, and learning that his name was Latif, I glanced down at his tapes and scanned the titles. Among all the love songs was one entitled "Ya Muhammad!" (O Muhammad!) I asked him what this tape was about. He said it was a praise song being sung to Muhammad, the founder of Islam.

I asked Latif to put this tape into his machine and play it for me. What I heard was mind-boggling. The words of the vocalist were in praise of Muhammad in the same way we Christians praise Jesus! Muhammad was being praised as divine!

"That is against orthodox Islam," I blurted out. "Do Muslim people think that deity lives in Muhammad?" He said, "Yeah. There are lots of tapes like these and they are very popular."

This was a turning point in my understanding of the Muslim heart. They were hungry for a "god" they could know—Muhammad—rather than a faraway unknowable God (*Allah*). And in their hunger to worship an ideal God-man, they had given Muhammad the place in their hearts that rightfully belongs to Jesus.

After that experience, I began to notice many things. The spirit in Islam is the spirit of imitation. If Jesus was sinless, Muhammad had to be sinless. If Jesus was infallible, Muhammad was infallible. If Jesus was an intercessor, Muhammad had to be an intercessor.

Where did it all start, this movement to deify Muhammad? It started with Muhammad himself and his own teaching. There was a discernible progression in his own self-perception. It goes something like this: In the beginning, Muhammad called himself merely a "warn-er" against pagan idolatry. Then he called himself an Arab prophet to the Arab people. Next, he said all prophets are equal. This was followed by saying he was the "seal" of the prophetic line. Then he put words in Jesus' mouth in which Jesus prophesies the coming of Muhammad. He then said that "in me, the prophet, you have an excellent example." It was not long before he said to one and all, "Follow me."

Out of this developed the Muslim creed, "There is no god but God and Muhammad is the Messenger of God." This led to Islamic law in which it is a capital offense if you speak against Muhammad or his book, the Quran.[2]

By these claims, Muhammad set himself forth as the only one people are to look to. If you are hungry for a human model that you could worship as someone knowable, infallible, filled with divine light, yes, even possessing deity, well then, Muhammad is the only choice that a Muslim really knows.

The human heart does crave a sympathetic Savior. Muslims have made Muhammad that savior. Yes, we can grieve over this blasphemy. But what I learned from Latif's music tapes that morning in Anarkali was that the *Muslim* heart, too, is hungry for a Savior. He is not satisfied with sterile orthodox Islam. There is hope, then, for what we missionaries do. The Muslim is hungry for the real Savior, and he or she will never know it is Jesus until we find a way to tell them. Thank you, Latif, for this wonderful insight.

1 Pakistanis never learned to pronounce my name.
2 But not if you speak against Allah!

ISKANDER'S QUESTION

Iskander was a fellow English professor with me at Forman Christian College in Lahore, Pakistan. We were sitting in the faculty lounge, drinking tea together, after a full morning of teaching.

As we were sipping our tea, Iskander mentioned that the night before he had gone to see the movie, *David and Bathsheba.* So he asked, "Don, how could God ever forgive David for what he did?" Iskander was a Muslim and he knew, of course, that I was a Christian.[1]

To understand Iskander's perplexity, one needs to know what Islam teaches about David in the Quran. David is mentioned in the following verses in the Quran:

2:251	David kills Goliath.
6:84	David is listed as a descendant of Abraham.
21:79	David celebrates God's praises with all creation.
34:10	David sings the praises of God.[2]
34:11	David invents chain-mail armor.
38:17	David is a man of strength.
38:18	Creation joins with David in praising God at dawn and sunset.
38:19	Birds assemble and turn to God in praise with David.

38:20   God strengthens David's kingdom and gives him wisdom.

38:21-25   Here begins a strange story in which two brothers break into David's private quarters and confront him with their problem. The brother who has ninety-nine sheep wants to take away from the other brother the one lone sheep of his brother. They ask David to judge what is right and fair. He judges correctly then bows down in repentance, supposedly for being proud of his wisdom. And God forgives him.

38:26   God warns David not to follow the lusts of his own heart.

That's it. This is all Iskander has to go on from the Quran for his knowledge of David. Muhammad apparently twisted Biblical stories to suit his own purposes. Notice what Muhammad leaves out: David commits adultery with Bathsheba while her husband is away at war. When she tells David she is pregnant, he arranges to have her husband killed in battle. Then he takes Bathsheba as his wife.

(As an aside, this story of David's sins closely parallels events in Muhammad's own life. In his own hometown of Medina, Muhammad killed all the Jewish men of the tribe of Quyrayzah and took the most beautiful young widow, Rayhanah, as his own concubine. Of course, all of this was legitimate for Muhammad because, according to the Quran, God approved of it.[3] But in the Bible, David's actions are labeled as sin. No wonder Muhammad did not want to repeat the Biblical story in detail. He would have implicated himself. So he lamely glides over the Biblical story by having God warn David not to lust.)

Back to Iskander. Being a somewhat nominal Muslim, he did not know the story of Muhammad's treatment of the Jews in Medina and his taking of the beautiful Jewish woman as his concubine.

Having studied at a Christian college for six years and teaching there for another two, Iskander had unconsciously begun to absorb Christian values. And so his question, "How could God ever forgive David for killing Uriah and taking his wife?"

Because it was an honest question, Iskander opened the door for what turned out to be a lovely two-hour discussion of the Biblical story in 2 Samuel 11 and 12. He was fascinated with the rich details in this account. Of course, he had never heard of Nathan or the parable of the rich man trying to take the poor man's one lone sheep away from him. From his scant memory of the Quranic material, he wondered out loud why Muhammad did not get the story right and why it looked so garbled and confusing in the Quran.

From the account in Samuel, we went to look at Psalm 51, which most Christians believe was David's prayer of repentance after being convicted of his sin by the words of Nathan the prophet.

We highlighted the following: "Blot out my transgression...Cleanse me from my sin...Create in me a pure heart, O God...Do not take your Holy Spirit away from me...Restore to me the joy of Your salvation...The sacrifices of God are a broken and contrite spirit." In the end, the conversation led to Jesus and His death on the cross for the sins of us all.

When our time came to an end, I asked Iskander if he had ever heard such an explanation before. "No, I never have," he said. Eight years in a Christian college and he had never heard an explanation of the Gospel!

Lord, forgive us for not reaching out to those around us who have never heard the wonderful news of Your offer of salvation through faith in Jesus Christ and what He accomplished for us all by His death and resurrection.

1 Our college occasionally hired Muslim teachers because so many of the Christian teachers migrated to the West.

2 Incidentally, Muhammad never sang.

3 Muslim men are allowed to take and "own" women as the spoils of war (Quran 33:50, 4:24).

BEYOND THE BORDERS OF WESTERN MEDICINE

Lahore is the capital of the heavily populated province of the Punjab in Pakistan. Forman Christian College and the United Christian Hospital were two of the outstanding mission institutions in that city. The tale that I am going to tell involves both the college and the hospital.

I taught English at the college and was chaplain to the Christian students. We lived on campus. One morning there was a frantic pounding on our front door. Standing there was a very agitated young man, Yunus, by name. I recognized him from the days when we used to live in Jhelum. His brother, Niamat, was the assistant postmaster in Jhelum and my good friend.

Yunus said, "Mister Dawn,[1] you have got to come to the hospital at once, my brother is dying and he is calling for you."

Hospitals in Pakistan have no central heating in the wintertime. Patients are often laid out on mattresses outdoors to benefit from the sunshine. And that's where I found him— outdoors on the ground in the glorious January sunshine. I barely recognized my old friend. His head was the size of a giant pumpkin. His hands and feet were grotesquely swollen. His arms and legs were shriveled to the size of mere sticks.

Utterly shocked by his appearance, I exclaimed, "Niamat, what happened to you?" He said, "Brother Dawn, I have advanced tuberculosis of the lungs and my kidneys have stopped working. The doctors tell me that the medicine for the TB makes the kidneys worse and the medicine for the kidneys makes the TB worse. They have just told me that there is nothing more they can do for me—that I am going to die."

Then Niamat looked up to me and said, "Brother Dawn, would you please pray for me?" I felt so totally inadequate. I had gone to medical school before my conversion. Science was the answer. And if the missionary doctors said he was finished—well, that's it. He's finished.

Disregarding the look of despair on my face, Niamat kept pleading with me to pray for him. Then I remembered that back at the college, Mrs. Hilda Sinclair, the wife of the principal, had a reputation for being able to pray for people's healing and many were healed. I said to Niamat, "I am going to the college to get Mrs. Sinclair and we will come back together and pray for you."

Having never been trained in seminary on how to pray for healing, I did what seemed obvious. We read many passages about healing from the life of Jesus. It was surprising to see how many times in these accounts there was also some reference to the forgiveness of sins.

When we were finished reading, I said to Niamat, "Now we are going to pray, but you are going to pray first." As he tried to pray, it became obvious that this brother was a nominal Christian. His words were dead. It was as though they tumbled out of his mouth and fell straight to the ground. I groaned in my spirit and silently cried out to God for help for this man.

Suddenly, in a loud voice, Niamat began to confess his sins—all of them! He went on and on. We were in a public place. I opened my eyes to see people stopping and star-ing at this man who was making these awful confessions. I closed my eyes to focus on the prayers. As I did so, inexpli-cably, faith was born in me to believe Niamat could be healed.

As soon as Niamat finished praying, we began to go over the simple Gospel message with him. Did he know that Jesus died for those sins? Was he truly repenting of his old way of life and surrendering to Jesus as Lord? Did he under-stand that by the power of Jesus' resurrection he now could have newness of life in the Spirit? When we were fully as-sured that Niamat understood and believed, then we felt free to pray for him.

We did the obvious. We placed our hands over the area of his lungs and asked the Lord to rebuke the disease and heal his lungs. We did the same with the kidneys, asking the Lord to open them up and cause them to work again. We went on and prayed for the edema to leave his head and hands and feet. Finally we prayed over his stick-like arms and legs and asked the Lord to cause the muscles to grow again.

When we were through, I had the faith to say to Nia-mat, "Now, brother, you are going to get well." We prayed prayers of thanksgiving and praise and took our leave.

A few days later, Dr. Dave Williams, one of our mis-sionary doctors at the hospital asked me to drop by and visit him. He asked, "What did you do to Niamat? He is getting better." I had the boldness to reply, "Dave, beyond the bor-ders of Western medicine is the Lord Jesus Christ—the One who is the same yesterday, today and forever. Jesus is healing him."

Niamat was completely healed. I wish I could say it was instantaneous. The truth is that it took six months for him to be totally restored. He was also a transformed man.

Not long after his return to work, he was transferred to the city of Narowal with a promotion to Postmaster General. He led a distinguished Christian life from that time onward.

Why did I have to go to Pakistan to learn that Jesus could heal today? Is it that the Western secular views of science and medicine have limited our faith to only what we can do? I thank God for a person like Hilda Sinclair, the wife of our Pakistani principal, who taught me to believe that Jesus could heal today. And I saw it happen before my eyes. Praise God! Jesus heals today.

1 Pakistanis could never say "Don."

UNDER THE FIERY UMBRELLA

Pakistan and India were at war again. This was their third.[1] We were living in Lahore at the time. Of course, in the middle of all of that carnage, we wanted to offer some kind of humanitarian relief. We volunteered to help in hospitals, roll bandages, give blood, anything that might show our concern. All of our offers were turned down. "We don't need any help from you Americans. We will win this war against the infidels as good Muslims should." Unfortunately, they lost the war. They suffered a bitter defeat at the hands of the East Pakistanis and the Indians who helped them. Bangladesh was born out of West Pakistan's defeat.

This was not the first time we had lived under aerial bombardments by the Indian Air Force. But this time was different. Lahore was only a few miles from the Indian border and the war front. The sonic booms shook the city. In the early days of fighting, we used to go up to our flat roof with the wall around it and watch the "dog-fights" between the Pakistani and Indian planes. That ended quickly when bullets whistled past our heads and buried themselves in the dormitory courtyard down below.

We were not as brave (or foolhardy) as some of our Pakistani neighbors who went to the edge of the city to put garlands of flowers around the necks of the anti-aircraft gunners who were firing away at the incoming bombers. India wanted to prevent the Pakistani army from bringing any help to the front across these bridges on the nearby Ravi River. They succeeded.

Meanwhile, we restless missionaries had time on our hands. Our offers of help were all refused. All schools and colleges were closed, including Forman Christian College, where I taught. What to do with all this time? Pray? Yes, we did that. But we didn't pray all day.

The leader of our mission, Dr. Park Johnson, was a golfer. So was my colleague at the college, Dr. Fred Ritzie. I was the duffer. The three of us decided to play golf every afternoon. The nearest public course was at the Railway Golf Club. And that is where we played.

Toward the end of the war, the Indian High Command decided to utterly destroy the nerve center of the Pakistani rail system there in Lahore. We were on the course—the *Railway* Golf course—when the first wave of planes came low over our heads to bomb and strafe the rail hub less than a mile away.

Having never been in a ground war and being unsure about what to do, I watched Fred, who had. He dove for the nearest dry irrigation ditch. I did the same with my face buried in the dirt. But my caddy didn't budge. He was nonchalantly leaning up against a keekar tree, watching the show. This made me feel ashamed. If this ever happened again, I decided I would stand beside him: be as brave (or as foolhardy) as he was and watch.

I didn't have long to wait. The next day, which happened to be the last day of the war, the Indian planes returned in full force. They were determined to inflict maximum destruction on the rail yards. I stood with my caddy under a keekar tree, riveted by the spectacle of fire and smoke around us.

What I hadn't noticed before was that we were inside a large circle of Pakistani anti-aircraft guns. As they fired away at the Indian planes, their tracer bullets formed a perfect, fiery umbrella right over our heads. We were as safe as a baby in its crib there in the middle of that circle.

The cease-fire took place that day at five o'clock p.m. We had finished our game and were back at the clubhouse drinking tea and enjoying the wonderful pastries on the outdoor patio. The skies were quiet but all of us were abuzz with excited chatter.

What stood out in all that talk were the words of one of our Pakistani Muslim friends, "You Americans didn't run away. You stayed with us right through our troubles. You are true friends. Why didn't you run away?"

These are the moments you wait for. Honest questions call for honest answers. We had toughed it out together through their war. Our war was different—it was a spiritual war. It was about bringing the light of life, not bullets of destruction, to these dear Pakistani Muslim friends.

We shared our own stories of how God had gotten a grip on our lives. They heard the Good News coming through our testimonies. Well, there are various ways of winning a hearing, aren't there? We won our hearing there in the middle of the guns under the fiery umbrella.

1 The wars have taken place in 1947, 1965 and 1971.

CHRYSANTHEMUMS HAVE CLAWS

Foreman Christian College was one of the most prestigious colleges in Pakistan. Many of the elite sent their sons there. The campus was gorgeous. The freshly painted cream-colored buildings sparkled against the setting of emerald green grass, colorful bougainvilleas, the graceful purple of the jacaranda trees and the brilliant red blossoms of the flame of the forest.

Since the college had grown beyond the capacity of the missionaries and the qualified local Christians to teach all the classes, the administration had resorted to hiring talented Muslims to teach. What a privilege it was to be invited to teach in that 50-50 mixture of Christian and Muslim faculty. Lifelong friendships grew out of these experiences.

Many of the best times of sharing Christ were in the faculty lounge where Christians and Muslims drank tea together. One of the most memorable was when someone asked, after seeing the movie *David and Bathsheba*, "Don, how could God ever forgive David for what he did?" This led to a two-hour discussion on God's whole plan of redemption and how Jesus' death on the cross was the basis for forgiveness.[1]

One of those sitting in on the discussion was Saleem Ahmad. He and his wife, Shummi, had become our dear friends. She also was well-educated and taught school part-time. Eventually she joined in a Bible class where Mary Jo saw her profess her faith in Christ.

Saleem was gifted. He led and acted in all of the dramas put on at the college. He also wrote poetry. One of his poems was entitled "Chrysanthemums Have Claws." He had noticed that within the beauty of the chrysanthemum were myriad petals that, on closer examination, resembled claws. Using this as a metaphor, he wrote a deeply moving poem about the beauty of love and the inevitability of pain. Little did I realize that one day I would experience the reality of both in my relationship with him.

Our relationship had its stormy periods, to say the least. He blamed Christianity for the Crusades.[2] I countered by calling his attention to the explosive wars of aggression that Muslims had committed against all others in the Middle East, North Africa, Spain, Greece, Europe, the Indian subcontinent and central Asia. He came back with the reminders of colonialism when Western powers subjugated 90% of the Muslim world. That kind of hot debate led nowhere.

The Lord convicted me of my folly. I invited Saleem to tea, confessed my foolishness in perpetuating a no-win debate, and asked for his forgiveness for provoking him to anger (and brilliant arguments). The atmosphere changed at once. Suddenly, we were able to talk about spiritual things: the things of Jesus, my own testimony and his needs. It looked like a promising new beginning.

My hopes were shattered when I learned he planned to emigrate to Britain. There were many reasons. As a free-thinking Muslim his life was becoming more difficult in Pakistan. The radical Islamic group, the Jamaat-I-Islami and their student wing, had penetrated our campus and our faculty.

We lost touch with one another. In the meantime,

the Lord had led Mary Jo and me back to the States for further study, a doctorate and teaching. Some years later, Saleem discovered where I lived. He wrote and asked if he could visit. Mary Jo and I were delighted.

Two nights after arriving, Saleem said to me, "Don, I want to become a Christian and I don't know how. Can you help me?" This was an answer to prayers that had begun fourteen years before. It was a time of great joy for both of us.

I wasn't prepared for what happened next. Two days later, somewhat out of the blue, Saleem announced that he wanted to become a Roman Catholic. I was stunned. "Why, Saleem?" His answer was devastating. "I have researched your little denomination. There are only three million of you in the whole world. I want to belong to something that is significant: a church that is authentically worldwide, a church that has a continuum of history from the beginning, a church that has a spokesman with world stature, the Pope, who can speak with authority for the wider Christian community." I was speechless. Pain, shock, even bewilderment rolled over me.

Consciously or unconsciously, what had I been teaching? Denominationalism? Sectarianism? Had I substituted an "-ism" for the Kingdom? Had I neglected to teach a truly universal Kingdom of God with Christ as the King? Obviously, that was not what Saleem heard.

God used the pain inflicted by my own "son" in the faith to show me what should have been the true focus of my teaching and preaching: the Kingdom of God and Jesus Christ as the King.

Out of this bittersweet relationship of both love and pain, I was called back to the "basics." I am thankful to Saleem, "the chrysanthemum who had claws," for focusing me more sharply on the Kingdom of God and Jesus the King.

1 See previous tale, *Iksander's Question.*
2 Most Muslims do.

I WANT TO BE BAPTIZED IN MY VILLAGE

While at Forman Christian College in Lahore, Pakistan, Muslim young men from other colleges and the local university in that city sought me out for private Bible study.

Muhammad Sherdil Khan was one of them. He was from a strong Muslim family in one of the major Pushtan tribes in the Northwest Frontier province of Pakistan. Having done his undergraduate work in Peshawar, he was now working on his master's degree in statistics at nearby Punjab University.

It was a joy to work with him. He was eager and faithful in preparing for our study times together. What was fascinating to me was to watch him learn to pray. His mother tongue was Pushtu. While he was a Muslim, he had to pray memorized prayers in Arabic. This did not set well with him. He wanted to pray in his mother tongue. He had never done it before. Haltingly at first, and then with ever more freedom, he learned to pour out his heart before God. It was beautiful to watch him grow.

There were many other things in Islam that did not set well with him. One of Islam's major failures was its inability to bring peace. All he ever knew as a child was the paralyzing fear of the blood feuds between the tribes and even within his tribe. Honor had to be avenged. Scores had to be settled. Fugitives were always on the run. He wanted out of that system.

Week after week, we studied the Gospels. One day, Sherdil said to me, "Brother Don, I want to be baptized." My heart soared with joy. We hadn't even discussed baptism. He came to it on his own. Then he added, "But I want to be baptized in my village among all my relatives and friends." My heart sank.

Years before, a missionary had won the son of a tribal chief to Christ. Having "lost" his own son, in retaliation the chief stalked and killed the oldest son of the missionary. The chief had avenged the "loss" of his son. Sherdil was from one of these tribes.

Astonished and apprehensive (for I thought I was going to be asked to do the baptizing), I blurted out, "Sherdil, why do you want to be baptized in your village? Surely they will kill you." What I could not bring myself to say was that I was afraid I would be killed along with him.

His answer was an incredible statement of courage. "All my life, I have seen men on the run. I am not going to give in to fear. I am not going to run. If I live, I live. And if I die, I die."

That night I did not sleep. The anguishing question that robbed me of sleep was, "Am I willing to die with my disciple?" Early the next morning, peace finally came. I had said to the Lord, "Lord, if this is what I must do, I will do it. My life is in Your hands."

I had never really faced death before. Yes, Mary Jo and I had left everything to follow Jesus: a promising career in medicine, family and friends, material goods and comforts. This was different. I did not really know what was in my own heart until the moment of truth came. Facing the possibility of death was not easy. But it was the best thing that had ever happened to me. It set me free from the fear of death. I was forced to this by Sherdil, my Pushtun disciple. He taught me to overcome the fear of death.

I suppose you want to know the rest of the story. After graduation, Sherdil returned to his village. He did not ask me to do the baptizing. Unknown to me, there was a Christian hospital in his town. The doctors had outstanding reputations of service to the community. They had saved hundreds of lives. Sherdil asked one of them to baptize him. And it was done in his village in front of all his relatives and friends.

There was an immediate uproar. Sherdil's father beat him up and disowned him. In response, Sherdil cried out to all the villagers, "I am a son of this village. I am one of you. I will not leave. I am going to sit at the village well until you take me back or until I die."

On the third night, his mother came secretly bringing him food. On the seventh day, his father stormed out, beat him up again, dragged him into his house and locked him up. His Bible and all his Christian books were burned. Day after day, the father brought leading Muslim scholars to try to convert Sherdil back to Islam. They could not break him.

Finally, at the end of six weeks the father broke. He said to Sherdil, "You are my son. I cannot change you. I cannot kill you." The father went and got him a job in a nearby factory.

Sherdil had won. He had broken the power of Islam in that village. He risked death. He refused to run. God honored the one who honored Him.

BROTHER, YOU SINNED

It all came about this way. I was fed up with these ethnocentric, prejudiced, inward-looking churches of Pakistan. It didn't matter which church or which denomination. They were all the same.

Historically, ninety-five percent of the members were third-generation Christians from a Hindu low-caste background. In our lingo, they would have been from the "ghetto," except the ghetto, in this case, was a social ghetto. It was called "untouchableness." Even though these "offscourings of the earth," to use one of the Apostle Paul's expressions (and that's the way Hindus and Muslims looked at them), had become "Christians," they were still treated as undesirable elements of society. The stigma of their former caste remained.

This persecution manifested itself in many ways. These people were often deprived of decent employment. The illiterate were often forced into menial street-cleaning jobs or working as laborers in brick kilns. The children were frequently denied admission into schools. In some strongly Muslim rural areas they were not allowed access to village wells. When hired as domestic servants, they were often abused, underfed and forced into generational debts. Their girls were frequently molested and sometimes raped by Muslim young men. Naturally, these Christians felt extreme animosity towards Muslims.

Missions had done a great job of helping this former "outcaste" community. They provided schools at every level: primary, middle, high school, technical training schools, nursing schools, and for the bright ones, scholarships to college. The most outstanding ones eventually got scholarships abroad. So missions did their part. But for all their uplifting work, they could not eradicate this "prejudice against Muslims" attitude from Christian minds.

All of this worked at cross-purposes with our mission's evangelistic efforts. The fruit of all of our tract and Gospel distribution, Bible correspondence schools, radio broadcasts and friendship evangelism got smashed up against the wall of Christian prejudice. Over and over again, I had seen new believers from Muslim backgrounds rejected in every way by Christians whenever they tried to join a local church. Questions popped out, like: "What do you want here?" "Have you been rejected by your father's second wife?" "Are you looking for a job?" "Are you planning to steal one of our girls?" "Are you trying to persuade the missionaries to take you in?"

I thought a lot about why God sent me to Pakistan. I was looking at the 97% unevangelized Muslims.[1] The Christians seemed to be looking out for their own protection and self-improvement. In utter exasperation, I made a lonely and drastic decision. Unless it unavoidably came my way, I decided not to seek Christian fellowship, but rather I would give all of my free time to Muslims.

The months rolled by. Old Christian friends slowly dropped away. They could not understand what was happening to me. Meanwhile, the time spent with Muslims did not fill the void in me. The sense of strengthening that came from genuine Christian fellowship was missing. At the end of six months I was utterly depressed.

Realizing I couldn't stand this self-imposed isolation anymore, I called up my old friend, Burkit Ullah Khokar. I had arranged to meet him in the air-conditioned Shezan's Restaurant there on the Mall Road. Away from the blistering light and dusty heat of a merciless pre-monsoon sun, we enjoyed mutton *biryani, dal-subzi,* and hot *nans* fresh from the tanoor. Following our normal chitchat over after-dinner tea, I began my confession, "Brother, I suppose you have been wondering where I've been for the last six months. Well, I decided not to seek Christian fellowship anymore, but to spend all my free time working with Muslims."

The words were barely out of my mouth, when he exploded in a burst of holy indignation. With blazing eyes and burning intensity, he said, "Brother, you have sinned!" If it had been anyone else, I would have brushed it off. But this was a man of exceptional integrity. His name was that of a Kashmiri Muslim family. He had chosen to identify with the suffering church (in spite of its faults). He had sacrificed a lucrative position with Burma Shell to head up InterVarsity Christian Fellowship, then after training his replacement, he accepted the presidency of the Pakistan Bible Society. Everything about this man spoke of integrity and his passionate love for Jesus Christ—and His Church.

He had called my behavior "sin." Scripture started flooding my shell-shocked mind: "By this will all men know that you are my disciples, if you have love for one another." "Do not forsake the assembling of yourselves together." "I was glad when they said to me, 'Let us go to the house of the Lord.'" "They devoted themselves to the apostles' teaching and to the fellowship, to breaking of bread and to prayer."

I really had sinned against the Lord and against His people. I asked brother Khokar for forgiveness. It was given. We prayed together. Fellowship was restored. Peace and joy returned. This brother helped me realize I could not make an "either-or" decision; it had to be both the Church and the mission.

1 There are 172 million Muslims in Pakistan today.

OKAY, THAT WAS FOR ME

The Pakistan government had just introduced brand new third-class-only trains. There would be no crowding. Every seat was reserved. No standing or sitting in the aisles. What a change.

Obligations back at Forman Christian College necessitated my traveling from Islamabad to Lahore, a journey of about eight hours. As I bought my ticket, I prayed, "O Father, please seat me beside someone with whom I may share my testimony and talk about You."

I got to my seat a few minutes early, wondering whom the Lord would put beside me. The seats were hard. There was no air-conditioning. The windows were wide open, great for viewing the changing scenery of the countryside from the rugged badlands of the north to the well-irrigated farms toward the south.

Departure time was near. The seat beside me was still empty. I heard many people offer bribes to the conductor. He refused to sell that seat. I was impressed. That was not what usually happened. The whistle blew. The train began to move. And I wondered why the seat beside me remained empty.

At the first stop down the track, a well-dressed, young government official got on. The seat was his. He was quite friendly. He knew all about my college, too. He attended our rival college across town, the prestigious Government College. We had a good laugh about our rivalry.

Mushtaq was not a good Muslim. His education had been more on the secular side. He wasn't sure about the meaning of life or the significance of religion. I told him that was the way I used to be—until my second year in medical school. He wanted to know what happened. I told the whole story.

When I was through, I asked Mushtaq if he had ever heard anything like that before. He said, "No, I never have. But I have been profoundly affected by someone who showed their Christian faith in a different way." I asked him to tell me about it.

He said he and his friend had gone up to Murree, the summer capital, where everyone goes to escape the heat. Murree is about 7,700 feet up in the Hindu Kush Mountains. It is a beautiful place perched on a ridge between ranges with slopes covered with pine and patches of terraced farmlands. Brilliant sunshine alternates with monsoon rains.

This particular evening Mushtaq and his friend were caught up in the living river of wall-to-wall people surging along the broad Mall Road. Off to the side, they spotted two young Roman Catholic sisters soliciting donations for their school.

Mushtaq and his friend were especially prejudiced against Roman Catholics. I asked why. He replied, "Because they practice celibacy. This is against God's natural order. The Holy Quran forbids monasticism. Every woman is supposed to have her husband. There are no single women in Islam. Islam is right. That's the way God made us."

He told me that he and his friend pushed their way

across the grain of this flowing crowd until they stood in front of these two pretty young nuns. One of them was holding her hand out for donations. To show his contempt, Mushtaq's friend leaned over and spit into the open hand of this sister. I asked, "And what happened next?"

At this point, Mushtaq had difficulty in talking. He said she pulled a handkerchief out of her sleeve and wiped the spittle off. Then she thrust out her hand and said, "Okay, that was for me; now what are you going to do for Jesus Christ?" He said, "We were both stunned and then became confused. My friend reached into his pocket, pulled out all his money and put it into her out-stretched hand. Then we walked away, thoroughly ashamed of ourselves."

I turned to look at Mushtaq. Tears were coming down his cheeks. I said to him, "Mushtaq, you are not very far from the kingdom." He said, "Yes, I know." He was very quiet and pensive. We talked seriously about the things of the Lord. I never knew if he ever came to saving faith because he got off the train unexpectedly before we reached Lahore. But I do know he was deeply marked by that selfless act of love on the part of that beautiful and, as it turned out, born-again sister.

I've asked many people what they would do if some-one spit in their open hand. Their answers are not worth quoting. It was the Christ-like gesture of this unique, love-filled, forgiving, young Christian woman who broke the hard hearts of these two young Muslim men.

How about you and me? Could we do that? Only with the Spirit of Christ living in us. He is the only one who can empower us in love to say, "Okay, that was for me; now what are you going to do for Jesus Christ?"

Lord, fill us all with Your Holy Spirit. Empower us all to demonstrate that same unquenchable love and that same boldly forgiving spirit as we ask our Muslim friends, "What are you going to do about Jesus Christ?"

JUST ONE SOUL

The question of whether or not we should have servants on the mission field bothered us a lot.

When we left the United States to go to Pakistan, we gave away everything we had: wedding presents, refrigerator, washing machine, electrical appliances, children's toys, etc. We thought we would be living in a mud house with few amenities.

Words fail to communicate the sense of awe we felt when we reached the ancient city of Sialkot, our new home. Long ago, this city had been the seat of an ancient empire. More recently, it had been a British cantonment city. Now it was occupied by the Pakistan army. It was in a lush area of the fertile farmland of the Punjab. To the east you could see the green foothills of Jummu-Kashmir ascending ever higher to give way to the majestic Himalayan Mountains.

Our arrival was also attended by a big shock. The house we were going to live in had a history. The British government had awarded it to a sister mission to compensate the death of one of their missionaries killed in an anti-British rebellion. They hated it and quickly gave it to our mission in exchange for other property. This *Lal Kothi* (Red Bungalow) was a fourteen-room sprawling, squat-ugly "castle" with twenty-foot high ceilings that we were going to share with a family and two single men. It was surrounded by a galaxy of servants' quarters—at an appropriate distance, of course.

Our missionary career was to begin here. We lived as the guests of an older couple while we did intensive language study. Out of the blue, our senior missionary supervisor stunned us one day with the announcement, "It is time for you to hire a servant to help with your housework." Tempestuous waves of protest, outrage and confusion swirled through our minds and emotions. This seemed like a betrayal of our missionary call. We came to serve, not to be served.

Cold logic ultimately prevailed. Six hours of language study a day with a private tutor, two hours of ministry, all those hours spent in preparation, plus trying to lead a normal family life, left no time for taking care of household tasks. We reluctantly acquiesced.

It was an unhappy experience. Salary or not, the prevailing ethos was that servants should be "maintained" by their masters. Towels, pillowcases, socks and underwear slowly and mysteriously disappeared. Later, when we tried a cook, it was sugar, flour, tea and whatnot. This kind of "help yourself to whatever you want" attitude among the servants drove us nuts. They saw it as the "given" of a normal symbiotic relationship; we saw it as a total lack of integrity on their part. "After all," we fumed, "why do we pay them a salary?"

In God's providence and as an answer to prayer, we finally found a lovely Christian widow with her infant son. We adopted them into our family. Mary Jo and she acted more like sisters than mistress and servant. They shared any task. How can I forget the image of them both drenched in sweat, with matted hair and clingy clothes, doing the wash together in 110-degree heat.

The children adored this diminutive *ayah* with a twinkle in her eye and a deep sense of right and wrong. She was their baby-sitter, their tutor in Punjabi culture and language, and their magic chef, the source of endless kitchen surprises.

Birkit Bibi was no ordinary helper; she was a fiercely committed Christian. We prayed together over all kinds of problems. She tackled community wrongs. She cared about the spiritual condition of those around us.

Unknown to us, at least in the beginning, she had a secret passion, a private goal. At the beginning of every year she prayed this simple prayer, "Lord, use me to bring one soul to you this year." Her humble origins, her meager education never deterred her. God had given her this marvelous, unquenchable faith.

I can still feel the intense excitement that consumed her as she sensed her lost friend coming to the point of accepting the Lord. You could tell the time was near when she asked for a gift Bible to have at the ready. For years we watched with wonder as God answered the prayers of this remarkable saint.

We had prayed for a Christian widow to be our helper in the home. We got much more than a helper. We got a Christian sister and, even more, a soul-winner. God planted Birkit Bibi right in the midst of our family to hold us up to a magnificent Christian standard.

Who of us has been as consistent? We, with our far more advanced educations, our unbelievable resources and our technical know-how? Looking back, I thank God for this passionate soul-winner, this teacher who taught us so powerfully through her life and through this relentless pursuit of her goal: "O God, give me just one soul this year." Just one soul.

THE FEARLESS QUILTER

The British meant well. From 1858 until the Partition of India in 1947, they were stewards of the lands that are now Pakistan, India and Bangladesh.

Five wonderful rivers fed the fertile plains of the Punjab[1] there in the heart of Pakistan: the Sutlej, the Ravi, the Chenab, the Jhelum and the Indus. Like fingers of a hand, they flowed down from the foothills of Jummu-Kashmir and the Hindu-Kush Mountains to form the mighty Indus River, the main waterway that runs into the Arabian Sea—a course of a thousand miles in all.

In late summer the clouds would begin to gather, billowing up from the Bay of Bengal and the Indian Ocean. Then for six weeks, the land would be bathed with the monsoon rains. Rivers filled, the land flourished—for a while. When the rains subsided and the easternmost rivers ran dry, the land withered. Potentially verdant soil lay caked and cracked under the blistering sun.

It was the engineers who first thought of shunting water from the heavy-volume rivers to the dry riverbeds of the others. And so great link canals were built there in the plains of the five waters.

Great ideas often have unintended consequences. These fabulous link canals did their job in the dry seasons.

But when the monsoon rains came, they hindered the natural run-off of the water. They acted as dams, which invariably led to flooding.

One particular year, the unimaginable happened. Heavier than usual monsoon rains overwhelmed the system. The floodwaters covered two hundred unbroken miles between the rivers. The photos in the local newspapers were heartbreaking. Mud houses have no resistance to strong flowing water. The devastation was mind-boggling. There were hundreds of thousands of homeless waiting for the waters to subside. And winter was not far behind.

Relief was quickly mobilized. There was grain to be had and most of the animals survived. The hapless tens of thousands would not die. Mud houses could be rebuilt; articles of wood and metal could be scavenged from the muck, but what about the bedding?

Let me explain the bedding. The most popular covering is a kind of quilt called *razai*. It is very simply made. You cut the bolts of printed cotton fabric to the size you want, make a matching piece for top and bottom, sew three sides together, stuff it with cotton, sew up the open end, and then run strong threads through this padding every few inches so that it is well joined together to keep the cotton in place. A very simple thing.

No one anticipated such a disaster. It would be a race against winter to mobilize ladies all over the Punjab to get enough *razais* put together before the near-freezing temperatures set in.

All other work stopped. Women gathered in clean, open spaces wherever they could and began one of the greatest quilting parties in the history of the Punjab. I can still see my wife, Mary Jo, on the open platform steps leading up to the classrooms in our seminary in Gujranwala: one white-skinned lady among her many brown-skinned sisters quilting away.

Lorries were rented. They were huge trucks with astonishing artwork in a riot of colors covering every inch of the outside of the vehicles. It took a while to make enough *razais* to fill a lorry. Finally, the first truck was ready. Then the question: Who would go to help in the distribution among these rural women sitting in the dried-out humps of dirt that used to be their village?

Yep. You guessed it. Mary Jo was the first to volunteer. One lone, foreign woman, wedged in between a fierce Pathan truck driver on one side of her and a goodhearted Roman Catholic priest on the other.

I had my misgivings. "Honey, are you sure you want to do this? We don't know either one of these men. And you are all alone with them." How could I ever forget her reply? "Where is your faith? God has promised to go with me. Of course, I am not afraid. I am doing what God wants me to do. He will take care of me."

I watched as they drove away, my wife seated between a Pathan truck driver and an Irish priest in a most colorful lorry, setting out to deliver quilts to the waiting women of the devastated land. With the greatest of admiration, I call her by the name she has so roundly deserved, "The Fearless Quilter."

1 Punjab is made from two words: *punj*, meaning five, and *ab*, meaning water.

WHAT DO YOU THINK OF MUHAMMAD?

No question is more crucial to understanding the relationship between Islam and Christianity than "What do you think of Muhammad?" Ancillary to this is the second question that is rocking Western civilization today: "Is Islam a religion of peace?" The answer to the second question depends on how you answer the first one. *And your life may depend on your answer!*

Islam sees itself as a theocracy (the rule of God), not a democracy (the rule of man). It believes that Muhammad was the last and greatest prophet. It teaches that Jesus was only a prophet for His age, not for today. Muslims believe that God sent Muhammad to correct the failures of the previous monotheistic faiths, Judaism and Christianity.

So from the mouth of Muhammad, we supposedly have the last words of God to the human race: not only the words preserved in the Quran, but also his words preserved in the written traditions called the *Hadith*. From these two sources, the Quran and the *Hadith*, legal scholars set out to articulate the "Laws of God." These laws are to be totally binding on the whole human race for all time!

In the development of these laws, the name of God and of Muhammad were so intertwined that to speak against one was to speak against the other. Of course, this then created an aura around Muhammad equal to that of God. In reality, *Muhammad's name became more important.* You see, in the Muslim world people use God's name (Allah) in profane ways all day long and no one notes it. But if you speak disparagingly of Muhammad, you are to be put to death.

Recently, in the United Nations, Muslims sponsored a non-binding resolution that if any one spoke disparagingly of another's religion he should be prosecuted. The Muslim interpretation of what this means is that if you put Islam or Muhammad in a bad light, you will be prosecuted. What does this include? Well, it could include anything from the Quran or the Traditions that would make Muhammad look bad, *even if they are true*; and it could include anything from Islamic history that would make Islam look bad, even if it includes wars of aggression, massacres of non-Muslims and any other atrocity.

In the same vein, in Australia, two young men were arrested under similar laws for this very thing. They were using only verses from the Quran that put Muhammad in an unfavorable light. This case went to the High Court: after six years they were exonerated.

What is so very interesting about Muhammad and the Quran is that they libel the Lord Jesus Christ. They regard Him only as a prophet for His age. They deny that He is the Son of God, that God is His Father. They deny His crucifixion. To them, He is only a man, not the Savior of the world.

Even though these above comments seem not to be germane to the main thrust of this tale, they do illustrate the utter hypocrisy of Islam. Muslims will not tolerate the slightest critical appraisal of the character of Muhammad or the Quran, while at the same time they seek to destroy the heart of the Gospel message of the Lord Jesus Christ.

Now, back to the question with which we started,

"What do you think of Muhammad?" Well, if you know the Quran, the *Hadith* and the biography of Muhammad, you are in a tough spot.

Mohammed was a man who mandated total warfare against all non-Muslims for the rest of human history! Even if Jews and Christians submit to Islam, they are relegated to the level of second class citizens. They are forced to pay punitive taxes and lose the freedom to propagate their faith, build new churches or repair old ones. Of course, they were expelled from what is today Saudi Arabia. If they resist Islamic law, they are to be put to death.

If you go on to dig out the details of his life and teaching concerning women, marriage, divorce, concubines, slaves and the annihilation of those who resist Islam, it actually is a very ugly picture. *And all of this based on their own sources!*

So what do you say when someone asks you, "What do you think of Muhammad?" Remember, you will be put to death in a Muslim country if you say anything negative. Even in your own country, someday you might have a case brought against you through the auspices of the United Nations.

This is all background information for what happened to me in a police station in Murree, Pakistan long ago. Because I was a foreigner, I had to check out with the police in the town where I lived, and check in with the police in the town where I was going to stay if longer than seven days.

The day I went to register at the Murree police station, the place was filled with the top police officers of the federal government. There had been a high-level political assassination the day before.

In front of this awesome array of the top police of Pakistan, the sergeant at the desk, who had known me for years, asked: "Mr. McCurry, you have lived in our country a long time. You know us; you know our people. What do you think of Muhammad?" Everyone in that room became deathly quiet. What would you have said?

I prayed and said, "Okay, Lord, it's your turn. Teach me what to say." This is what the Lord gave me: "I have read the Quran and I have studied the life of Muhammad. I have read the *Injeel*[1] and I have studied the life of Jesus Christ, and I am in love with Jesus Christ."

After a few moments of eerie silence, everyone went about their business. I had not fallen into the trap of speaking against Muhammad. And, I might add, I did bear witness to my faith and love for the Lord Jesus Christ. God gave those words. Blessed be His Name. And may He do the same for you when the time comes.

---

1 The quranic word for the Gospels.

IF YOU ARE THE LIGHT OF THE WORLD, THEN…

He stood there in the midst of the mustard fields on the edge of Gujranwala Town. It was 4:00 in the morning, the time he would normally be going to the mosque to recite his prayers. So what was he doing there so early that particular morning?

For secularized Western readers, what happened next may be hard to believe. For people living in the non-Western world, it would not be such a surprise.

However, before telling you what happened, you need to know a little more about this unique man. Aslam had memorized the Quran in Arabic. This Muslim holy book is about two-thirds the size of the New Testament. By our standards this was a remarkable feat of memory. In Pakistan, this was ordinary. Those who have done this are called by a special title: *Hafiz*. Aslam was a *Hafiz*.

In addition, Aslam had a beautiful voice. He was often asked to chant Quranic passages at the central mosque on Muslim holy days. The whole city knew that voice.

From his knowledge of the Quran, Aslam had reached a strange conclusion: Jesus was greater than Muhammad *in the Quran!*[1] Aslam had put it all together: Jesus was born of a virgin. He was called "Holy Son." He was born sinless. He was all-righteous, among those nearest to God. He could heal the blind, cure leprosy and raise the dead. The Quran even says He created birds of earth, breathed His spirit into them and they flew away. He was called "a Spirit from God" (*Ruhullah*) and "a Word from God" (*Kalamatullah*). The Quran says He was to be "a sign for all peoples."

Aslam wanted to know more about Jesus. For three days, he walked the streets of our city of four hundred thousand people asking everyone where he could find a Christian or a copy of the *Injil* (the New Testament). God providentially arranged for him to meet Caleb, a young man I had been discipling from the Christian Technical Training Centre. Caleb got him enrolled in a Bible correspondence course. Aslam eventually got a copy of the New Testament.

It was when he got to the words of Jesus in the Gospel of John that he was stopped dead in his tracks. Jesus said, "I am the Light of the World. Whoever follows me will never walk in darkness, but will have the Light of Life" (John 8:12). From his knowledge of Sufi (mystical) Islam, Aslam had heard of divine light dwelling in the Sufi leaders. But Jesus, almost two thousand years earlier, claimed to be the "Light of Life— the Light of the World."

This is why he was in the mustard fields at 4:00 in the morning—praying: "O Jesus, if you really are the Light of the World, appear to me, so that I will know it for sure and never doubt." That morning Aslam was enveloped in a supernatural light that shone on him from heaven. From that moment on, he never doubted.

Soon God opened his mind to fully understand the Gospel. For two years he sought baptism in the local church. It was of a different cultural background than Aslam's. The pastor and people ignored him.

One day there were riots in our city. Members of the

Jamaat-i-Islami (the Party of Islam) had heard that the Pakistan High Court had declared members of the Ahmadi sect as non-Muslims.[2] They began to kill Ahmadis wherever they found them. Muhammad Aslam watched twelve Ahmadis die in the house across the street. He asked himself, "Am I ready to die for Jesus?" He said, "No, I have not completed my obedience to Him. I have not been baptized."

In this agitated state of mind, he came to me. "Uncle, I watched Ahmadi Muslims die today. I want to be ready to die for Jesus, but I am not baptized yet. No one here will baptize me. Would you arrange for my baptism?"

Knowing full well the hostile attitude of the local Hindu-convert church to Muslims and Muslim converts, I reluctantly arranged for Aslam to be baptized in Lahore, a nearby city, by a Presbyterian pastor who himself was a convert from Islam.

It was a wintry January day. The large tank of water outside Bethany Church was ice-cold. When Aslam came up out of the water, he was ecstatic. Shivering and smiling at the same time, he shouted, *"Al hamdallilah."*[3] I have never seen a man so happy, so fulfilled. We sang all the way back to Gujranwala.

He had completed his obedience to the Lord. He had finally been baptized. Now, if need be, he was ready to die for Jesus. What an example of perseverance and courage he was to me.

1 It's true, by the way.

2 See "A Fox in the Chicken Coop".

3 "Praise to the Lord!"

WHAT? USE THE QURAN—IN EVANGELISM?

For decades, missionaries have learned how to attack the Muslim's holy book, the Quran. They could show the contradictions, the abrogated verses, and misunderstandings that Muhammad had about the Bible characters and stories and scientific errors. If we studied the Quran at all, it was usually to learn how to tear it apart and discredit it in the eyes of Muslims. This approach seldom, if ever, helped Muslims come to Christ.

Every once in a while, someone tries something new. In this case it was Muhammad Aslam. He is the man who had memorized the Quran and, in doing so, discovered that Jesus was greater than Muhammad—in the Quran.[1] This ultimately led him to personal faith in Jesus Christ and later to his baptism.

What happened next, however, turned out to be one of the most profound lessons I have ever learned from a national brother. This is Aslam's story.

He had just returned from his baptism in the nearby city of Lahore. When he entered his family home in Gujranwala, his relatives wanted to know where he had been. Without a moment's hesitation he said, "I've just returned from my baptism in Lahore."

The explosion inside the family was instantaneous.

His stepmother began shrieking, "Why are you trying to destroy our family?" His father said, "We will have to kill you." His brother, who knew the Islamic law said, "Take him to the mosque. Let the *Imam*[2] talk to him. The *Shariah* (Islamic) law says he has three days to repent."

On the way to the mosque, his stepmother kept on screaming hysterically, "Aslam has become a *kaffir* (blasphemer). He is destroying our family. Kill him." A crowd began to grow. Word of his apostatizing (conversion to Christ) began to spread like wildfire through that part of the city.

By the time he was dragged inside, the mosque had completely filled up with angry Muslims. The *Imam* and two *maulvis*[3] were there. The interrogation began: "How could you do this? What did the Christians offer you? A better job? We'll get you a better job. A woman? We'll get you a woman. How did they get you? How much money did they give you? Tell us," they screamed.

Calmly, Aslam took out his handkerchief, tied it neatly into a four-cornered covering for his head, folded his arms and began to chant verses from the Quran.

The crowd immediately quieted down. Everyone recognized his voice for he had often chanted the Quran publicly at the mosque on special holy days. In the hush of that sacred hall, soon all that could be heard was Aslam's voice chanting beautiful Arabic verses from the Quran.

When he sensed that the audience was totally with him, he stopped chanting and began to explain in the Punjabi language what these words meant. The crowd was captivated—up to a point. He had been quoting verses that mentioned *Isa*, the Arabic name for Jesus in the Quran. Then he explained what these Quranic references to Jesus meant from his newfound knowledge of the *Injil* (the Gospels).

As soon as he sensed the crowd getting restless, he began reciting another Jesus-passage from the Arabic Quran. When everyone was quiet again, he then explained what it meant from the Gospels. He was able to do this for about forty-five minutes.

It finally dawned on one of the *maulvis* that Aslam was using the Quran to bear witness to his new faith in Jesus. The *maulvi* began to shout to the crowd, "This man has a demon. We do not know how to control him. Everyone must leave the mosque at once." When the mosque was cleared, the *maulvis* and the local *Imam* took Aslam into a side chamber for private "treatment."

After enduring a tirade of abusive threats, Aslam asked one of the *maulvis* to bring him a Quran. Taking it respectfully in his hands, he held it out to them and said, "*Maulvi Sahiban* (respected scholars), if you can show me from this *Quran Shareef* (the Noble Quran) how I can receive the forgiveness of my sins, I will become a Muslim again right now." One of the *maulvis* snatched the Quran from his hands, cursed him, struck him and threatened that in three days they would kill him unless he renounced Christ and became a Muslim again. Then they drove him out of the mosque.

The next day, twelve young men came to his house. Fearing the worst, he was wonderfully surprised to hear them say, "Aslam, yesterday we heard you bear witness to your new faith in the mosque. We want you to tell us everything you know about *Isa*." Knowing he couldn't entertain them in his father's house, he took them to a local teashop and began to teach them about Jesus.

In the days following, many attempts were made by various authorities to bring Aslam back to Islam. He remained true to his new faith in Christ. Fortunately, he was not killed but he was kicked out of his home. He found lodging with sympathetic Christians.

A few months later, Aslam brought two other *huffuz*[4] to me. He had led them to Christ beginning from the *Isa* material in the Quran and by fully explaining to them what the Gospels really say.

It took a while for all of this to sink in. Eventually I realized this approach of starting with Quranic material about Jesus—and He is mentioned ninety-three times in the Quran—and urging Muslims to look at the Biblical material to which it alluded, just might be one of the best approaches ever, at least for those Muslims who are familiar with the Quran.

Time has borne this out. I have had many Christian workers, even Arab Christians from the Middle East, who formerly detested the Quran, come back to me and say this teaching revolutionized their approach to Muslims. It gave them a new, positive way of relating to Muslims.

It was Muhammad Aslam who first opened my eyes to the possibility of this approach. He showed me how to take the book I formerly detested and use it to explain Jesus to devout Muslims.

1 See "Caring for God's Own" and "If You Are the Light of the World, Then..."

2 The recognized leader of the prayers.

3 Muslim religious experts on the law.

4 Plural of *hafiz*, one who has memorized the Quran.

A NEW WORK AMONG MUSLIMS?

The pastor was late that warm Sunday morning. The chapel bells had long since rung. Christian grandmothers, wives, little girls, all decked out in their highly colorful *shalwar* and *qameez*, with graceful head veils, were taking the seats on the *zanana* (female) side of the sanctuary. The Punjabi men and boys, some in plain-colored *shalwar* and *qameez*, and others in Western shirts and trousers, were taking their accustomed places, too.

This chapel had no screens at the open windows or doors. Birds, too, attended church every Sunday. They flew in and out at their own pleasure from their nests high in the rough rafters. How often in Pakistan we found customs and scenes that reminded us of biblical pictures. Today was one of those days. The words of Psalm 84:1-3 came to mind:

How lovely is your dwelling place, O Lord Almighty!
My soul yearns, even faints, for the courts of the Lord;
My heart and my flesh cry out for the living God.
Even the sparrow has found a home,
And the swallow a nest for herself,
Where she may have her young—a place near your altar,
O Lord Almighty, my King and my God.

My reverie didn't last long. A talented group of teenage students from the nearby Christian Technical Training Center had seated themselves on the floor. Spontaneously they formed themselves into a musical ensemble. One of them began to squeeze the bellows of the small harmonium with the two-octave keyboard. Another began to tune the *tabla*—the "male and female" drums for which India is so famous. Another picked up the tambourine and began to pick up the rhythm of the drums. The young man with the *chimta*, the fire tongs, completed the group. The *chimtas* were a pair of three-foot-long flat iron strips joined at one end that could be made to clack musically.

A few others sat with them to form a choir. They began to sing. We all joined in as we sang those old familiar psalms, hymns and choruses, mostly in the Punjabi tongue. This was the mother tongue of these sons and grandsons of Hindu converts from earlier decades. Since I love to sing, I was really "into it" with them. Gradually I began to focus on the words. Suddenly I became conscious of these strange sounding Hindu words of worship. I was intensely aware of where we were. We were in Pakistan, a land that was then 97% Muslim.

Music is never heard in Muslim mosques, much less music sung in the language of hated India! Pakistan and India had already fought three major wars. And the guerrilla infiltration of Pakistani *mujjahadin* into Indian-held Muslim Kashmir was still going on. These boys were singing in the language of the enemy!

I abruptly stopped singing. Inside I began to seethe with anger. Unvoiced words were raging inside of me: "You stupid sons and grandsons of Hindu untouchable converts! What do you think you are doing? You are singing in the language of the enemy as we sit here in Muslim Pakistan!" And then the Lord rebuked me. Deep in my spirit a conversation began that went something like this:

The Lord: "Don! Be quiet! What do you do when you feel

spiritually dry and want to be revived?"

Me: "I seek out dear American missionary friends and I pour out my heart and then we begin to sing in our mother tongue from a common repertoire of spiritual songs and choruses."

The Lord: "That's what these boys are doing. They are pouring out their hearts to Me—in their mother tongue. This is their cultural background. Join them, but I am going to do a new work among Muslims."

I sat bolt upright. "A new work among Muslims?" What did that mean? No one had ever thought of such a thing before. We had always sought to integrate Muslim-background new believers into the existing church. They had to leave their people and their culture. They had to adjust to what is. They had to learn our ways.

What was the Lord trying to say? Was He saying Muslims who came to Him didn't have to embrace the Hindu-ish culture of the existing church? Was He saying that a church would emerge that fit the cultural background of Muslim Pakistan? These were new and strange questions.

Life was never the same after that. New ideas were in the air. New approaches could be tried. New churches could form that would fit the culture of Muslim Pakistan. The vision was born of a door opening for thousands of Muslims to come to Jesus who would be able to worship in forms congenial to their culture.

Inadvertently, it was that beautiful group of young men from Hindu-ish background, singing to Jesus with all the passion of their souls—in their mother tongue—that set the stage for those words the Lord spoke so deeply in my spirit that Sunday morning, "I am going to do a new work among the Muslims."

A BROTHER HAS FALLEN

It was two o'clock in the morning. There was a persistent knocking on our verandah door. Who could it be at such an hour? Half awake, I made myself decent and stumbled to the door. "William, what are you doing here, so far from home and at this hour?"

We were living in Gujranwala, Pakistan, at the time where I taught in the Theological Seminary. William Gill was from a Pakistani Christian family. His parents gave him an English first name. "Gill" is actually a Kashmiri tribal family name.

He replied that a brother in their Rawalpindi assembly had fallen into sin and had run away. He said that he had been searching for him for three days. He asked if he could have a place to sleep for just a few hours before pushing on. We welcomed him in, of course, gave him a bed and a great breakfast later that morning.

William had been won to Christ while in the Pakistan air force. The discipleship training he had experienced in Kohat gave him a good grasp of the Bible and a level of commitment that was exceptional.

Some background information on the Pakistani church scene may be helpful here. Before the British quit the Indian subcontinent in 1947, Pakistan, India and Bangladesh were all part of one great country, British India. The caste system was pervasive throughout India. This sharp stratification of society was there before the British came. It was still there when they left.

At the very bottom of this system were the "untouchables," the *achoot*. These were a people who were not allowed to even let their shadows fall across the path of the upper classes. Greetings were done in such a way that no two bodies ever touched. The church grew out of this system.

Protestant Christianity rode into India on the coattails of the British. Under British rule, these unfortunate *achoots* saw a way to escape the intolerable cruelty of their caste. Beginning around 1890 and continuing for the next 40 years, a mass movement of about five hundred thousand untouchables became nominally "Christian." This tidal wave of humanity overwhelmed the puny missionary force with their tiny fledgling churches.

Enormous problems now faced the Christian movement. How do you disciple such a vast flood of these tragic victims fleeing from Hinduism? The sad truth was that discipleship failed to keep pace with the number of "conversions." These new "converts" brought their illiteracy, their ethics and their morals with them. Four out of every five could not read. The results were predictable. The unconverted church members overwhelmed those who genuinely believed. Party spirit, power struggles, lawsuits eventually ran rampant in the churches. Church discipline was a farce.

The small indigenous Brethren movement was different. There was strong emphasis on repentance at the time of conversion and firm discipling followed. All were expected to know the Bible well. Faithfulness to the teaching and example of Jesus was expected. When he retired from the air force, William Gill chose not to return to his nominal home church but to become part of this new vigorous indigenous movement.

It was against the background of moral laxity in the other denominational churches that made William's example so outstanding. I can never forget those burning words tumbling out of the lips of this exhausted man, "A brother has fallen. In shame he has run away. I must find him and bring him back." Village to village, town to town, city ghetto to city ghetto, he relentlessly pursued this frightened sinner. Little rest. Little food. Snatches of sleep here and there. What love, what energy, what spirit drove this leader? It was Jesus.

On the fourth day, William found his man—guilt-laden, confused, self-condemned, running, running, running.

William's example reminded me of the concluding words of James' letter:

> My brothers, if one of you should wander from the truth and someone should bring him back, remember this: Whoever turns a sinner from the error of his way will save him from death and cover over a multitude of sins (James 5:19, 20).

Do you remember how Jesus described the love of God? "If a man owns a hundred sheep, and one of them wanders away, will he not leave the ninety-nine on the hills and go to look for the one that wandered off?" (Matthew 18:12). William left his flock to go looking for the one that wandered off.

If ever there was a man in this world who taught me what Jesus' love for a fallen brother was like, it was my friend William Gill of Rawalpindi. He could not rest until he had found his "lost sheep" and brought him back, back to the Lord, back to the flock, back to his family.

JATS OR RAJPUTS?

In Pakistan, being a land of great political instability, it was not uncommon for the president, in this case, Zulfiqar Ali Bhutto, to make political appointments for his own reasons. The new Senior Superintendent of Police in our District of Gujranwala was such an appointee. Only we did not know it at the time.

One day this new SSP, Captain Nafaq Khan,[1] called me to his office. On my way to meet him, all kinds of wild thoughts were going through my mind: "What have I done?" "What kind of trouble am I in?" "This has never happened before." "Lord, give me grace in the eyes of this man."

Nothing had prepared me for what really happened. This was the gist of what he said: "Don, I am the newly appointed SSP for Gujranwala. One of my jobs is to keep you under surveillance. You and I are both educated men.[2] I propose that we become good friends. Let's enjoy one another's company while we are here."

He then asked, "What do you like to do for recreation?" Thinking back on previous pleasures as an accomplished badminton player, I said, "I like to play badminton." He said, "Great," and he gave instructions for his orderly to set up a badminton court in his yard.

This turned out to be a stupid choice on my part.

This man had been a university champion player and he was ten years younger than I. I remember the day when I finally scored one point on him. It was not an enjoyable experience, although I did enjoy the tea and pastries we always had afterwards.

At one of the teas, I said, "Nafaq, I think I made a mistake in choosing badminton. I am past my prime. I am really not offering you any competition. Could we do something that would include our wives?" He said, "What did you have in mind?" I said, "We live in a beautiful district with lovely government rest houses along these picturesque canals. I wonder if we could do picnics together." He thought this was a good idea. So we had picnics in rest houses along the Punjab's gorgeous tree-lined canals.

What did we talk about? I told him all about the different things I was doing in and with the local churches and in the seminary where I taught. I omitted the references to the evangelistic activities. He actually admired the spirit of dedication: the hard work of cycling into the inaccessible villages, the facility we showed in the local languages and, most of all, being willing to work with a largely illiterate population. No problems.

Eventually, my wife and I felt bold enough to invite him and his wife into our home for dinner and to play parlor games. *Clue* turned out to be the most interesting one.

It was during one of those relaxed evening tête-à-têtes that Nafaq shared something that he really shouldn't have. He said, "You know, Don, President Bhutto appointed me to this post for only one year. The first six months I have been instructed to give a hard time to the mafia belonging to the *Jats* and to be tolerant of the mafia belonging to the *Rajputs*. Then at the end of the six months, I am to reverse the policy. Mr. Bhutto, in this way, hopes to keep the Punjabis divided so that they will never unite against him in an election."

Jats? Rajputs? What was he talking about? I thought all Punjabis were the same! Then somewhere in the dim recesses of my mind, the memory of the Muslim conquests of the peoples of the Indian subcontinent awakened.

The Hindu *Rajputs*, the fiercest of the high caste Hindu warriors, were those who killed their women and children before they went into desperate battles. Eventually they were won over to Islam by being awarded high offices in the Muslim government.

The *Jats* were a more rebellious Hindu caste against whom the *Rajput* Islamic converts fought. Eventually they too were subdued, but by force, at the hands of the *Rajputs*. The rivalry between the *Rajputs* and the *Jats* lives on to this day. How devilish of the Pakistani *Sindhi*-background President Bhutto to know about and exploit this ancient rivalry to keep the Punjabis divided.

It was then I began to link this information with some disturbing recent events.

Through one of my students at the Gujranwala Theological Seminary, I had gotten in with a group of Punjabi Muslim businessmen in the city. That was quite an accomplishment.

However, when it became known that I was the friend of this particular businessman and his circle of friends, others in the city avoided me like the plague. Previously, I thought that it was simply because I was a Christian. Now I wondered if it was this *Jat-Rajput* thing.

Armed with my new insights, the next time I met my friend, I casually got around to asking what his ancestral background was. He proudly shared that he was from *Rajput* stock. Then I began to ask him how things worked in the city, like, "Was there a *Rajput-Jat* rivalry going on?" He just glared at me and said, "You better believe it."

Then I knew. The men in the city who looked daggers at me were *Jats*! They knew I was in with the *Rajputs*. The lesson God was teaching me became crystal clear. If you have a burden on your heart to win eighty-eight million[3] Muslim Punjabis to the Lord, you will have to have two teams: one for the *Jats* and another for the *Rajputs*.

Captain Nafaq Khan, you played a devious game with your compatriots. But you were also a good friend. God used you to teach us vital background information for developing an adequate strategy for reaching the Punjabis—both kinds—the *Jats* and *Rajputs*. Thank you, sir.

---

1 Name has been changed.
2 His education included a degree at the Sorbonne University in Paris.
3 The census figure at the time.

GOD IS NOT MOCKED

All "Tales That Teach" are not necessarily uplifting. Occasionally one teaches by way of warning. This is one of those.

As you know, Mary Jo and I served as missionaries in Pakistan for many years. John Meadowcroft, my colleague at Gujranwala Theological Seminary in Gujranwala, Pakistan, opened a Theological Education by Extension center in a nearby city. When he returned to his homeland, it fell to me to step in and carry on with the program.

In the class to which I fell heir, there were several Christian leaders who were lacking seminary education. They now wanted to take advantage of this opportunity to get a seminary degree.

At the time, we were doing an inductive Bible study on the book of Jeremiah. We used a brilliant textbook prepared by Ross Kinsler, a missionary working in Latin America. Ross had gone to the trouble of sorting out the messages in the book of Jeremiah according to the chronology of events going on in the lives of the kings of Judah. The book came alive for most of us.

Spiritually, the condition of our denomination of some 250 churches in Pakistan was not healthy. Not only was there a satanic spirit of divisiveness destroying the churches, there were also cases of theft, lying, power struggles, and occasionally immorality. It was a return to the world characterized by "the lust of the flesh,[1] the lust of the eyes[2] and the pride of life."[3]

We hoped that by introducing this profound study of the book of Jeremiah in the seminary and in the extension centers, God would be pleased to bring a revival to the churches, starting with those who attended our classes.

Often in the past, God sent prophets to his wayward people to warn them of dire consequences if they did not cease their rebellions against Him, repent of their sins and turn back to Him with all their hearts. More often than not, the prophets were ignored or worse. Do you remember the long list of atrocities against God's servants mentioned in Hebrews 11:35-38a?

Some were tortured, others faced jeers and flogging, while still more were chained and put in prison. They were stoned, they were sawed in two, and they were put to death by the sword. They went about in sheepskins and goatskins, destitute, persecuted and mistreated—the world was not worthy of them.

Things had not gotten this bad in the churches in Pakistan. But I was reminded of the teaching of my favorite professor when I was in seminary, Dr. James Kelso, professor of Old Testament, Hebrew and archeology. He said, in commenting on the apostatizing of the people of God in the days of the prophets, "The priests always killed the prophets." Priests often degenerated into worldly bureaucrats, the prophets were the great visionaries and the defenders of the honor of God. Our church had killed its visionaries.

When God sends His Holy Spirit to anoint His teacher, His teaching then becomes "...the aroma of Christ among those who are being saved and those who are perishing. To the one we are the smell of death; to the other, the fragrance of life" (2 Cor. 2:15, 16).

Who can forget the tragic event in the life of the early Church when a man and his wife allowed Satan to fill their hearts and lie to the Holy Spirit? First, Ananias was confronted by Peter, who said, "You have not lied to men but to God." Ananias fell down and died. Later, his wife, not knowing what had happened, came in and was tested by Peter. She too lied and fell and died under the judgment of God (Acts 5:4-10).

There was a student in my class who was a leader of great power. He had risen far above all rivals. He was in a sense "untouchable," beyond the reach of the words and deeds of ordinary men. His adulterous relationship with the wife of one of his workers was known more widely than he thought.

One unforgettable night, we were in Jeremiah's famous passage on the denunciation of the lying prophets. In this passage were the words, "The land is full of adulterers; because of the curse the land lies parched" (Jer. 23:10). Because each student was to write a paper on some theme in the book of Jeremiah, this prominent leader, in a mocking spirit, asked, "Would you like me to write on the theme of God's judgment on adultery?"

What would you have done if you had been in my shoes? Before I knew it, these words were out of my mouth, "Tatabaz,[4] you don't have to write that paper; the judgment of God has already come." At that moment all the color drained out of his face. Within one week he died of heart failure. Did I kill him? I think not. The Lord struck him down for his arrogant and mocking spirit.

It is one thing to fall into sin and Jesus surely knew how to recover any of us in that classroom from such a state. It is another thing to mock God—to be so intoxicated with your own power that you think no one can touch you, not even God!

Paul's words in Galatians are so *apropos*, "Do not be deceived: God cannot be mocked. A man reaps what he sows. The one who sows to please his sinful nature, from that nature will reap destruction" (Gal. 6:7, 8).

1 Immorality.

2 Materialism and love of money.

3 For example, turning the church into a battle ground, creating rival parties and striving for power. See 1 John 2:16 (KJV).

4 Name has been changed.

THE SAVIOR OF PAKISTAN

Zulfiqar Ali Bhutto came to power under a cloud. East and West Pakistan at that time were one country. The election for president was won by the wing with the most votes—East Pakistan. Bhutto, being from West Pakistan and in control of the army, nullified the election, took control of the government, had his rival jailed and set the stage for the civil war that divided the country in 1971.

Bangladesh was born out of the ashes of that war. East Pakistan was no more. West Pakistan no longer needed the word "west" and assumed the straightforward name of Pakistan.

Broken political promises always lead to cynicism and flagging popularity. President Bhutto could not deliver on his campaign promises of *roti, cuperda aur mukan* (bread, clothing and housing). During the post-election period of disillusionment, as often happens, this politician created a crisis and then proclaimed himself as the one person who could solve the problem.

This culminated in a full-length photo of the president, from the top to the bottom of the front page of the Sunday paper, with this banner headline, *Zulfiqar Ali Bhutto: The Savior of Pakistan*.

After spreading the paper out on the dining room

table, I found myself saying out loud, "Goodbye, Mr. Zulfiqar Ali Bhutto. God can read your newspaper and He does not agree with your assessment of yourself."

Things went from bad to worse. President Bhutto invited all the heads of Muslim states to a convocation in Lahore, Pakistan. Leaders from forty-four Islamic countries showed up. The agenda was to unite these countries in the cause of advancing Islam in the world and deal with the hindrances. You guessed it. Christianity in all of its multi-form activities was singled out as the enemy.

Resolutions were drafted to the effect that visas should be denied to Christian missionaries who want to come into Muslim countries. The Christian school systems should be taken over by Muslim governments and the same for Christian hospitals.

In Pakistan, they did take over all Christian schools and all but one of the Christian colleges. When it came to the action of taking over the Christian hospitals, the general population rose up in protest. The people knew the quality of service in the Christian hospitals was vastly superior to that in the government ones.

The net effect of the confiscation of Christian schools was a disaster. They were deliberately allowed to deteriorate in quality of teaching and in maintenance of the properties.

To this, Mr. Bhutto added one more crime. He had one of his political rivals assassinated. This was his undoing. A military dictator took over, General Zia-ul-Haqq. Bhutto was imprisoned, virtually starved to death and then hanged. This self-proclaimed *Savior of Pakistan* was hanged. His legacy was demolished. And there has been no resurrection. It has been thirty-three years since all of these events transpired and Mr. Bhutto's voice is silent in the grave.

What a contrast to another hanging. Jesus was hung on the cross at about the age of thirty-three, paid for all the sins of humankind, conquered death and Satan, and then rose unchallenged from the grave to give life to all who believe in Him.

And, miracle of miracles, God raised up another general, Pervaiz Musharraf, to give the schools back to the Christians. Being a grateful graduate of our own Forman Christian College, he even gave a grant of five hundred thousand dollars for its restoration.

There is much to ponder here. Men continue to want to play God, even taking one of His sacred names, such as "Savior." But their claims are always false. There is only one Savior of Pakistan and it is the Lord Jesus Christ.

The Lord is still on the throne. When we are tempted to despair, dramatic events like the hanging of this would-be savior, Mr. Bhutto, are modern-day reminders that the Lord does hear the cries of His persecuted people. His answer may take time in coming, but we have lived to see Him triumph over such a false savior.

AMERICANS FIRST AND CHRISTIANS SECOND

It happened in the chapel of our Christian Technical Training Center in Gujranwala, Pakistan. A shouting match was in progress. Two hundred and fifty brown-skinned Pakistani pastors and elders were pitted against twelve white American missionaries. What could possibly have caused this fiery debate?

In those days our mission field was divided into districts. Each missionary administered a district, which included superintending schools, an adult literacy worker, sometimes a "Bible Woman" and dispersing various financial subsidies and scholarships.

The system looked so good—in the beginning. But it expanded beyond the number of missionaries who could administer it. Most of us were doing the work of two or three men. At that time, there was talk of nationalization in the air. Why not try a well-qualified Pakistani pastor as a District Missionary? One was appointed.

Then an economic crunch came. Inflation hurt everyone. Salaries of the national employees were raised. But no additional funds came from the States. Hard decisions had to be made. Which schools should be closed? Which teachers should be let go? Somehow, foreign missionaries had been able to make those decisions. Not so with the new Pakistani District Missionary.

Any decision he made would involve his friends, even his relatives. Where would he find the courage to fire a relative or slam the door on scores of students or dismiss a teacher? In this case his courage failed. A check was written on a bank account with no money in it. He thought the missionaries would intervene to save the situation. On the contrary, the missionaries were enraged at this irresponsible cop-out, which they perceived as outright dishonesty.

The matter finally reached the highest assembly of the church. Pakistani pastors, elders and American missionaries were all there. It was fairly easy to predict what was going to happen. The Pakistani pastors and elders were sympathetic to the plight of their Pakistani District Missionary. They would defend their man, while the missionaries, who wanted this man prosecuted and removed, would go down in defeat when the vote was called for.

Before the matter could come to a vote, one of the missionaries lost his temper and, with blazing eyes and a reddened face, stood up and said, "It is now obvious to us that this church no longer has any ethical or moral standards. I hereby declare this church apostate." He then resigned from all his offices in its presbytery and synod and walked out. Eleven other missionaries did the same.

What happened next blew me away. The oldest Pakistani pastor present stood up and in a resounding voice said to the retreating backs of those twelve missionaries, "Yes, this is what we have always thought about you. You are Americans first and Christians second."

If I had been writing the script for this highly charged drama, I might have had the Pakistani pastor say, "You missionaries have exalted judgment above mercy," and quoted from the Bible. Considering the evident dishonest conduct of the Pakistani District Missionary, I was amazed at the searing words this venerable pastor hurled at those exiting missionaries. They ricocheted around in my brain, "Americans first and Christians second!"

What was he thinking? That the Pakistani system of *panchayat*[1] is superior to the parliamentary one introduced by Americans? Or Pakistani concerns for family, friends and community are paramount, whereas Americans who had already left all these behind really didn't care? Did he perceive American missionaries as heartless and unfeeling administrators? Or was he venting long, pent-up frustrations over the disparity in lifestyles between the missionaries and nationals? I did not know. It didn't matter. His words burned in my mind.

I stumbled out of that meeting, asking myself, "Why do I do things the way I do?" Do I just automatically act like an American, dress like an American, eat like an American, go to the bathroom like an American and think like an American? Had I ever even considered an alternative?

Life was never the same after that. Mary Jo and I decided to change our lifestyle. We began to wear Pakistani clothes and to eat like Pakistanis. We rearranged our living room. We learned to entertain like Pakistanis. We even put a spouted water pot in our bathroom as an alternative to toilet paper.

More and more doors began to open to us and to the Gospel. Pakistani friends began saying things like, "When you visit us, we don't feel like we are entertaining foreigners. And we feel at home when we visit you."

The words of that elderly pastor who so forcefully expressed his perception of us, "You are Americans first and Christians second," changed our lives and, we believe, raised the level of our effectiveness.

1 Discussing an issue until a consensus is reached.

IF I DON'T COME BACK

Of all the reasons why Muslims don't come to Christ, the greatest is the fear of death. A second reason closely allied with this is the fear of fellow men and what they might do to one who converts to Christ.

Jesus saw this among the people during his own days of ministry. "Many even among the leaders believed in Him. But because of the Pharisees [here we could substitute *Muslim clerics*] they would not confess their faith for fear they would be put out of the synagogue; for they loved praise from men more than praise from God" (John 12:42, 43).

This is the issue, isn't it? Who takes first place in your life? Jesus' teaching seemed so severe when He said:

Anyone who loves his father or mother more than me is not worthy of me; anyone who loves his son or daughter more than me is not worthy of me; and anyone who does not take his cross and follow me is not worthy of me (Matthew 10:37, 38).

We all wrestle with these life-and-death questions. Who takes first place in my life? Do I love Jesus more than anything else in the world?

In Afghanistan, this was all played out in the life of a very courageous man. His name was Zia ul-Nudrut. Let me tell you his story and perhaps you too will be mightily encouraged in your own walk with the Lord. Most of what I am about to tell was commonly known in our Christian community in Pakistan and Afghanistan. Nevertheless, I am indebted to the late Dr. Christy Wilson for confirmation of these following details.

As a young boy, Zia had memorized the whole of the Quran in Arabic, even though that was not his mother tongue. In his mid-teens and because he was blind, he became a student in a Christian school for the blind. In the same period of time, by listening to Christian radio programs coming from abroad, he learned English, but more importantly, he became a confirmed believer in our Lord Jesus. Then, as today in Afghanistan, for a Muslim to convert to Christ could mean he would be killed as an apostate. Islamic law mandates this.

After shifting to a regular school, Zia graduated at the top his class and gained entrance in Kabul University to study Islamic law. His purpose? To be able to defend Christians in court.

His ability with languages led him to study German while still in Afghanistan. He was so good that he won a scholarship to do advanced study in Germany where he graduated at the top of his class.

Upon his return to Afghanistan, he translated the New Testament from Iranian Persian into Afghan Dari. His ability with languages was so great that the Afghan government sent him to Saudi Arabia to compete for the grand prize as the best reciter of the Quran. He won, the first non-Arab person to do so, and this was after he became a Christian. Astonishing. Truly amazing.

In 1978, the Communists overthrew the Afghan monarchy. At first, the new rulers were favorable to Zia and other blind students who had become Christian. But when they refused to become communists, they were arrested. In prison, Zia learned Russian.

He was freed in December, 1985, and migrated to Pakistan. There he learned Urdu and founded a school for the blind. He also wrote storybooks for children in Dari and preached locally in the Urdu language.

Sometime in the early part of 1988, I met Brother Zia in Rawalpindi.

We had both heard of one another, but this was the first time we had met. After tea and long discussions, Zia said to me, "Brother Don, I want you to pray for me. I feel that the Lord is leading me to meet my former classmate from Kabul University, Gulbuddin Hikmatyar. I want to share my testimony with him and pray that he will come to Christ." I gasped in astonishment!

For those of you who may not know, Gulbuddin Hikmatyar is the most feared of all the Afghan warlords. He was instrumental in helping drive out the Russians and was known for his ferocity in dealing with his enemies.

Many times Zia had faced death and threats of death and had shown that he was not afraid to die. He often asked his tormenters if they were afraid to die. So when I asked him if he was not afraid that Gulbuddin might kill him, he said he was ready for that but he had to share Christ with him.

Before we parted, Zia said to me, "Brother Don, if I don't come back, please see that my wife and children are taken care of." He didn't come back.

And I did alert those closest to him about his request to take care of his family. That was done. They are in Canada today.

Zia's courage, his love of the Lord and his fearlessness have left an indelible impression on me. He held onto the words of Jesus, "Be faithful, even to the point of death, and I will give you the crown of life." He has that crown now! What about you? And me? Yes, Lord, by your grace, we will be faithful to death.

THE INTERCESSOR
OF OSLO

My first and only pastorate was that of the First United Presbyterian Church of Colorado Springs, Colorado. The year before we arrived, The Navigators, in a prodigious leap of faith, bought the famous castle that General Palmer, the founder of the city of Colorado Springs, had built for his English wife. The estate was called Glen Eyrie, which has now become world famous as the headquarters of The Navigators.

It was at one of The Navigators' conferences at Glen Eyrie that I met two remarkable people, one of whom has much to do with this tale. She was Kari Torjessen, a Norwegian MK (missionary kid) from China who had linked up with The Navs and was now home on furlough from her assignment in Taiwan. At The Glen, she met the man she was going to marry, Robert Malcolm, a Presbyterian pastor of Swedish lineage, who had missions in his heart too.

As the Lord would have it, they asked me to perform their wedding ceremony in the Rose Garden at Glen Eyrie, during which Dawson Trotman, the founder of The Navigators, would be preaching a sermon. This was to be my very first wedding as an ordained pastor. What a beautiful and an unforgettable way to begin that part of what it means to be a pastor.

After their wedding, the Malcolms went overseas to

Davao City in the Philippines on their first assignment together reaching out to Muslims. In due time they returned to
the States where Bob accepted a call to a church in Min-
neapolis—a church that took an interest in our ministries.
We kept in touch down through the years.

From time to time, Kari and Bob would visit their relatives in Norway and Sweden. It was on one of these visits
that Kari learned of the growing presence of Pakistani immigrants in Norway. The Norwegian church was at a loss to
know how to respond to this unusual development. That was
when Kari thought that, because of my years of ministering in
Pakistan, I should visit the interested church leaders in Oslo
and also visit the leaders of the Pakistani immigrants and see
what could develop.

Thanks to Kari, I found myself giving a seminar at the
historic Mission Hall in downtown Oslo, Norway. Sometimes, in order to surprise an audience, I will ask an outra-
geous question such as, "How many of you have ever
memorized the names of the twelve sons of Ishmael in Genesis, chapter 25?" Up to that point in time, no one had ever
raised their hand.

This was going to be different. To my surprise a white-
haired lady raised her hand. I said to her, "Dear Sister, after
this lecture is over I want to meet with you and find out why
you have done this."

What she shared was amazing. She said that at the
present time she was seventy years old. She went on to explain that when she was thirty, the Lord spoke to her about
becoming an intercessory prayer warrior for the Muslim world.

Not knowing a single thing about Muslims, she in-
quired in church circles about this and learned of the Santal
Mission, a Norwegian group working in Bangladesh. From

them she learned that Muslims relate to Abraham through Ishmael and his descendants rather than through Isaac. From that moment on she decided to memorize everything in the Scripture about Ishmael and his descendants and to pray over their descendants wherever they were today!

What commitment to this assignment from the Lord. I think she was allowed to see some of the results of her prayers. It occurred to me that those Pakistani immigrants were in Oslo because of this lady's prayers. When the time was ripe, I too was drawn to that city to share helpful tips with the church on how they could reach out to these immigrants.

Among the passages that she prayed over were Isaiah 42:11-12, "Let the desert and its towns raise their voices, the settlements where Kedar [Ishmael's second son] lives rejoice....Let them give glory to the Lord and proclaim His praise...," and Isaiah 60:7, "All of Kedar's flocks will be gathered to you, the rams of Nebaioth [Ishmael's first son] will serve you."

Wow! One woman praying faithfully for forty years for a people she had never seen before and God brought them to her doorstep. Then He brought a field worker from the same country to help her and the church minister to them. What a woman—the Intercessor of Oslo!

If you are wondering why there are so many Muslim immigrants in your cities, in your countries, look for the intercessors. It's their fault. And you had better find the field workers to minister to them.

GUESTS NEVER PAY

It was my first time in Istanbul, Turkey, and I was visiting three of my former students. Late at night the four of us hailed a taxi to take us from the Asian side of Istanbul, across the Bosphorus Bridge, into that half of the city that lies in Europe.

At that hour of the night, "beggars can't be choosers." This taxi looked like bailing wire was holding it together. When I piled in next to the driver, I just happened to glance at his face. If ever a man looked menacing, it was this man. From his looks, I was sure he was a serial killer.

My three friends were in the back. I twisted around in the front seat to join in the happy chatter. They began telling stories on themselves, remembering all the stupid things they had said when trying to learn their new language. Pretty soon, we were all roaring with laughter. The problem was that the more we laughed, the meaner the driver looked. In fact, now he was scowling. This was not good. I turned to the best Turkish speaker among the missionaries and said, "Please translate for me."

Then I apologized to the driver for not speaking his language. I also apologized for not being able to include him in the laughter at our mistakes. We shared with him a few hilarious booboo's. He began to join us in our laughter. Then he told us some jokes. Soon we were all lost in uproarious laughter.

The only problem was that the more the driver laughed, the heavier his foot got. By the time we descended that long bridge ride into Europe, the car was vibrating as if it were going to disintegrate. We decided to get off at the bus stop rather than risk any more jokes, laughter and lead-footed driving.

However, when we got out to pay, he would not take our money. By including him, we had transformed a most certain villain into the happiest of friends.

The second experience was in East London where I was attending a Strategy Working Group of the Lausanne Movement. To economize on airfare, I stayed over three extra days. I was lodging with friends, but took my meals at different ethnic restaurants each mealtime. This "tale" happened in a Turkish restaurant.

There were no customers, only a miserable looking old man at a front table and two young men behind the counter. Rock and roll blared on the sound system. Though they tried to seat me in the back, I chose to sit with the old man. I soon learned that his name was Mehmet. He was the proprietor and the two young men were his sons. Ever since the Bengali restaurant opened up down the street, all the customers went there.

His story was typical. There had been no work in Turkey. So his sons were the first of the family to come to London. They earned enough to buy this restaurant. At that point I asked Mehmet if he would ask his sons to turn off the rock and roll and put on Turkish folk music. He was delighted.

So we began to talk about Turkey, where he lived, where I had visited. He became nostalgic. We talked for a couple of hours. Then it was time for me to go. The old man would not let me pay. I had become his personal guest.

The third "tale" happened on the taxi ride from Dulles Airport in Washington, D.C., to my mother's home in Alexandria, Virginia. A long ride indeed. I learned my driver had been the former Afghan consul in their embassy in Islamabad, Pakistan. There had been a change of regime in Afghanistan, a civil war and a new government. Now he was a political refugee on the run.

We talked a lot about both countries: Afghanistan, which I had visited several times, and Pakistan, where we had lived for eighteen years. We both lamented the destruction of his beloved country. We reminisced about the times we had picnicked in Paghman, the almond trees in the spring, the *shashlik kabobs* (cooked minced meat) and giant tear-shaped *nans* (bread) that were available in tea shops along any road.

He obviously was homesick. I tried to enter into his sorrow: the loss of relatives, the split-up of the family. The tragic economic loss. His shameful reduction in status from consul to taxi driver. His sorrow was a bit overwhelming. We talked of spiritual things and the hope we have in Christ. These were all new thoughts for him. He was pensive and promised to begin reading the Scripture I left with him.

When we got to my mom's house, he insisted on carrying my bags up the steps and then refused to take any money for the fare. I insisted but to no avail. I had become his guest because I had entered into his sorrow and showed him how to have hope in Christ.

A taxi driver in Istanbul, a restaurant owner in East London, an Afghan ex-consul taxi driver in Virginia. The keys to friendship were: 1) including one in the fun and jokes in his language; 2) entering into an appreciation of Turkish culture, music and country; and 3) entering into the sorrow of a true refugee, with a shattered family, who was starting life over in a new land.

I was not looking for free rides or food. But by showing an appreciation for their lands, cultures and languages, and becoming a friend, as I believe Christ would do, in each case I was transformed from a stranger and "customer" to a friend and "guest." And guests never pay.

COME HOME WITH US

Mary Jo and I were on a return trip to Pakistan. We would be visiting friends in Karachi, then going up-country to Punjab, where I would be speaking in various city conventions and teaching for a month as a guest lecturer back at my old seminary in Gujranwala. To get a flavor of the country again, we decided to travel by rail.

The train from Karachi to Lahore is always an ordeal. Pakistan is decades behind in upgrading its rail system. Therefore, most passengers for this 24-hour trip would carry their own food, water and bedding, plus washcloths, towels and toilet paper.

Mary Jo and I decided not to take food and water, but rather to eat and drink from the tea stalls and vendors that are found on every station platform. We decided to wear our Punjabi *shalvar* (baggy pants) and *qameez* (loose shirt hanging out) instead of Western clothing. It would be good to be "back home" after years in the States.

We chose to travel first class in an air-conditioned compartment. Hopefully, it would make the endless hours through the dusty desert more endurable. We were joined in our compartment by a young Muslim couple with a baby and the young mother's sister. As soon as they saw us dressed as Punjabis, and learned that we spoke fluent Urdu, they adopted us as part of their family. They gave us each a new

name: Gulab Khan (Rose King) for me and Roshen Bibi
(Mother of Light) for Mary Jo. What fun!

The miles clickity-clacked away. In spite of the air-
conditioning, the compartment grew warm. Dust began to
seep in. We grew drowsy with the heat. A few hours later, the
train began to slow. We were pulling into a station. As soon
as the train stopped, Mary Jo and I jumped onto the platform
to forage for snacks and something to drink. Our newly
adopted family looked at us through horror-stricken eyes.

"What are you doing?" they exclaimed. "Where is
your food? Where is your water?" "We didn't bring any," we
answered. "We lived in Pakistan for many years. We know
how to survive like the local people."

They were shocked. "You can't eat that filthy food.
Flies have been all over it. The soft drinks have been adul-
terated. How could you, being educated people, risk your
health like that?" they asked. "Look, Gulab Khan and
Roshen Bibi, you are part of our family. We have lots of food
and boiled water and tea. You will eat and drink with us.
Don't ever jump off the train like that again. Stay with us.
We will take care of you." Wow! We were experiencing that
fabulous Middle-Eastern hospitality for which the Muslims
are so famous.

By the way, for those of you working with Muslims,
this is exactly where you want to be—their honored guest or,
better yet, adopted members of their family. It is inside the
family that you reach those intimate times of sharing.

So it was on this trip. It wasn't long until we were
sharing our testimonies of how we became followers of our
Lord Jesus Christ. Which points to another lesson: Always
share your testimony. There is no argument against your personal testimony. There would be plenty of arguments if we

had gotten right away into those theologically charged areas that so upset Muslims.

While we are talking about sharing our faith with Muslims, there are also cultural concerns that make a difference. Personally, I often read about the traditions of Muslims and how they like to mimic Muhammad in every way possible. Much of this material was fresh in my mind at the time we made this trip. One of the traditions said, quoting Muhammad, "It is okay to use three fingers when eating chicken, but it is much more refined to pick the meat off with only two."

And lo and behold, our new family offered us chicken. I whispered to Mary Jo, "Don't eat directly off the bone; pick the meat off with just two fingers, not three!" We performed well.

In a whisper that I overheard, the wife said to her husband, "Look how cultured these people are. They use only two fingers in picking the meat off the bone." I barely restrained a smile. To think that such a tiny bit of knowledge about their cultural ways would raise their estimation of us in their eyes—and our credibility, too.

Throughout this day and night journey, our sense of camaraderie deepened. We were able to share more intimately what we really believed about Jesus, about God as Father and about the unique role of the Holy Spirit in bringing about new birth and teaching us how to walk with God.

But alas, all journeys sooner or later come to an end. As it turned out, our destination was Lahore and theirs was beyond. As they saw us making preparations to get off the train, they begged us not to do it. "Please come home and spend a couple of weeks with us!" Of all the decisions we make in missions, the hardest are those where you have to turn down an invitation like this one because of some prior commitment. And there is always that "What if…?"

Yes, our speaking the language fluently and our wearing Punjabi dress helped open the door. But it was that "two fingers, not three" that was the clincher. We were truly accepted as cultured people. "Come home with us," they said.

Oh, Father in heaven, we did what we could. Remember our witness and cause them to remember, too. May it bear fruit in the lives of these lovely, openhearted Muslim friends. Remember them, Father; they served your servants well. May they, too, come home to You.

WHAT'S A HOME?

From time to time, God burns indelible images into our memories. One of those that haunts me to this day happened in a dimly lit street on a summer evening in Calcutta, India. But before getting to it, let me share the background of how this trip came about.

It all began with a trip home to the States after eighteen years in Pakistan. This was to be a study furlough. Friends at Fuller Seminary invited me to come and work on my doctorate in missions. Our mission vocational counselor advised it, too. Based on credits earned elsewhere, I was told by friends at Fuller that I could get my doctorate in one year.

But it didn't work out that way. After arriving at Fuller, the Academic Affairs Committee took a hard look at those credits I had accumulated elsewhere. The number of credits was adequate, but the subject matter of courses taken did not match the requirements at Fuller. I was doomed to take two years of residency.

The question arose of what to do with an "empty" summer between those two years of study. Co-opting two brilliant young friends as research associates, I decided to tour the Muslim world from the Pacific to the Atlantic.

Our trip turned out to be one of those "bench-mark" experiences. From Singapore to North Africa and many countries in between, we traveled across the middle belt of the world where most of the Muslims live.

What do you talk about with two young single companions for ten weeks? One of the subjects was marriage and what it's like to have a home. My young friends learned that in Pakistan, our family life was an endless cycle of moves: from the plains to the mountains every year; changes of assignments from station to station over the years; plus many other times away from home, whether in Pakistan or on furlough.

They asked, "How do you maintain stability as a family? In a life like that, where is your home?" I thought to myself, "Where is my home?"

It came to me that, wherever we had lived, it had become "home" because Mary Jo was there. It was her love, her caring presence that made it "home."

Then came that summer's evening, walking down a dimly lit street in Calcutta.

Our day of interviewing was over. It was time to go home to our cots in the Salvation Army hostel. That's where we were staying at seventy cents a night. We were keeping within our budget of five dollars a day. We ate off the streets. Yes, we were survivors and proud of it.

The hostel was in the poor section of town and, while walking, I saw in the shade of a sycamore tree a young mother in dirty, tattered clothes. She was seated on a patchwork of burlap about ten feet by ten feet square. Two small children were playing by her side. She was cooking the evening meal in a cheap aluminum *dekhchi* placed on top of a small portable *chulha* (mud stove) into which she stuffed scraps of wood and small dead tree branches to keep the fire burning.

Her husband was just arriving "home." He was either working as a day laborer carrying backbreaking loads or as a rickshaw puller. He was obviously bone-weary. I saw him put a fistful of crumpled *rupee* notes and coins into his wife's hands—his earnings for the day. Then he lay down and put his head in her lap. She began to untangle his matted hair and to stroke his head. In a matter of seconds, he was asleep, too exhausted even to eat.

I stood a few paces away in the shadows, riveted by this family portrait. Never before had I come face to face with such grinding poverty. But what amazed me even more was that poverty had not destroyed them. They had kept their family together. She had a place, an all-purpose square of burlap on the pavement. And his home was his wife's arms.

What irony, I thought. In the wealthy Western world, we are watching family values crumble: broken homes, deadbeat dads, one-parent families; and even worse, abandoned children.

In Calcutta, I saw a family—a "home"—held together by a faithful mother and wife. For them, having a "home" had nothing to do with the size and shape of shelter. It was about love and loyalty.

And central to it all was a woman of noble character.

In Proverbs, we read, "A wife of noble character is her husband's crown...She is worth far more than rubies" (Proverbs 12:4, 31:10). Yes, I saw it that night on the burlap carpet under the sycamore tree there on a street in Calcutta.

And with the same eyes, I see it in the life of my own dear wife.

Thank you, Father, for faithful wives, who, whether in poverty or wealth, create that atmosphere of love and acceptance that goes to make a home.

Thank you for the wife of that nameless coolie, who, long ago, there in that dimly lit street of a Calcutta slum, taught me that my real home, in this life, is found in the arms of my faithful wife, Mary Jo.

CAN GOD EVER FORGIVE ME?

It happened in Calcutta. It could have been any-where in India but it was Calcutta. Dr. Ray Bakke of Chicago Urban Ministries and I had been invited to teach evangelism. Calcutta is 10% Muslim, about one million people. That's why I was there, to help Christians learn how to reach Muslims.

Calcutta is where the first Protestant missionary to Muslims began his work. His name was Henry Martyn. He worked there only seven years, from 1806 to 1812. He began his career by setting out to debate the top Muslim scholars in the city. In no time at all, the Muslim community was in an uproar. I went to visit the gazebo on the bank of the Houghly River where Henry used to hold his debates.

From the gazebo you could see, not far away, the home of William Carey. It was Carey who cautioned Martyn, "Henry, don't debate. That is counter-productive. You are only making the Muslims angry. Be their friend." He accepted Carey's advice.

By 1810, Martyn had worked out a strategy that is the best I know. What an irony that almost 175 years later, I should be in Calcutta, teaching these long-forgotten principles to a new generation of Indian Christian workers. Here are his suggestions:

1. Always be a warm, supportive friend to your Muslim neighbor.

2. Appreciate the best in the culture and religion of your Muslim friend.

3. Change the atmosphere from hostility to receptivity by doing some kind of good deeds or service for the community. Martyn used medicine.

4. Learn to share your own testimony. People can argue theology, but there is no argument against your personal testimony.

5. Steer your conversation in such a way that it is always Christ-centered.

6. At the appropriate time, lead your friend into a study of Scripture.

7. Trust the Holy Spirit to help you in the communication process, working in both of you, the communicator and the one listening.

While I was teaching these ideas to our Indian Christian friends there in that famous Baptist church on Circular Road, something very extraordinary happened. A young man literally fell off the end of his bench and collapsed on the floor, sobbing. I stopped my lecture and went and knelt beside him. "Brother, what happened?" Over and over again, through his sobs, he was saying, "Can God ever forgive me? Can God ever forgive me?" I asked, "Brother, what have you done?"

This is what he said: "Recently, I got a new job with a Christian radio station here in Calcutta. Just yesterday, I found an apartment for my family. As we were moving in, neighbors from down the hall approached me and said, 'We hear you are Christians. We are Muslims. We have always wanted to have Christian friends. Can we be your friends?' I told the man, 'No. We never make friends with Muslims.' And I shut the door in his face."

I told this young man, whose name was Manohar Lall, that he could not stay in the meetings any more. I said he had to go home and find that Muslim neighbor, that he was to apologize for his rudeness and was to begin his friendship with him. Only after doing that could he come back to our meetings.

The next day, there he was—in the front row. His face was shining. He had begun his friendship with his Muslim neighbor. You could see that the old hatred was gone. He was now a liberated man. I have never seen a conviction of sin so profound, nor an obedience so immediate and a change of attitude so complete.

To better understand the significance of what happened, you need to know something about India. It is a very old country that has been invaded by many different races of people. Long ago, these races stratified into what is called the "caste system" today. Hindu religious priests were at the top. The military caste was second. Then came the whole business community. At the bottom were the "unclean." They did the street sweeping, the hauling away of dead animal carcasses, the cleaning of latrines, etc. They were called "untouchables."

Historically, Christian converts have come largely from the untouchable caste. Their stigma came with them. Since they did not fit anywhere in the Indian caste system, they were identified by their roots. They are still called "untouchables." Even Muslims, who had no caste system, have imitated the Hindus in calling Christians "untouchables."

Indian Christians, of course, have resented this social discrimination. And they in turn, unfortunately, have rejected those outside of their "caste." Sad to say, this is an all-pervasive attitude. Consequently, Indian Christians never even try to reach their Muslim neighbors.

What happened to Manohar Lall lives vividly in my memory, especially his burning question, "Can God ever forgive me?" How many of us, not born in India, have the same problem? Have we been bent away from reaching Muslims for Christ by events in our social, racial, political and military history? Do we have an anti-Muslim attitude?

Perhaps, like Manohar Lall, our hearts need to be pierced by the teaching of God's Word, "Anyone who does not love his brother, whom he has seen, cannot love God, whom he has not seen" (1 John 4:20). Can God ever forgive us? Yes! But then we, too, have to change and reach out to our Muslim neighbors.

LOVE WILL FIND A WAY

In 1993, Samuel P. Huntington of Harvard University shook the academic world in the West by his decidedly *not-*politically-correct article under the title of "The Clash of World Civilizations." In his discussion of the fault-lines between major civilizations, he predicted, among other things, major clashes between Islam and the West. This, of course, jarred the minds of those who were thinking in terms of other metaphors, such as, "all the world is a village" and "we are all interconnected" and "the world is flat."

If we, who live in the West, perceive ourselves as merely Westerners and if Dr. Huntington's prediction is accurate (and there is much to indicate that it is), then we are in for a rough ride and a bleak future.

What the esteemed scholar left out of the discussion was God and the expansion of the Kingdom of God through the presence of Christians in every civilization and every country under the sun.

There are certain manifest truths that give us cause for great hope, *no matter what the political pundits say.* Our God is a very-much-alive sovereign God who is building His kingdom in the midst of all other kingdoms and political entities, none of which are destined to last. When the time is ripe, this will become dramatically apparent to those who love Him and those who don't.

The challenge for the Christian living in any one of these civilizational blocs and the countries that comprise them is: How do I relate to my non-Christian neighbor? For my Christian reader, the answer is so obvious. From the days of Moses (1400 B.C.) to this present moment, God has revealed His will for His children. "Love your neighbor as yourself" (Leviticus 19:18, quoted by Jesus in Matthew 22:39). And just in case you were looking for loopholes to excuse yourself from this, Jesus added, "Love your enemies, do good to those who hate you, bless those who curse you, pray for those who mistreat you" (Luke 6:27, 28).

Sad to say, history is filled with illustrations of Christians who disregarded Jesus' teaching. But there are many beautiful believers who have taken His teaching to heart and lived it out with wonderful consequences. This tale is about such a friend, the late Fouad Elias Accad (died 1994), who rose to prominence in Lebanon as the leader of the Middle East Bible Society.

Briefly, here is his story. Fouad came to Christ early in life from a nominal Christian background. He had the good fortune to be able to study at a Bible institute in Switzerland where he met the woman he later married. Upon his return to Beirut, he began work in the local Bible House. Step by step, he rose to the position as the General Secretary of the Bible Society in Lebanon and then for the Middle East. His passion was to find a way to get the Bible into Muslim hands, the majority people of the Middle East.

When I first met Fouad, it was in the crowded quarters of the old Bible House in Beirut. Later, under more leisurely circumstances, we met while he was vacationing in Switzerland with his family. It was here that I began to catch up on the amazing things this man was doing through his love for Muslims and his passion to see them come to Christ.

Here was a man who knew the Bible very well, not just in Arabic, but in Hebrew, Greek, Syriac, Aramaic and Armenian. He could well have rested on his laurels with all of that, but his love for Muslims led him to one more achievement. He read and became well acquainted with the Quran.

Through friends working with Campus Crusade for Christ in Lebanon, he became aware of CCC's famous "Four Spiritual Laws." This triggered in his creative mind the thought of adapting the concept to what he subsequently called, "Have You Heard of the Seven Muslim-Christian Principles?" Later, this was further refined in a book entitled *Building Bridges*.[1]

What was so unusual about this approach was Fouad's unqualified use of the Quran. Others among my acquaintances had used the Quran either to degrade the Quran[2] or as a starting point for presenting a Christian theme.[3] Accad was the first to use Quranic verses (as well as the Bible) in the development of his seven principles. In fact, he used 187 verses from 45 chapters of the Quran in this fashion (and even a larger number of Bible verses).

This went contrary to the current Christian practices mentioned above. Since the Bible and the Quran are diametrically opposed on crucial Christian doctrine, and both can't be right, the Quran has been rejected by Christians, out of hand, as not being from God. Therefore it was never used to "proof-text" a biblical theme. Moreover, to use it this way made the user vulnerable to the Muslim's use of the rest of the Quran to refute the Bible, the idea being that if you counted any of the Quran as valid, then the Muslim could insist all of it is valid. So Fouad's approach was risky indeed.[4]

Having said all of the above, the astonishing thing is that Fouad claimed that eighty percent of those Muslims who completed this study, using the seven themes in *Building*

Bridges, have put their trust in Jesus Christ as Lord and Savior. How does one account for this success? Let's have a look.

Love found a way. Love led Fouad to deep friendships with Muslims. Love moved him to use appropriate material from the Quran. But most important of all was Fouad's overriding love for the Lord and His Word, the Bible. This the Lord used to draw Muslim men and women to Himself through His servant, Fouad Accad, a man of relentless love.

1 NavPress, 1997.
2 Abdul Haqq, Chaudhry Inayat Ullah Mujahid.
3 Barkat A. Khan.
4 Many would say unwise.

THE WATER OF LIFE

The setting for this tale is in Pune (poo-nah), India, a city of about a million and a half people. It's about a four hour drive east of Bombay (now called Mumbai). We heard that Pune was in the hills, with a pleasant climate and was known as a vacation city for Bombay-ites. I was looking forward to a new and pleasant experience.

The road from Bombay to Pune was of the devil's own design and a major trucking route. Every size and shape of vehicle you ever saw or imagined was on that road, bumper to bumper. Every driver had to be first, including the driver of our rented mini-van. Hair-breadth passes, braking and racing, horns and the roar of behemoth-like engines. Fumes, dust, chickens, pedestrians, bicyclists, pushcart vendors all scattering like wind as we hurtled through.

Pune at last. City vehicles are now downsized. By far, the blue-fumes-shooting, three-wheeled rickshaws were the norm, sometimes six abreast at the lights. You stretch out your finger and touch another in the rickshaw a fraction of an inch away. What glorious pandemonium. And pollution? You could scoop it out of the air by the cupful.

We arrived at last into a semi-residential neighborhood. I would be the guest of an Indian couple who both worked for Youth With a Mission. He was the bookkeeper and accountant for the two hundred-plus Indian YWAM-ers scattered in teams all over India. She worked with Mercy Ministries. He was in his early forties; she in her late thirties.

Living Indian style again was fun. Eating with your fingers, bathing from a bucket, no toilet paper—just a good water pot. The food was wonderful, better than any Indian restaurant in the States. And the fellowship with this good-natured couple was hilarious.

She was an orphan. He was an ascetic—until he decided to marry her. Children? She was the mother of six thousand Muslim families in the worst slums I have ever visited. Maybe it was because she had been an orphan that she took on the problems of the slums.

Early one morning I had the joy of following Sunum through the neighborhood where she daily ministers mercy. The slum was along the side of a thirty-foot wide canal. At some point near the origin, the water may have looked normal. As I stood there on the edge of this canal, what I saw was bluish water bordering on black with every describable and indescribable kind of refuse being swept along.

Until Sunum began her work there in the slum, this was the only source of water for those six thousand families. It is too horrible to think about. Sunum is medically trained. She began her work in a ramshackle room for her "clinic." She soon realized that it was the lack of clean water that was the cause of so many diseases she was treating.

It was then that the war began—Sunum's war with the municipal authorities. Her only weapon was the sense of moral outrage at a government that would allow this. Scolding, badgering, persistent shaming, whatever it took, she battled through the endless red tape, from office to office until she won.

As I tramped through the narrow gullies, avoiding

scum, cesspools and scurrying children, I began to notice the water faucets in front of every tenth house (hovel would be a better word). This was the fruit of her victory. She had won the war over drinkable water for maybe up to thirty thousand souls. A formidable lady indeed.

Then I went to the "schools," one-room affairs scattered here and there in the various alleys. She had recruited and trained the teachers. But they were so pitifully few in the face of the swarms of gutter kids I saw everywhere. Slowly but surely, her effort was making a difference in the quality of life in these slums.

I followed Sunum on this tour through her Muslim mission field and I thought how different this is from what I would have chosen. We made our way through the serpentine, unplanned walkways in this warren of ramshackle, make-do shelters. Everywhere we went, I heard Sunum greeting her friends by name, inquiring about their children and scolding any kid who played hooky from school. She was a woman greatly loved and a woman who loved greatly.

Along the way, Sunum would tell me which ones were believers in the Lord Jesus Christ. Yes, there was harvesting going on there in that Muslim slum.

Here was a side of Muslim work I never even dreamed of: the slums. So different from teaching and training programs that I normally did in relatively nice settings.

After our tour, I sat there in one of those clinics, guiltily sipping a Pepsi someone provided, and my heart was breaking. Sunum showed me the love of God for Muslim people with a depth of love I had never seen before. I was convinced the Lord Himself had led me into this experience, to show me the mercy ministry side of Muslim work by this dedicated Indian sister.

She had not only brought clean drinking water (and many other benefits) to these people, she was the living carrier of the "water of life," the Good News of Jesus Christ. From now on the "water of life" will have a new meaning for me because of Sunum, the grown up orphan girl who has given her life to ministering to these cast-off Muslim "orphans" in the slums of Pune.

Thank you, Lord, for Sunum, who showed me what Your love could do in the most hopeless of places.

PRAYER WALKING IN THE LION'S DEN

Deoband! The fiery center of the Muslim Freedom Movement of India. Their slogans tell it all. "No Muslim should ever live under non-Muslim rule!" "The Quran should be the only constitution of the people of Islam!" "Allah (God) should be the only ruler; *Shariah* (Islamic) law should be the only law; and the *Ulema* (Islamic legal scholars) should be God's agents in government." The founding of De-oband was a reaction to the events listed below.

After the crushing of the great Muslim Sepoy Rebellion in India by the British in 1857, the remnants of the shattered Moghul empire split into two groups. The modernists decided to come to terms with the British who ruled all of India. These Western-educated Muslim elite, under the leadership of Sir Sayyid Ahmad Khan, founded the Mohammadan Anglo-Indian College in Aligarh, India, in 1875. Sir Sayyid and his faculty attempted to reconcile Islam with modernity and the Quran with science. Upper class Muslims flocked to this new university in Aligarh. It produced many of the well-know Muslim intelligentsia and politicians during the following decades.

In violent protest against the British and the Muslims who sided with them, militant Muslims founded a fundamentalist seminary in Deoband, in 1876. Muslim *Ulema* set out to reassert the supposed immutable doctrines of Muhammad as taught in the Quran and *Hadith*.[1]

The Deoband Movement targeted the young men of the lower classes. Here in this hotbed of fundamentalist Islam, these largely poorly-educated young were taught how to become teachers in the *Madrassahs*[2] scattered throughout the Muslim enclaves of India. They were also taught how to preach militant Islam; to bring wayward Muslims back into the fold of the true believers; and how to offer non-Muslims the opportunity to convert to Islam.

As a result of this impassioned teaching, thousands of downtrodden Muslim youth were given a new identity and a great cause to live and die for—militant Islam—supposedly, the glory of God—and the rewards of paradise for martyrs.

Deoband was also the heartbeat of the agitation that grew to be the Muslim Independence Movement in British India. The result of this was the partition of India in 1947 into three separate wings: Muslim West Pakistan, Hindu-secular India in the middle, and Muslim East Pakistan.[3]

What has all of this got to do with us today? Plenty! It is out of Deoband that the Taliban movement of Afghanistan and Pakistan was born. In time, this movement coalesced with the Wahabbi movement of Saudi Arabia, a movement that is violently anti-Western and anti-American, a movement backed by Osama bin Laden.

Shortly before 9/11, I was asked by the leader of a major mission to visit their evangelists in a town only thirty miles from Deoband! These young men were assigned to work with Muslims. After arriving, I discovered their first mistake was that they chose to live in the Hindu section of town, thus alienating themselves from all Muslims. The second, which soon became apparent, was that they were afraid of Muslims. What would you have done under these circumstances?

I suggested we rent a taxi and visit the Muslim seminary in Deoband! The looks on their faces showed that they
were not quite ready for this. Finally, they agreed. We parked
our taxi on an empty lot near Deoband Seminary. What a
sight! Before our eyes unfolded a forest of exquisitely beautiful minarets. Many of them were brand new and more con-
struction was underway. Money—oil money from Saudi
Arabia and the Gulf oil states—was pouring into this boiling
cauldron of Muslim fundamentalism.

We asked God to lead us. Immediately, a young man
appeared and asked if he could help us. We told him we were
visitors who had come to see this famous school. He was totally at ease with us. We did not tell him our other purpose—
namely, to "spy out the land"—and to prayer-walk every nook
and cranny of Deoband Seminary.

Muhammad Salim, the young man who was leading
us on this tour, was a fountain of information. From him we
learned that there were three thousand young men in training here from all over Asia. We took turns walking beside
him as he spoke. While one of us was at his side, the other
three were off praying over every pavement we walked, the
dining hall, every dormitory we visited, every lecture hall and
mosque:

> O God, may your spirit begin to work here. Every time
> a Muslim opens the Quran, may he turn to the Jesus pas-
> sages and begin to wonder who Jesus really is. O God, may
> these young men begin to hunger to read the Injil (the
> Gospel) mentioned in the Quran. O God, may the Gospel
> come to Deoband. May these Muslims see Jesus as Lord
> and Savior. May they believe in Him and be saved.

Does this kind of prayer walking really help? You bet.

First of all, *God hears our prayers.* Secondly, these three young men came away with a new sense of love and boldness for reaching Muslims. They had been in the lion's den and they came out unafraid and renewed.

1 Written traditions of all that Muhammad did and said outside of the Quran.
2 The schools attached to the mosques.
3 To become Bangladesh in 1971.

THE PERILS OF PRAYER

Praying for the unevangelized in faraway lands can often seem so…distant. Yet sometimes, God's answer can hit very close to home.

That's the way it was with me. Way back in 1979, I joined a small group of intercessors at the U.S. Center for World Missions in Pasadena, California. The focus of our prayers was the Muslims of Central Asia locked behind the "Iron Curtain" in the Soviet Union.

We researched these people. We identified their languages. We even made computer maps of all of them. We prayed, first of all, that the Iron Curtain would come down. In Acts 12:10, we read that God opened the iron gates for Peter to go free. He would open these "iron gates," too. We were comfortable in these audacious prayers, never believing that God would choose us as part of His answer.

Yet in 1983, two Dutchmen walked into my office and invited me to do the unthinkable. They asked me to go behind the Iron Curtain with a translator and begin ministering in Central Asia. They were crazy. Unfortunately for me, they belonged to an organization that had been doing similar things for years: smuggling Bibles. They were authentic "smugglers," very successful ones, too. But this was a different matter. This involved *me*—a living commodity!

These men actually thought I could get a visa to go in and meet Christians who were already being persecuted and begin training some of them in the "registered" and "unregistered" Baptist churches of Central Asia. It sounded preposterous—even hazardous—to me. As is often the case with me, my first reaction was negative. I began to think of ways to squirm out of the invitation.

The issue was settled in a dramatic and incontestable way. The chairman of my board, who had been a Marine chaplain during the Vietnam War, and was never troubled by fear, volunteered me. He said, "Oh, Don would love to go!"

Oh, why did I ever agree to pray with those radiantly believing, enthusiastic young people? If they wanted this to happen so badly, why didn't the Lord choose them?

Well, there were reasons why I was chosen. But not being able to argue with the chairman of my board, nor willing to admit that I was fearful, I consented to go.

And so it was that I found myself in London, rendezvousing with three other people in an obscure section of town in a non-descript, drab apartment. There was an experienced British "smuggler" who had been working behind the Iron Curtain for years. What a tough lady she was! Then there was a younger Scottish woman who, three months before, had gone in, scouted out the land, and had set up all our contacts in Uzbekistan, Tajikistan and Kazakhstan. She was the one with the maps—all in Russian. And then there was Richard, who was to be my companion and translator. He had studied Russian for four years including one year living in Russia.

The Russian alphabet is made up predominantly of Greek letters, thanks to two early Greek-speaking missionaries who evangelized Russia a thousand years before. I was so thankful for my two years of seminary Greek. In no time at all, I was reading these Russian maps. This was going to be easy. I could see where we were going and could learn to read the names and addresses of the people we were going to meet.

Then the tough lady dropped her bombshell, "You will have to go in clean. You may be strip-searched. They must find nothing on you. We cannot betray our friends. You can't take these maps with you, nor any material with the names and addresses of your contacts on them!" She added, "You will have one day, here in this apartment, to memorize these maps and the people's names and addresses—in Russian!"

Richard and I sweat it out. Our Scottish friend drilled us over and over again on the names of streets, rivers, important buildings, color of key houses, even the location of landmark trees, the numbers on doors and apartments. On and on it went. She taught us how to use the modes of transportation available in each target city. Most important of all, she taught us how to detect and avoid surveillance. Finally, she said, "Don, you are in charge. If you have to abort a mission because you cannot escape surveillance, it will be your choice. You must not betray our contacts!" This was 1984, seven years before the Soviet Union collapsed.

And so the "great game" began, on the ground, behind enemy lines. We were never apprehended. We had to abort two goals in Tashkent but God led us to the key woman, Robiyya, whose story is told in another "tale." The Lord frustrated our every attempt to find several contacts in Dushanbe but these men were in all our meetings without revealing themselves. They got it all. And, in spite of the frightened church in Almaty, we found the key convert and his local Christian adoptive family.

Since then, many trips have been made into Central Asia, both before and after these countries became free. It is one of the great chapters in the annals of missions.

All of those young people in that long-ago prayer group in Pasadena, California, are now in these fields. In spite of persecution, converts number in the thousands.

Was the prayer worth it? Would I pray that way again? Yes. Would you? Is it worth all the perils of prayer to see the fruit of that intercessory passion? Yes. God is seeing the harvest of His children in Central Asia: Uzbeks, Tajiks, Kirgiz, Kazakhs and Turkmens. Keep on praying, no matter what the risk. The perils of prayer are great. Risk it—even if you personally end up as part of God's answer.

GOD SENT YOU

This tale took place in the Soviet Union seven years before it collapsed. I flew to London to meet Richard, my British traveling companion, a brother totally fluent in Russian. Our ministries would be in the Central Asian Republics.

In London we were briefed by a team of two women who had gone in ahead of us to set up our ministries. We had a day to memorize maps and the names and addresses of our contacts. We were not allowed to have any written information on us in case we would be searched. Our first stop was Dushanbe, the capital of Tajikistan. The flight from London to Moscow gave Richard and me further time to get acquainted with one another.

An Intourist guide was waiting for us at the Sheremetyevo airport, outside of Moscow. From there, in a black limousine, we were sped off to the domestic airport, Domodedobo, several miles on the opposite side of the city. Then a long wait in a dingy airport for our old Tupelo plane to be serviced. Sleep came easily on the flight from Moscow to Dushanbe.

Somewhere over the Pamir Mountains, I awoke. The view out of the window startled me. It seemed as though the bottom of our plane was scraping the tops of these gorgeous, snow-covered mountains. The majestic Pamirs, twenty-two thousand feet high, permanently covered with snow, were awesome in their sharply chiseled, dazzling white beauty.

Shortly after landing, we were whisked away, again by an Intourist car, to the well-bugged Tajikistan Hotel. My companion and I found an ingenious way to talk to one another: a scrabble board where we made words for our eyes only. Better yet, we saved our conversation for walks in the open air, hoping their surveillance equipment could not pick up what we were saying.

We found our contacts on the first try. Then we walked to the registered Baptist church. It was strange not to be introduced by anyone in church. If anyone of them had introduced us, it would have meant endless interrogations of that person by the KGB. My translator and I stood in the pulpit and said, "We bring you greetings from your brothers and sisters in the West."

No one had prepared us for the "sonic boom" of their return greeting. In perfect unison the entire congregation leaped to their feet and in one glorious united voice shouted back at us, "And we send our greetings to them."

My eyes teared up. I knew what this meant to them. By our very presence, we were saying to them, "You are not forgotten. We know what you have suffered and are suffering. We know who has been martyred. We know who is in prison. We know the hardships you are going through for your faith. You are remembered and we have come to tell you so and to stand with you."

Following the church service, there was a communal meal. The entire courtyard, inside the compound and under the grapevine canopy, heavy with lush grapes, was filled with tables laden with food. But before the meal, there was the reception line.

The handshakes I had expected. The kiss on the lips

by every one of the three hundred Russian and German men there, I had not. Kissing men? Never! Men with mustaches, light kisses, heavy kisses, wet kisses and kisses from men who had not shaved for days. I died a thousand deaths (well, three hundred, anyway). But because I knew what this meant to them, I did not shrink back.

The evening after our fourth and last message, we were kneeling and praying with the inner group of leaders. The man next to me began to weep. When we were through praying, I asked him why he was weeping. This is what he said: "Two years ago, I was visiting my son who was studying in the conservatory of music in Moscow. While there, I went to a church meeting. In that meeting a person stood up and said there was someone in the audience who was going to help give birth to a church of Tajik believers. I knew that couldn't mean me. It absolutely could not mean me because all of my relatives had already immigrated to Germany and I was planning to do the same.

"For years, my requests for a visa have been denied. Now I know why. God brought you here to speak to me. I am in charge of a farm commune of five hundred Tajiks. I know their language. I solve their problems. I go to their weddings and their funerals. We have suffered together: I as a Christian, they as Muslims. God has held me here because of His love for the Tajik people. I am to help give birth to the Tajik church."

Tears came to my eyes again. This was why we had come. I said to Richard, "We have scored. God has led us to the key man. Eduard has embraced his call. Now there will be a church of Tajik believers."

THE ILLUMINATED QURAN

Tajikistan is in Central Asia. It is bordered by Afghanistan, China, Kyrgyzstan and Uzbekistan. Up until the twelfth century it was part of the Persian empire. Its national language is Farsi, similar to the language of Iran.

As you look at the map, it reminds one of Louisiana, only it is slightly larger. But it is as different as day and night from our southern state. The Pamir and Tien Shan mountains cover ninety-three percent of the land, many of them twenty-two thousand feet high! Most of the people live along the great river valleys.

Dushanbe, the capital city, holds close to a million of the seven million people who live in what is one of the most unreached parts of the world. Our visit there was in 1984, seven years before freedom came to the fifteen states that made up the Soviet Union, of which this was one.

During our ministry trip there, we took time out to visit the Firdausi Library. Firdausi was the name of a very famous Persian poet. Around the top of the library was a frieze with the figures of other famous poets such as Sheikh Saadi, Hafiz, Rumi, Jami and Khayyam. This was going to be interesting, as these were poets I had studied in Pakistan. Once inside, we discovered the library was totally dedicated to Soviet accomplishments and not a sign of the great poets. A quick inquiry revealed that these works were all shut up in a special archival room and one could only go there after paying a special fee for a guide.

Our "guide" turned out to be an atheist who was not at all interested in our interests. After much insistence from us, she sent for the archivist. I could tell by the way Suleiman greeted the receptionist with the traditional "As-salam-alayikum," meaning "Peace be with you," that he was a Muslim and would be our friend in this situation.

To our surprise there was not much about the poets, but what a collection of ancient Qurans from so many different periods of history. The different styles of calligraphy reflected the ages and places from which they came: *Kufic, Istaliq, Thuluth, Divani* and *Nasky*.

One especially caught our eye. In it the name of Allah (God) and Isa (Jesus) were the only words written in brilliant, vermilion-colored ink. Immediately, I asked Suleiman, "Are there Muslims here who consider Jesus divine?" Without saying a word, he smiled and nodded his head in the affirmative. Wow! What a discovery. I shared it with everyone I knew. This awakened great interest in the local church members in Dushanbe, as well as among our students at the Zwemer Institute, some of whom subsequently went to Tajikistan after finishing their preparation.

What did these Tajik Muslims know about Jesus from their knowledge of the Quran? Following is a brief overview.

- *His titles*: a Sign, a Mercy, a Witness, an Example, Son of Mary,[1] the Messiah,[2] a Prophet, an Apostle, a Servant, a Word from God, a Spirit from God.

- Chapters 3 and 19 of the Quran contain stories of *His birth*.

- In Chapter 5, you can read of the mention of *His miracles* of giving sight to the blind, curing lepers and raising the dead.

- *His being put on the cross* is mentioned in chapter 4, but it says He was not killed; that God took Him alive to heaven and someone else who resembled Him was crucified.

- *His second appearing* is hinted at in 43:61 and in 89:22, in which He will come with rank upon rank of angels to judge the world.

Suleiman, the Tajik archivist mentioned above, gave us an indication of the hunger of the Muslim heart to know Jesus. With that illuminated Quran in which the names of God and Jesus were both highlighted in bright red ink, he intimated to us the longing of some of the Muslim Tajik people to know Jesus.

That information, relayed to enthusiastic young people in the West and to faithful Russian and German church people in Dushanbe, led to a movement of people to Jesus in an obscure, unreached part of the Muslim world. Today there are growing churches in certain areas of the country.

How thankful we are to God for Suleiman, who signaled to us Christians, both locally and from the West, that there were people in his land who were hungry for Jesus.

1 His virgin birth is attested in the Quran.
2 With no understanding of what "Messiah" really means.

"SPASEEBA"

The story of the formation of the Kazak people in the middle of the sixteenth century is one of the most fascinating in the history of Central Asia. As a pastoral people, they were unable to hold their own against their better-organized and more warlike Kalmyk neighbors. In desperation they turned to Russia for help. By 1731, the leader of the Kazaks had pledge his loyalty to the Russian Empress. From that time on the Kazaks were to be under Russian domination.

In the late eighteenth century, the Empress Catherine the Great made a tragic mistake. She concluded Islamic, rather than Christian, missionaries could better civilize the Kazaks. This opened the door for the complete Islamicization of the Kazak people.

Following the Bolshevik Revolution in 1917, the Kazaks found themselves liberated from the tzars, but then ended up with new masters: the Russian communists. Their hopes for religious freedom were cruelly crushed.

Our part in this story began in 1984. We were asked by Open Doors to visit the Baptist church in Almaty, the capital of Kazakhstan. Our goal was to impart a vision for, and teach concepts of, winning Muslim Kazaks to Christ.

Locating the church turned out to be very frustrating. We had memorized our instructions perfectly. Our landmark was a river on the edge of town. We got there easily. But there was no street by the name we were searching for. In blistering sun, we gridded the entire area, then walked every street. We came up empty.

As a last resource, we went to the local fire station and asked where this street was. The answer? "The street you are looking for is just two blocks this side of the second river." No one had told us there was a second river!

When we finally got there, we were not welcome, thanks to our "friends" at the fire station who had alerted the secret police. They, in turn, had phoned the church and warned them not to receive us.

Because we arrived after church had started, we had no chance to meet our contact ahead of time. Fortunately, he was at the church waiting for us. Afterward, we hung around chatting. Then, at his urging, we jumped into a car that had just pulled up. Circling through the city a half hour later, we ended up back at the church! The crowd was gone—except for this fifty-voice choir of young people!

We were invited to speak to the choir on the concept of missions and the need to win their Muslim neighbors to Christ. At the end of my talk, a hard-faced young man asked in a sarcastic voice, "Sir, have you ever met a Russian missionary?"

I was momentarily stunned. His question spoke volumes: "Mister, don't you know where you are? We live under Soviet Communism. The KGB has eyes everywhere. Do you think we could get away with this? What do you think you are doing, challenging us to evangelize Kazaks?"

Jesus said the Holy Spirit would help us know what to say. I asked for His help and this is what He gave me. I looked at the young man who asked, "Sir, have you ever met a Russian missionary," gave him a big smile, and said: "Yes! I am looking at a whole room full of Russian missionaries."

There in the front row, a young woman, her face radiant with joy, looked up and spontaneously spoke out the word "*Spaseeba*" (thank you). After our meeting, we met her and asked her why she said that.

This was her reply: "I was utterly disillusioned with communism. After long searching, I found Christ. Last night I was baptized. This was my first worship service as a baptized Christian. Thank you for believing God could use me in His work among the Kazak people."

What was the significance of her "*spaseeba*," her "thank you"? I believe she spoke on behalf of all Russian believers when she spoke that "thank you." I believe God began to move among the Kazaks when He saw a person of faith say "yes" to His call. Since then, many others, locally and from abroad, have joined in this tremendous effort.

Today there are several hundred Kazak believers. Perhaps it began with prayer by many of us on the "outside." Then it took a risky trip "inside." And finally, an embracing of the vision by a local believer.

Thank you, Father, for what you began that day. Thank you for Katya, whose *spaseeba* opened the door. Yes, Lord, from the bottom of my heart, *spaseeba*!

THE TOMBS OF THE LIVING KINGS

Samarkand, the most attractive of all the Muslim cities of Central Asia and located in present-day Uzbekistan, is one of the oldest cities of the world. It was built on the site of ancient Afrosiab, whose ruins date back beyond the time of the Egyptian pyramids. Later it became the chief city of Sogdiana, a part of an ancient Persian Empire.

After Alexander the Great conquered it in 329 B.C., it became the meeting point of Western and Chinese cultures. By the sixth century A.D., Nestorian missionaries had established churches in the region. During the eighth century, it fell to invading Muslim armies. Over the course of time, it became the center of a Muslim civilization. In 1220 Genghis Khan devastated it. Gradually these Mongol invaders converted to Islam.

Tamerlane (1336-1405), a descendant of Genghis Khan, established Samarkand as the seat of his vast Islamic empire. In spite of his reputation for cruelty in the sack of Delhi and destruction of Persia, he encouraged the arts and sciences and built vast public works and great mosques with Muslim theological schools attached. Many of these architectural masterpieces have been restored and draw thousands of tourists every year.

Today Samarkand is almost totally a Muslim city. But there was a small underground church there. "Underground" means it was not registered with the government. Our assignment in this city[1] was to find the pastor and his leaders and begin to train them in Muslim evangelism. During our time of briefing in London, we had memorized the map of the city and had instructions on how to find our man.

The temperature was not our friend. With blistering heat, there was precious little shade as we searched for our rendezvous house. After ten hours of walking on the first day, we retreated to our hotel to assess our situation. The second day was equally frustrating. We even entered a Muslim house that we were sure was it, spoke our password greeting and drew nothing but blank stares.

Having exhausted all our options (and ourselves), I finally said to my companion, "Richard, for whatever reason, God has sent us a spirit of confusion. For some reason we are not supposed to find this man." This being the case, I suggested that we make the best of it, become tourists and hire a guide. But before proceeding with the story, I need to jump ahead and tell you what we learned on our return to London. The pastor we were looking for had been arrested before our arrival and the church members were praying that we would not find them and cause them even more trouble.

And so we rented a tour guide. As soon as Ludmilla got in the car with us, she said rather saucily, "You know I am an atheist." From the way she spoke, I knew she was lying. Since her driver had to spy on her as she fraternized with Westerners, she had to say this for his benefit. *This tour was going to be interesting.*

After visiting the grand mosques and attached *madrassahs* (theological schools), she insisted we visit the tombs of the *Zinda Shahi* (Living Kings). It was a pilgrim center for Uzbeks and Tajiks. We stood back and watched the steady stream of seekers-of-blessing come to the waist-high, rounded tombs, each in its own room, and pray to the spirits of the "Living Kings" for their desperate needs: healing, a job, guidance, fertility, protection from evil.

Ludmilla was entranced. I asked if she knew what was happening. She didn't. So I explained that orthodox Islam does not let a Muslim get in touch with God, so these hurting people had turned to the spirit world for help. Then I added, "Isn't it a shame that they have come to the dead instead of the living." She replied, "I am glad you said that. I believe in the living, too." Then she added, "You are an optimist, aren't you?" "Yes, I am," I replied, "but I didn't used to be." Then I shared my testimony.

Later she took us to the impressive building that housed the tomb of Tamarlane. There, like the other pilgrims, she knelt and touched the brass grillwork around the tomb. I gasped and asked, "Ludmilla, what are you doing?" Her answer astonished us, "Everyone knows there is great power here and I want to get some of that power."

Then we talked about the One who has all power in heaven and on earth: about Jesus, His death, resurrection, ascension and the pouring out of the Holy Spirit of power on all who believe.

Unwittingly, this would-be atheist betrayed her own hunger to get in touch with the real God by taking us to the tombs of the Living Kings and the tomb of the most powerful of them all, Tamarlane. And there she learned of the one and only Living King, Jesus. The Lord took her from the tombs to His throne. No, we never found that pastor, but the Good Shepherd led us to one of his lost sheep there in Samarkand.

1 Seven years before the collapse of the Soviet Union.

THE CRY OF THE UZBEK PEOPLE

My British Russian-speaking companion and I were going on assignment behind "enemy lines" in Central Asia. These nations were still under Soviet control. It would be seven more years before these republics would become free countries.

Before we left London, we had been briefed on how to tell if a KGB agent was following us and how to evade him—if possible. We also had to memorize maps of four key cities: Dushambe, Almaty, Samarkand and Tashkent. This "tale" took place in Tashkent, the capital of present-day Uzbekistan.

In each city we had two or three objectives. That was because if, for any reason, you couldn't succeed in one objective, you would go on to the next. In Tashkent we had to abort our first two objectives because of the very close surveillance of our contacts.

The problem with our third objective was that we did not pay enough attention to the details in the briefing session. Consequently, we got lost. For six hours we crisscrossed Tashkent in every kind of transportation available: buses, streetcars, underground railways, taxis, mini-buses and finally on foot. By the time we found the right apartment, no one was following us.

So often in the former Soviet Union we found that

Christians tend to live on the upper floors of apartment house buildings, especially the ones with no elevators! (This is how the Lord keeps me in shape.) As we approached our target apartment, we met a lady sweeping the stairs. Without bothering to use code words for identification, she beamed and said, "Where have you been? We have been waiting for you for three days."

She "swept" us inside her cozy apartment. Immediately she phoned for her daughter and son-in-law to come. They appeared in no time. While the son-in-law went off to fetch two more guests, the mother and daughter prepared the meal.

The two guests turned out to be a divorced Uzbek woman and her six-year-old son. She was the key contact we had been looking for all along! She was one of the very first Uzbek Muslims known to turn to the Lord.

It happened this way. Her brother-in-law worked in a hotel kitchen beside two zealous German Christian young women. They witnessed to him daily. One day they gave him a Russian New Testament. Eventually, this Uzbek young man accepted the Lord. Then he led his wife to Christ. She, in turn, led her sister, Rubiyya, to the Lord. And it was this very Rubiyya who was sitting at the table with us with her son Turilbek.

Rubiyya was an important government translator and a well-known poet. After her conversion, life became increasingly difficult for her. First she lost her job. Then the harassment by the KGB began. She thought she might have to flee the country.

After dessert, Rubiyya said she wanted to recite a poem. It was in Russian. As she spoke, we could feel her emotion and at the end we saw her tears. Poetry was hard to translate on the spot. So I asked Rubiyya to write it down in my pocket diary. This could have led to big trouble if the immigration authorities searched us. And they did! But the Lord shut their eyes. In looking through all the pockets of my daytimer, they never noticed what was written on one of the pages.

After returning to London for debriefing by the European Mission agency that set up this trip, my companion translated this "smuggled-out" poem into literal English. I then took this wooden translation and tried to shape it into something that rhymed without losing the meaning.

Rubiyya's poem, at the time, became well known in Europe and North America. I believe many Western Christian young people were touched by this passionate prayer plea for the Uzbek people and are working there today because of how God touched their hearts through this cry. Here are the words of Rubiyya's poem:

The Cry of the Uzbek People

Salvation to a people! How precious a gift!
Happy are the people who thus are blest.
Freedom from bondage and joy in the Lord,
A people made holy by Jesus' blood

My cry for you all is to pray to God.
O friends, near and dear, think it not odd
That God would reach down to the Uzbek people
And create for Himself a Church most noble.

Lift up your eyes on the fields so white.
Uzbeks are thirsting for life and light.
They're a people made ready for full salvation.
O, who will come to my Uzbek nation?

Friends, don't you hear this plaintive call?
Let's join in prayer and lift that pall
So sons of the Uzbeks can taste God's grace
And find acceptance before His face.

Earnestly, zealously, pray to the Father
That workers be sent the harvest to gather.
God awaits your prayer; His ears are open
To release His love to the Uzbek nation.

As I write this "tale" today, we know of several hundred Uzbeks who have become believers. Rubiyya's cry is being answered! But we have so far to go! What are a few hundred Muslim background believers among sixteen million Uzbek people? Will you let Rubiyya's prayer-cry-poem speak a word to you?

THE CIRCLE OF TEARS

It was winter. Icy slush covered the muddy roads. We bundled up to keep warm as we made our way through the dimly lit streets of Tashkent to our friend's house. Soon others appeared out of the dark and joined us in the warmth of this friendly home.

During dinner around the table of this loving missionary family, we heard the testimonies of the other guests—the ex-Uzbek and Kazakh Muslims who were now part of our heavenly Father's family.

Each story was harrowing. One person's house was fire-bombed. Another had his wife and children taken away by angry Muslim relatives. The others were kicked out of their families and fired from their jobs. These men were the miserable victims of the followers of the intolerant religion of Islam. They were fortunate to be alive because Islam teaches that anyone who leaves Islam should be put to death. They found a temporary haven here in this missionary home.

Following supper, the mother took her children to another part of the house for their family time of prayer. The men gathered around the fired-up, pot-bellied stove in the living room. The after-supper tea was a time to get better acquainted.

So many burdens were shared. There was so much to

pray for. We formed a circle there on our knees. As we began to pray, first one and then another began to weep. I could not understand their language and did not ask for translation during those holy moments. Even though we did not know what they were saying, in our spirits we sensed the cry of their hearts. Tears came to my traveling companion's eyes and to mine as we prayed in our mother tongues (Dutch and English) with, and for, our Central Asian brothers.

After our extended time of prayer had ended, I asked my host to tell me what these Asian brothers were weeping over. It was tempting to think they were weeping in self-pity, but that was not the case. They were weeping for lost relatives. I was astounded. They had every right to be bitter, angry and resentful after the harsh treatment they had received from the very ones they were praying for. The grace of God had been working mightily in them.

Where did they learn this? From Jesus, of course. It was Jesus who wept over Jerusalem because they "did not know the hour of their visitation." It was Jesus who prayed from the cross, "Father, forgive them for they know not what they do." It was Jesus who modeled His own teaching, "Love your enemies, do good to those who hate you, bless those who curse you, pray for those who mistreat you."

What I learned, what I heard in that "circle of tears" has been reinforced over and over again by the triumphant spirit of forgiveness that our Lord Jesus Christ has given to those who have lost everything because of their testimony to Him.

Most recently, the wife of one of the three men who had their throats slit in eastern Turkey in April, 2007, was interviewed on national television in that land and openly, before the nation, forgave the fanatical Muslim young men who killed her husband. The dastardly acts of those Muslim young men stunned a nation. But what was infinitely more stunning was the beautiful spirit of love and forgiveness that Christ gave that brave, young widow.

This is reminiscent of a similar incident that happened many years ago when a Muslim young man killed a missionary who was discipling him. That man's widow, in love, named her newborn son after the name of her husband's killer. This was her way of expressing that divine love and forgiveness that could only come from the Lord in heaven. No root of bitterness can linger in such a heart.

These are reflections that should cause us to stop and think. For we live in a day of growing violence. One by one, the five top leading pastors in Iran have been martyred. We cannot count the tens of thousands in the south of Sudan who have been sacrificed on the altars of Muslim hatred. The same could be said of the many bold Koreans and Filipino brothers who have been martyred in present day Saudi Arabia. Added to this is the bombing of churches in Pakistan *with the worshippers inside*. The list could go on for a long time.

Satan does not easily give up his clients. He knows his time is short. And he is enraged. Behind all of these killings of God's precious children is his destructive hand. Those he uses to do his evil bidding are the most to be pitied. For Muslims have been deceived and enslaved by him. No wonder Jesus prayed, "Father, forgive them for they know not what they do."

With us who do believe, Satan has other tactics. It is to stir us up to feelings of hatred and revenge, even to violence against his clients. Peter was the one who thought he was being magnanimous when he questioned whether he should forgive one who sinned against him seven times. Jesus put no limit on it with his figurative answer—seventy times seven.

God's way is so different from ours. His is the way of forgiveness. In this sense, "we are more than conquerors through Him who loved us." We bathe ourselves in His love and we learn to forgive.

That early experience in Tashkent has left an indelible imprint on my memory and, yes, even on my spiritual development. It was in that "circle of tears" that I learned from every Muslim convert in the room the power of forgiveness and how to pray with tears for those who did them so much harm.

THROUGH "CHINA CRY" EYES

I first met Julia Nickson Soul on the screen. She was that attractive Asian-American actress who played the lead role in *China Cry*, a Billy Graham Association film. This film was about the suffering of a Christian couple under the Chinese communists. It was based on the true-life story of Sung Yeng Lee and her family.

In the film, Julia lived through Sung Yeng Lee's arrests, interrogations and the endless writings of her "confessions," the beating and kicking while she was pregnant, the cruel work on the rock pile. Julia saw how the communists used Sung's father as a guinea pig with medicines designed to kill.[1] She saw how people suffered and died in the labor camp. Even though Julia was only acting in a film, the portrayal of human suffering was forever etched in her memory.

When I met Julia in person, it was in a Baptist church in Bishkek, the capital of the newly liberated country of Kyrgyzstan. This was one of the six Muslim republics that had suffered under the heel of Soviet (read: Russian) communism. Julia and her team were in this lovely mountainous country on the border of western China, looking for potential sites for filming a new movie.

Since Julia is a Christian and this was a Sunday, it was quite normal for her to attend church. And that was where we met. Before I tell you what happened that Sunday morning, let me fill you in on the description of the church and some of its history.

This was a church that had been registered with the communist government. As a registered church, it was allowed to build its own building and had a certain degree of freedom to worship at government-appointed times. Informants attended every service and reported back to the police about what went on, what was said, the names of the leaders and guest speakers, if any.[2]

Just because it was a registered church did not mean that the local believers were free from the usual communist harassment, attempts to get them to deny their faith and become communists and the threats of dire consequences for not complying.

On the contrary, because they were Christians, many young men were denied the privilege of going to a university. This meant that they were given the meanest of jobs, unless, of course, the communists desperately needed their talents. If they were too strong in their faith, at the whim of a communist official, they were sent off to the local prison or to the notorious Gulag Archipelago. Many never came back.

The church building itself was of a unique design and figures into the events as they unfolded when Julia was asked to speak. Let me describe it architecturally. It was a long rectangular building of three floors: a basement built deep in the ground, a ground floor and a balcony that ran down the two long sides of the building and wrapped around the far end opposite the platform.

In the front, positioned half way between the ground floor and the balcony, the platform spanned the space from one balcony to the other. When you stood to speak, you were almost at eye-level with the people seated in the first row of the balcony. As you can imagine, you looked down, way down, on the people on the ground floor.

Since this event occurred after 1991, when the country became free, newcomers started coming to church. The pattern of how people seated themselves was most interesting. Under each of the balconies were the Christian families. These Baptists did not believe in "family planning," so there were lots of kids. Above them in the balconies were the newcomers of all kinds: some families, some singles and a variety of ethnic people who were curious. In the rear balcony was the choir. One form of witnessing under communism was through these highly-talented, large choirs. The soul of suffering Christian Russia came through that music.

It was the main floor of the sanctuary that caught Julia's attention and mine. White-haired ladies occupied the entire area. This large body of women, occupying the entire main floor of the church, was comprised of the widows. The congregation had put them right in the middle, as though to protect and honor them. Families were on either side, forming a kind of loving shield and honor guard around these godly widows.

Julia had lived through it all in China—on film. Now she was on the other side of the border in real life, staring down at these tragic survivors of Russian Communism. She burst into tears. At almost the same moment, sensing what Julia was thinking and feeling, tears started rolling down my cheeks too.

Through Julia's "China Cry" eyes, this Westerner, who had never suffered under either form of communism, saw with heart-breaking realization, the price that these Christians had paid for their faith in the Lord Jesus Christ.

Thank you, Julia, for helping me see more clearly and

feel more deeply the pain and the sorrow of those widows. Thank you, Father, for these brave people who stood the test, endured the pain and are still standing—your faithful witnesses.

1 He died in a hospital room in her presence.
2 My file in that country is now about three inches deep.

A NIGHT IN KARA-KUL

It was a short flight from Bishkek to Osh. The daz-zling white, permanently snow-covered Pamir Mountains were an awesome sight, scudding close under our plane. In Osh we were met by Russian brothers. After a hearty supper and much discussion over tea concerning the Lord's work in that area, we rolled out the bedding for a night's rest.

Tomorrow was going to be a full day's drive with stops along the way to visit small groups of Christians. The journey would take us around a long sliver of Uzbekistan land that jutted into western Kyrgyzstan. Our objective was to reach Kara-Kul by suppertime.

Traveling through the lush Ferghana Valley, slowing down as we passed through sleepy villages with their sprin-kling of mosques, old and new, and then wending our way through the sheep-covered, sloping pastures, we ascended the foothills to the base of the mountains on this road of breath-taking beauty.

Arriving in the town of Kara-Kul, we located the apartment house block where our key contact lived. This sixty-year-old Kyrgyz woman, Gulzar, found Christ while working in Bishkek. Immediately, she realized she needed to move to Kara-Kul to win her younger relatives and their friends to Christ. Her ne'er-do-well, alcoholic, un-protesting husband was dragged along by this indomitable lady.

If I had not known I was in a concrete apartment house room, I would have thought I was in a typical Kyrgyz *yurt*. The main difference is that *yurts* are larger and round, with a dome. Adorning every wall were these beautiful, highly colorful, rug-like felt wall hangings. There were artistic floral motifs in many colors on a brick-red background. Long, round, colorful *goltuckis* (pillows) were scattered around the edge of the bright Kyrgyz carpet. There was no other furniture.

In no time at all, we were assembled for a pre-supper worshipping and teaching time. Seated on the floor, with our backs to the walls and leaning on our *goltuckis* for support, we worshiped in both the Russian and Kyrgyz language. I, as the guest of honor, was then asked to teach. Since most of the young men and women were not yet converted, all our efforts went into presenting Christ as the Savior and Lord of the Kyrgyz people.

Meanwhile, Gulzar mobilized a couple of neighbors to prepare food for this roomful of about twenty people. At the conclusion of the teaching, a large white sheet was spread on the rug. It served as the *dusterkhan* (tablecloth). During the meal, questions and answers flew around the room. Some questions seemed naive; others were profound. All came with great intensity from young men and women earnestly wanting to know the truth.

Since Gulzar had already been witnessing near and far, the local *imams*, (the teachers at the *masjids* or mosques), feeling that Islam was now in danger, had openly begun to attack these young inquirers with Quranic ideas that totally contradicted the message of the New Testament (*AlInjeel*): "God is not three." "God does not have a son." "God could not become a man." "No one can die in the place of another." "Jesus did not die on the cross." "God is not our Father; He is not like us, He is totally other."

By ten o'clock, our hostess had compassion on us. The dishes were removed and the *dusterkhan* folded up. Bedding was brought in. The men were given the room of honor and the women were placed elsewhere. Of course, we all slept on the floor—well, on the wall-to-wall carpet. Even then, no one stopped talking. On and on, questions and answers, questions and answers. By midnight, I couldn't keep my eyes open any longer. I asked to be excused from the conversation and fell asleep.

At six o'clock the next morning I awoke to find that everyone else was still awake and talking! As we took turns washing up, the relentless question-and-answer session continued. The bedding was taken away. Back came the *dusterkahn* and, voila! these tireless ladies served breakfast.

Needless to say, this teaching by Q&A never stopped. Eventually it was time to leave. As we packed our things and loaded up the cars, it was under the constant stream of more questions and answers. No one wanted to say goodbye. As we were pulling away, young men were running alongside the car still asking more and more questions. Finally, they couldn't keep up and reluctantly released us to head back to Osh.

Today there is a church, a house-church to be exact, in Kara-Kul. One of those young men came to Bishkek, got trained in the bible college there and returned to be the pastor to the growing number of believers. An awesome story!

SONG IN THE NIGHT

The church in Osh, the second largest city of Kyrgyzstan, is one of the healthiest I have ever seen. It solved the bi-racial problem, in this case, between Russian believers and Kyrgyz believers. It also vigorously pursued church-planting goals.

The Unity of the Spirit

Easter Sunday the church was packed with people: Russian (about two hundred) and Kyrgyz (about fifty). The three-hour service alternated between the use of Russian and Kyrgyz languages. The choir director was Kyrgyz! And he functioned equally well in both styles of music. He could play the piano for the Russians and the *kumus* for the Kyrgyz. New songbooks had been printed in the Kyrgyz language with both Russian and newly composed Kyrgyz worship songs.

The rhythm of the worship service alternated evenly between the two languages and styles of music. It was fascinating for me to watch the Russian quartet taking its turn with the Kyrgyz group during the times for special music and then later to see and hear them sing together with the larger combined choir.

The pastor, by the way, was half Dungan[1] and half Russian. His wife was Russian with a touch of gypsy. The assistant pastor was pure Kyrgyz and the leading elder was Russian. This was a very interesting display of the unity of this multi-ethnic mixture of people that is so common in these former "Russi-fied" cities of Central Asia.

Church-Planting Activities

This mother church in Osh had a superb outreach church-planting program. One example was in a city far to the north, on the other side of the Uzbekistan protuberance of land thrusting into Kyrgyzstan. Let's just call it Khush-bagh.[2]

In the house church there everything was pure Kyrgyz. The worship was in a large central room of an apartment. Colorful Kyrgyz rugs were spread wall to wall. The walls themselves were covered by beautiful one-piece rugs for each wall. Everyone sat on the floor. There were special cushions to lean on. The music was purely Kyrgyz—quite different from the Russian.

When it came time to eat, the musical instruments were put away. A tablecloth was spread on the carpets covering all space not occupied by those seated and then the food was brought in.

Sleeping was done in the same room for the men and an adjoining room for the women. The tablecloth was picked up and then mattresses were brought in, filling the room. The problem was that no one wanted to sleep. The room was filled with not only our team of five, but all kinds of young Kyrgyz believers and inquirers. Questions, questions and more questions. I ran out of steam at midnight. My younger Kyrgyz team members kept on answering questions all through the night, through breakfast, right up to the time of leaving. I felt like I was living in the time of the book of Acts with Paul and his team.

Space will not permit writing about all the other

churches in which we ministered. But it should be mentioned that they fell into two types: a) those where the leadership was Russian but the congregations were mixed, and b) those where the leadership was Kyrgyz and the congregations were purely Kyrgyz.

The Birth of a Baby Church

Of all these successes in church-planting, there was one that caught my attention more than all the others. It happened in the town of Cheraghpur[3]— a town of about five thousand souls—with no church. Our team had learned that there was a handful of old Russian believers to whom no one ministered.

We piled into two old Russian Ladas and began the torturous journey over pot-holed roads. Arriving in town, we found one of the old widowed believers. She led us to an elderly couple. And finally, one more was rounded up. Four. That's it. Four old Russian believers.

Our team had a music ensemble of four Kyrgyz young men and women and one young Russian girl. A talented young Kyrgyz man was the leader of the team. He led us in singing in both Russian and Kyrgyz.

After singing, teaching from the Word about reaching out to our Kyrgyz neighbors, and prayer, the elderly couple prepared our meal. Just as we were beginning to eat, there was a knock on the door. Two lovely young Kyrgyz Muslim women were asking to come in. They said they lived across the street and had heard us singing Kyrgyz songs and they wanted to listen.

We invited them to join us for the meal. As we finished eating, our young Kyrgyz leader began singing with his team—right there at the table. The new songbooks were put into the hands of our guests. They began to read and then lip-sync the words, words of God's divine love for them. They were completely captivated by the music. We sang on into the night.

Eventually, it was time to leave. The Kyrgyz Muslim young women left first. Then we had a final prayer with the elderly Russians and went to our cars for the long drive home in the rain and the dark.

But before we could get started, the mother of these two young Kyrgyz neighbors came out in the road and stopped us. She said, "Next week, you must come and sing in our home and eat with us."

Dear friends, that night, there in the road between two houses, one Russian and the other Kyrgyz, a baby church was born. The Kyrgyz neighbors had heard our "songs in the night." They were drawn by their kind of music and the words in their mother tongue telling them of God's love for them.

---

1 A non-Kyrgyz type of person, supposedly descended from a people who were the result of Arab Muslim men, invaders of long ago, who intermarried with local Chinese women.

2 Happy Garden, not its real name.

3 The City of Light, not its real name.

DIRT UNDER THEIR FINGERNAILS

By the light of the flickering candle, I followed the cup as it moved around the table. As each man lifted the cup to his lips, I was shocked to see irremovable black grease in the creases of their hands and under their fingernails. I studied their faces as they broke the bread and drank the wine in remembrance of the Lord's death—His body broken for them, His blood shed for them. These were the survivors. Strong men, resolute men, men who risked three years in prison just to be in this meeting.

In those days, Christians were treated harshly. Many were shipped off to the Gulag Archepelago for various prison terms. Some never came back. Others died under torture in local jails. It was not uncommon, in such Christian meetings as there were, to see the women outnumber the men by large numbers. These were the widows; their husbands were no more.

No wonder our driver took forever to deliver us to this grim looking building on the edge of town. Finally, after taking all of those evasive measures to make sure we were not being followed, with headlights out, we arrived at this nondescript building with the shades drawn. We parked our car in the rutted street and hurried in.

This was no ordinary meeting. My Dutch companion

and I had come on a double mission. His was to arrange the exact details for the delivery of Gospel portions in the Tajik language and the delivery of a printing press. No small adventure here in the Soviet Union, under the nose of the dreaded KGB.

Poppe had done this many times before. Maps were memorized in Russian. All significant landmarks were duly noted. Street names and house numbers were part of the game, even the color of people's houses, their gates and the kind of trees in front of their houses. No detail was overlooked.

Since the brothers who would deliver these items were not with us, we would have to convey precise details on everything. Most important of all were the passwords. Unusual ways of greeting were agreed upon. There must be no slip-ups.

My assignment was different. Never before had a teacher on Muslim evangelism come to teach about sharing the gospel with Muslims. Even though these men lived in a Muslim state, Tajikistan, then part of the Soviet Union, they did not know Islam. They were all from Russian and German ethnic groups. Most had never seen a Quran before, never been to a mosque, nor had they figured out the basics of the worldviews of the different kinds of Muslims in their area: the Sunnis, the Shiahs and the Sufis.

As I sat with them and listened to their experiences, it was obvious that they had run into the buzz saw of Muslim attacks on the Christian faith. They heard Muslims quote such passages as these from the Quran: "Say not three" (denial of the Trinity), "God has not taken to Himself a son," "No one can atone for the sins of another," and "Jesus did not die on the cross; God took Him alive to heaven. Someone who resembled Him died in his place," and "All prophets are equal.[1]"

And of course, the Muslims repeated the accusation that they had developed after they had conquered the Christian Middle East. For it was then they had discovered the Bible and the Quran didn't agree on major points and, without any proper investigation, assumed that the Christians (and Jews) had changed and corrupted their Scriptures.

My assignment was quite clear. These men had to be prepared to answer these attacks and find the best way to share the Gospel. Time was of the essence, no matter how long it took. There was a palpable sense of urgency. I might never come back. This night might be their only chance to learn. The deep earnestness written in their faces was reciprocated by me as I sought to equip them. Working into the night, we went over point after point, until they got it.

When it was apparent to all that we had finished our work, the table was cleared and the bread and the wine were set before us. But first there were the prayers—the prayers of those in the testing fires. Then came the familiar teaching on the meaning of the broken bread and the blood of Jesus. How could I ever forget that night with those brave men?

Forever etched in my memory is the image of the worn and battered hands on the communion cup, hands of those who had suffered much for their faith—yes, with dirt under their fingernails from the grimy jobs assigned them by cruel taskmasters. Hands of men who will later, with clean hands and pure hearts, drink the cup anew with Jesus in our Father's Kingdom.

1 Thus, Muhammad attempted to make himself equal to Abraham, Moses, David and Jesus—meaning Jesus was no more than a prophet for His age and not for today.

A DIVINE DISRUPTION

The Uighur (pron. we'-gr) people live largely in north-west China. They are a core remnant of a once-powerful empire that we in the West call "Greater Turkestan." Their ancestors migrated into the area from Mongolia in the very early part of the Christian era.

By the sixth century, Persian Nestorian missionaries made their way among these people. Some have even thought they were largely converted to Christ. A famous stone monument was found in the region dating to the eighth century that said something like this:

> The country that formerly was filled with the smell of blood and characterized by barbarous customs has now become a land of peaceful farmers. The land has been changed from killing fields to a place where good deeds are fostered.

Some time later, tragedy struck. In the tenth century, the ruler of the Uighurs embraced the religion of the Arab and Persian merchants who were Muslims. Of course, the Muslims, with the Islamic teaching about *jihad* (holy war) and subduing all non-Muslims, proceeded to kill those who did not convert to Islam. By the fourteenth century, the churches in this area had all disappeared.

From around 1892 to 1938, Swedish missionaries

arrived in northwest China to work among the Uighurs. The Lord blessed their work, which resulted in the planting of Uighur churches. Then, for the second time, the Muslims mounted a *jihad* against the Christians and the Uighur church was wiped out once again.

From that era to the present time, Islam has flourished among the Uighur people. Old fallen mosques have been rebuilt. New ones with *madrassahs* (mosque schools) are flourishing.

Here, of course, as everywhere else in the world, Muslims are not supposed to live under non-Muslim rule. The current re-awakening that is going on throughout the Muslim world has touched the Uighurs in northwest China, too. The government of China has responded to these Muslim uprisings with great harshness. The result is that many Uighurs have fled west across the borders of China into neighboring Kazakhstan.

After the collapse of the Soviet Union in 1991, missionaries began to arrive in the area. Many focused on these Uighur refugees. Uighurs started coming to Christ.

I was invited to meet with the first gathering of these new believers in a lovely conference center in Almaty, the former capital of Kazakhstan. About eighty were gathered for our very first meeting.

Because these new Christians were under attack by their Muslim friends and relatives, I was asked to go over the basics with them so that all would clearly understand the relationship with the Lord and then equip them for dealing with the various charges Muslims made against the Christian faith.

In the middle of the very first lecture, a woman burst out in a loud voice, saying, "Stop, stop! I want to accept Christ right now." Of course, we stopped. Mature believing

Uighur ladies gathered around this weeping woman. They carefully made sure she understood the Gospel, was truly repenting of her sins, believed that Jesus had died on the cross for her and that henceforth she was going to follow Jesus as her Lord. After this, tears gave way to joy and many shouts of "Hallelujah" went up.

When things quieted down, I resumed my lecture. I couldn't have been happier. My own joy knew no bounds as I continued teaching.

That evening after supper, these young believers, with their newest sister among them, spontaneously broke forth into song. Later they began to dance. This went on until midnight. Uighurs, by the way, are known as the most musically gifted of all Muslim peoples. That night, the joy of the Lord was unmistakable and irrepressible as they used their great gifts in singing to the Lord and dancing for His glory.

A few days later when it was time to say goodbye, these dear believers presented me with a copy of one of the most famous paintings of the Uighur people. It portrays fifty Uighur musicians, each playing a different instrument and all are singing their hearts out.

To make the gift all the more precious, each of those new believers signed their names on the back of it. Now, each time I look at this painting, I am filled with joy. I see the new believers singing and dancing before the Lord. And I remember especially the face of that intrepid Uighur sister who disrupted my meeting so that she could accept the Lord right then and there.

Thank you, Father, for the joy of salvation. Thank you, Lord, for visiting the Uighur nation. And grant me more of these divine disruptions!

PRAISE HIS NAME WITH DANCING

Many *Tales That Teach* grew out of experiences that took us by surprise. The following is a composite of three experiences. But they all demonstrate a spontaneous bursting forth of joy and praise in a way that I was never taught. So, for me, they were a surprise. Maybe they will be for you, too.

What makes this "tale" so interesting, at least for those who work among Muslims, is that orthodox Islam, the so-called straight-path-Islam, forbids music in the mosque and, of course, dancing. The reasons are not hard to find.

Muhammad was intolerant of poets who mocked him. On his orders, two were murdered when his forces conquered Mecca in 630 A.D. He also wrongly assumed all music and dancing were associated with prostitutes. When the fundamentalist Taliban controlled most of Afghanistan, they went so far as to smash every TV and piece of video equipment in the country.

The truth is that Muslims around the world love music, poetry and, yes, even dancing. To talk about it is one thing; to get caught up in it is quite another. In previous "tales" we have taught much about music and poetry. This tale will focus on dancing.

The first experience was when I was up in the uranium-rich mountains a few hours drive from Tashkent, the capital of Uzbekistan. The setting was in an old run-down, former vacation camp for high communist officials. Now it was virtually abandoned, except for occasional brave souls like us who didn't mind the broken plumbing, the doors off their hinges and the decrepit beds. The setting was gorgeous: majestic mountains, ancient trees and a mighty rushing river.

This is where one hundred new Uzbek believers, former Muslims, gathered for a week of teaching, training, praying and hiking. On the last evening, after the foot-washing and the communion service, an unplanned spontaneous movement began.

A music ensemble began to play and sing. Suddenly, chairs were pushed up against the walls. The large auditorium floor was cleared. We found ourselves in a huge circle with hands joined. We all began to sing in Uzbek, newly-composed songs that we had learned that week. Then the movement began: rhythmic movement to the right and then to the left, singing with arms now locked together. Then the circle broke. One end began to curl inside the other. Two circles formed—one inside the other—going in opposite directions. Someone began smacking his or her left hand against the left hand of someone coming in the opposite direction. It caught on. We were all doing it—singing, moving in sync with the music and clapping hands in moving circles.

The second time this happened was late at night under the spreading arms of the huge chenar trees in Almaty, Kazakstan. Training classes were over. The Uighurs were not used to going to bed before midnight. Music filled the air. Singing and clapping of hands began. Then there was the spontaneous formation of a circle that began to move.

My companion and I were just coming back from a late dinner at the home of a friend. Hands reached out and grabbed us as we attempted to walk by. We were swept into that beautiful, rhythmically moving, singing, dancing circle. The joy on the Uighur believers' faces was so evident. Their joy would not have been complete without us. This was the joy of those who had recently come to Christ, discovered one another and could not think of a better way to praise God. No one taught this to them but the Lord.

The third time was different. It was mid-morning at another run-down, ex-communist vacation camp, this time high in the mountains of the western Caucasus in southern Russia. Buses were late in coming to pick us up to take us home. An ex-cabaret singer broke out her accordion and began to play. Again, a circle formed. But this time, couples from each of these people groups represented among these seventy believers took their turns in spontaneous, joyous dancing in praise of the One who had so recently saved them. Again, against my wishes, I was drawn into this spontaneous celebration. I felt like a clumsy bear among light-footed gazelles.

Was God trying to teach me/us something in all of this? What did this outbreak of dancing among these newly born believers mean? In each case this was unplanned. It was a spontaneous bursting forth of joy with one's whole being in culturally accepted ways of dancing for each group.

Have we lost our joyous spontaneity in expressing our praise and thanksgiving to God our Savior? Did these joyous, freshly-born Uzbek, Uighur, Chechen, Adegey, Daghistanis, Lurs, Karakapak, Adzarian, Ossetian, Nogay believers know something from the Bible that some of us had long forgotten? Maybe. Ponder anew the words of the psalmist (Psalm 149:1, 3, 4a):

> Praise the Lord. Sing to the Lord a new song,
> His praise in the assembly of the saints...
> Let them praise His name with dancing
> And make music to Him...

INTO THE NIGHT

Martyrdom is not something we think about very often, at least in the States. The closer you get to the Muslim world, though, the more relevant the topic becomes. Islam is not a peaceful religion. Officially, it prescribes death for anyone who wants out. Fortunately, that law is not enforced, at least not yet, in the majority of the fifty-five Muslim countries of the world. Nevertheless, it is a very real threat, even for those who do not come from territories under Islamic law. And there are just enough documented cases of ex-Muslim Christians being killed for their faith these days to make the possibility very real.

This was what made our assignment in Russia so momentous. Muslim background believers had gathered from various parts of the former Soviet Union. We were gathered for a week of meetings at an undisclosed location on the outskirts of Moscow. This was considered a safe place to meet: far from the Muslim enclaves inside of Russia like Tataristan and Bashkordistan and farther still from the newly independent (1991) Muslim states of Central Asia and the troubled tribal region of the Caucasus area of southern Russia.

Even before our arrival, Russia was attempting to put down fresh Islamic uprisings in Muslim Chechnya and neighboring Deghistan. Retaliatory terrorist bombings occurred during our visit. Yet that did not deter these brave brothers and sisters from attending these strategic meetings outside of Moscow. Some had already been threatened with death before they came. What is at the root of this persecution?

Some Muslim countries and territories espouse the idea of religious freedom. It doesn't always work that way. The problem is the Muslim mentality. Even if at the highest levels of government a constitution guaranteeing human rights and religious liberty has been enacted, at the local level the Muslim police and judges are a law unto themselves.

The struggle, again, is with the Muslim mentality. Here is a bit of how they think: Islam is the last and greatest expression of the monotheistic faith. Judaism and Christianity have both failed. God, in His mercy, sent Muhammad as the last and greatest prophet.[1] Islam is a correction and purification of all that went wrong before Muhammad came. Since Islam is the final expression of God's will, there must not be any toleration of any competing religion or ideology. All of them must either be crushed or contained. To try to spread Christianity, therefore, is to fight against God!

So even if the leaders of a country have accommodated to Western ideas and tried to introduce some kind of secularism or democratic ideas and religious freedom, the true Muslim believer, at the grass roots, knows that this is not right. It is not uncommon to have former Muslims who become Christians to be arrested and jailed. The case is appealed to a higher court, sometimes even the highest court in the land. Finally the judgment is made according to the constitution and the Christian is set free. Even then he can be rearrested at the local level, sometimes by the same policeman, and re-sentenced to jail by the same lower court judge—because they know that Islamic law, not government law, is on their side. Wasn't this the same kind of problem faced by the early Church? Peter and John were warned not to speak any more in the name of Jesus. Their response was most remarkable: "Judge for yourselves whether it is right in God's sight to obey you rather than God. For we cannot help speaking about what we have seen and heard" (Acts 4:19, 20).

The Church in the Muslim world today is plunged into the same kind of controversy with Islam. How are these tiny persecuted groups of believers facing this challenge? In two ways: The first group uses scriptures like Joshua 1:3, 5, 9, "I will give you every place where you set your foot...I will be with you. I will never leave you nor forsake you...Do not be terrified; do not be discouraged, for the Lord your God will be with you wherever you go."

We have heard them also quoting from the story of Joshua and Caleb in Numbers 14:9, "Do not be afraid of the people of the land, because we will swallow them up. Their protection is gone, but the Lord is with us. Do not be afraid of them."

Sad to say, on the other hand, we keep hearing about missionaries who are teaching people to say, "We are Muslims," and even to say, "We are not Christians." And they give some explanation of how they read the Bible, believe in Jesus and still can remain Muslims. Some even justify this by saying the purpose of the strategy is to avoid persecution. Does the Bible teach this? We think not.

During these meetings outside of Moscow, we heard the personal accounts of Avars, Chechens, Tajiks, Nogay, Uzbeks, Turkmens, Azeris, Balkar, Kabardin, Adegy, Tatars and Bashkirs, all testifying to God's faithfulness to them through their times of sufferings.

There were many occasions for tears during these meetings, especially at prayer times. Tears not for themselves but for their unsaved relatives. At such times we all wept and we joined in these "acts of love in prayer," asking God for the lost relatives.

Yes, there were discussions and teaching on leadership development, planting churches, training curriculum and the possible formation of new training institutes for those who have come from Muslim backgrounds. But that was not what impressed us the most.

It was after the Lord's Supper that we saw a sight we can never forget. Mary Jo and I were opposite the door that led down a long corridor and out into the night. As these brave men and women walked out, they turned and smiled and gave us who were watching them leave a "thumbs up"— you know, the symbol that says, "We are going to make it. We are going to prevail whether we live or die. Be encouraged. We will meet again—either here or there."

Oh God! Thank you for these brave brothers and sisters in Christ. Wake up, you sleeping church in the West. Lord, put fresh fire in all of us. No matter what it costs, Lord, we will extend our hands, as our brothers and sisters did, and gesture "Thumbs up!"

---

1 Jesus, in their system, is no more than a prophet.

THE FUTURE BELONGS TO FREEDOM

In 1984, three prayer chains of a thousand people each, organized by Open Doors in Holland, covenanted to pray around the clock for the next seven years for the dissolution of the Soviet Union. In 1991, the Soviet Union fell apart. The fifteen countries that made up the former Soviet Union were now free. What an incredible testimony to the power of prayer.

During that period of time, the then-foreign minister of the Soviet Union secretly flew to his own country of Georgia and was baptized there. Ever since, to remind himself that he belonged to Christ, he has worn a cross around his neck.

During that same period of time, we in the outside world read such words as *perestroika* and *glasnost*, referring to a new sense of openness in the thinking of men like Gorbochav and Shevardnadze. Of the two, Gorbochav remained the atheist and Shevardnadze became a Christian. It was Eduard Shevardnadze who then penned the book, *The Future Belongs to Freedom*. The "tale" that follows was made possible by the amazing wisdom and courage of Mr. Shevardnadze.

Shortly after freedom came to the country of Georgia, I was invited to go there and minister. My contact was another one of God's amazing men, Professor Malkhus Songalashvili, the professor of Church History at the University of Tblisi. Malkhus was also the son of the head of the

Baptist Union of that country—a position that he later would step into when his father retired. It was through him that the doors were opened to minister from one end of Georgia to the other.

Our journeys took us from the borders of Azerbaijan and Armenia in the east to the Black Sea in the west. Georgia is on the border of the southern part of Russia, including the troubled land of Chechniya, and in the south, the border is shared with Turkey. Historically, Georgia has been occupied by many other powers, most of whom were Muslim. Today about twenty percent of the population is Muslim. Many live in the east on the border of Azerbaijan, some live in the south on the border of Turkey and others live in enclaves on the coast of the Black Sea. It is because of the Muslim population and the strategic location of Georgia that I was invited to minister there.

And what a ministry! It took our team to the village of Ulianovkov in the east from where we crossed the border into Azerbaijan to distribute beautifully illustrated children's Bibles and to pray for the sick. In the west, we ministered in the area surrounding the town where Josef Stalin lived as a child. In fact, we actually visited the original home where he was born. It was a ramshackle place that bore witness to the wretched poverty of his family.

Among the amazing things that happened on this trip was an interview with the patriarch of the Orthodox Church, Elias II. He actually requested the interview. He was concerned about the millions of Georgian Orthodox Christians who had been forcibly converted to Islam by the Turks and absorbed into Turkey. The patriarch knew why we were there, that is, to train Christians how to work with Muslims and lead them to Christ. He asked for help in winning those Georgian ex-Christians back to Christianity. He also was intensely interested in the book I wrote, *Healing the Broken Family of Abraham: New Life for Muslims.* He knew it existed in the Russian language.[1]

Later, when I asked permission to lecture in the Orthodox seminary in Tblisi, I was denied. Even after much persistence, the answer was no. The reason? The authorities were afraid I would teach or preach from the Bible and undermine their system that was based on the veneration of icons and intercession to their saints. How sad. The best we could do was to stand outside and share our testimonies with these black-robed students who swarmed us with questions and actually wished we could have come inside to lecture. This seminary, by the way, Josef Stalin attended before he left to join the Communist Party.

On our first visit to this country, we unknowingly walked right through a protest march that was headed for the central government buildings downtown. No sooner had we passed through, when we heard gunshots. This was the beginning of a revolution—one of four civil wars. We were unscathed.

By the time of our second visit, Mr. Shevardnadze had become the president of his own country. Also by that time, the book mentioned above (*Healing the Broken Family*) had been translated into the Georgian language and it was dedicated to him. After all, it was his courageous stand that opened up all of these countries to freedom. We requested an interview with him and it was arranged.

Before going to meet him, we had all read his book, *The Future Belongs to Freedom.* During the interview, we were able to explain to him what we were doing in his country, namely, preparing Christians to learn how to work with their Muslim neighbors and win them to Christ. He was greatly intrigued. When we presented the Georgian language copy of the book which was dedicated to him, he was over-whelmed. He said, "Nothing like this has ever happened to me before."

And then he blessed us. He said something like, "I don't know everything you are doing in my country, but may the Lord bless you." And then one of those show-stopping requests: "Could you stay with me over the weekend?" How I wish I had had the courage to say to the team, "Hey, guys, I am not flying back to Moscow with you; I am going to spend the weekend with Mr. Shevardnadze." But the Western dictates of time and schedules won out over my desire to stay and it never happened.

As a kind of stamp of blessing on our visit, I learned just before leaving the country that two Muslims on the eastern border had become Christians from reading *Healing the Broken Family of Abraham*. These strategic visits, initiated by friends from Open Doors in Holland, marked the beginning of wonderful things that are happening in that turbulent land.

---

1 By the way, it was translated into Russian long before it was ever printed in English.

HAMLET

Hamlet. What an improbable name for an astonishing man. He was on the cutting edge of the revival that had come to the Armenian Apostolic Church following the great earthquake of 1988. Hamlet was also a member of the "Brotherhood," the evangelical arm of that church.

Armenia, by the way, is a tiny land-locked country of 3.5 million people, surrounded by Turkey, Georgia, Azerbaijan and Iran. In the year 301 A.D. it was the first nation to ever become Christian. Through the centuries, it has suffered indescribable cruelties at the hands of its Muslim neighbors.

In the midst of the revival going on through the "Brotherhood," a special organization was born called *Gtutiun*, which means "Compassion." Hamlet was its leader. *Gtutiun* promotes evangelism, distributes literature and Bibles, and does children's work and medical work in hospitals and old people's homes.

In 1991 *Gtutiun* invited us to minister in Armenia, and Hamlet became our guide. Our assignment was multi-faceted. We were bringing in relief goods and medicines for the victims of the earthquake and the Nogorno-Karabakh war.[1] We also had brand-new picture Bibles for children. But most surprising of all, I was asked to come to teach Armenian Christians how to evangelize their powerful Muslim neighbors.[2]

Under the circumstances in Armenia at that time—poverty, war and the destruction caused by a powerful earthquake—the training for Muslim evangelism seemed like a preposterous venture. As if to reassure me that I was supposed to be there, on our first day in the offices of *Gtutiun*, I had an unusual encounter. A bearded and bespectacled young man named Aram (and that's as Armenian as you can get) rushed up to me and gushed, "God has called me to evangelize Turkish Muslims. I am so excited. How long do you think it will take me to learn the Turkish language?"

And that was the beginning of a wonderful ministry in Armenia, a ministry that took us from one end of the country to the other. Everywhere we stopped, while the other brothers did the relief and Bible distribution, I was asked to share on Muslim evangelism.

One of those trips took us to Stepanavan where the destruction from the earthquake had been quite severe.[3] To complicate things further, the coming of independence in 1991 led to a general economic collapse. Add to that the ravages of war and you have a three-fold disaster. Armenia was devastated and could not help itself. Nothing had been rebuilt. People were living in Quonset huts, abandoned railroad cars and makeshift dwellings of boxes and tin.

Life was hard on us, too. Food was scarce. At night we slept on the kitchen floor of a dilapidated wooden frame house that was still standing. This was our "headquarters" for all the different ministries we did in that area.

One of those ministries was a little out of the ordinary for me. Hamlet was also into reopening and restoring ancient churches that the communists had shut down and abandoned. It was awesome for me to be present at the re-opening of a thirteenth-century chapel and then to be the first to preach in it in fifty years or more.

In the audience was a young couple with their two-year-old son. He had never walked. At the end of the service, they asked me to pray for their son. I don't look for this kind of ministry, but when it comes my way, I do it.

First, I asked if they knew the Lord. Did they really understand the Gospel message? They didn't. So carefully and patiently we went over the basic truths of Jesus' death on the cross for our sins and His resurrection from the dead. We asked if they wanted to repent of their past sins and believe in Christ for their salvation. They did. They prayed and invited the Lord into their lives.

Afterwards, they reminded me that they had asked me to pray for healing for their son. I hesitated. The boy looked normal to me. But I agreed. God gave me intuitive feelings about what to do. I turned to the parents and asked them if they had taken their son to a non-Christian spiritistic "healer." They had. We talked about the enemy—the other power—the power that is not from God. They understood. Then I asked if they were willing to repent of turning away from God to the other "powers" in their time of need. They did. They renounced them completely. Then I felt free to pray. As I prayed for this little boy, while anointing him with oil, faith came—faith to believe that the Lord would heal him.

When we were through praying, the little boy jumped out of his mother's arms, ran out of the church and down the road—his arms outspread—as if he were an airplane zigging and zagging through the sky. We were all amazed. I still look back in wonder at what the Lord did that day.[4] But when the Spirit of God is present, unusual things, *wonderful* things, sometimes happen.

When we returned to Yeravan, I was asked to speak in a former communist youth hall. It was now packed with born-again Christians, priests and laity alike. I talked about their history, their suffering at the hands of Muslims down through the centuries. I asked if they would be willing to forgive their enemies, yes, even love their enemies and pray that God would use them in bringing their Muslim neighbors to Christ. The Spirit of God seemed to be moving among them. At the end of the message, the presiding priest felt led to give an "altar call." Scores came forward. Many were weeping as they offered themselves for training in winning Muslims to Christ. Only the Spirit of God could move people to do that.

It was the willingness to forgive and work with ancient enemies that impressed me the most. What a lesson for all of us. To believe God for the winning of our enemies—but only after we have confessed our hatred and have forgiven them.

1 Azerbaijan attacked Armenia.
2 Turkey, Iran and Azerbaijan.
3 Fifty thousand people died throughout the country!
4 This is not my normal ministry: I am a teacher and trainer for Muslim evangelism.

HOW SHOULD WE THEN PRAY?

Jesus' disciples were bothered by this question. Let's look in on a scene in Jesus' life with his disciples: "One day Jesus was praying in a certain place. When He finished, one of His disciples said to Him, 'Lord, teach us to pray, just as John taught his disciples.' He said to them, 'When you pray, say…'" (Luke 11:1, 2).

We all know what came next. Today we call it "The Lord's Prayer," or the "Our Father" prayer. But He only taught the content of what to pray; He did not say anything about the posture of prayer. Should we stand or sit? Should we keep our eyes open or closed? Should we fold our hands or raise our arms? What about kneeling or falling flat on our faces?

It is the question of posture that concerns us in this tale. My own anxiety over this question first arose when I was a young believer in seminary. My dear wife, Mary Jo, was in the hospital delivering our second child. Friends invited me to supper. It was what happened after the meal that was so disturbing.

My host read a passage from a devotional book and then said, "Let's pray." All others rose from their chairs, turned them sidewise, then knelt on the floor and put their elbows on the seats of their chairs. I had never seen this done before, but with some awkwardness and embarrassment imitated them.

That night, after arriving back at our apartment, I turned to my Bible with this question: "What is the correct way to pray, that is, what do you do with your body?"

Into the wee hours of the morning I read noting what the Scripture said about how various people prayed. The list of possibilities was amazing:

- Abraham *built altars* and called on the name of the Lord.

- Isaac *went out to the field* to meditate.

- Jacob *set up a stone pillar*, poured oil on it and made a vow (at Bethel).

- Moses was commanded to *take off his sandals* in the Lord's presence.

- Under the Lord's direction, Moses introduced the priesthood and rituals.

- David, *standing*, led the whole assembly in praise. Later, the whole assembly *fell prostrate* before the Lord.

- Solomon *stood* before the altar and spread out his hands toward heaven.

- When Ezekiel saw the glory of the Lord, he *fell facedown*.

- Daniel *knelt* before an open window and prayed toward Jerusalem.

- Jesus *knelt down* and *sweat, as it were, great drops of blood* as He prayed.[1]

- Paul *knelt down* with all the Ephesian elders and prayed.

- In his letter to Timothy, Paul said to *lift holy hands* when you pray.

- To the Thessalonian church, he wrote, "Pray without ceasing." This, of course, means that you could find yourself in *any posture* as you pray!

The above are samples taken from various episodes in the lives of some of the Lord's servants and from the life of Jesus Himself, plus some instructions from the apostle Paul. What a great variety of postures!

Years later, at our own supper table in Altadena, California, all of these memories were revived while listening to an Iranian sister, who had recently come out of Islam, tell of her experiences concerning postures of prayer.

Sameem was converted in a Brethren Assembly in Los Angeles. So I asked, "How did you pray there?" She replied, "We sat on the floor and raised our hands slightly as we prayed."

Then she went on to share that she had left that assembly because of internal strife and joined a Pentecostal church. Again, I asked, "How did you pray there?" The reply: "We stood and lifted our hands over our heads." She left that church also because of leadership problems.

Next, she joined a Lutheran church where they stood and bowed their heads and folded their hands. For whatever reason she left that church also. Finally, she ended up in a Presbyterian church. There, she reported, they didn't do anything. They just sat there while a pastor prayed. Hmm!

When supper was over, I suggested we could all go into our living room where we could kneel down and pray the way she learned as a little girl. And that is what we did— with our foreheads touching the rug. Afterwards, she exclaimed, "I feel like I have prayed for the first time since becoming a Christian." How odd, I thought. Forms or postures should not matter, but this is the posture she felt most comfortable with.

Later I did research on prayer in the early church. To my surprise, I found that this "Muslim" posture of prayer had been borrowed from Sabian Arab Christians. Wow! It was a "Christian" form long before the Arab Muslims borrowed it.

Today, this is a burning question for those who are seeing Muslims come to Christ. Is it okay for those who have left Islam and come to Christ to retain this posture while praying? What would Jesus say?

"God is spirit, and His worshipers must worship in spirit and in truth" (Jn. 4:24). That is what really matters. Jesus did not say a single word about posture.

Paul's words seem so *apropos* today: "... [W]here the Spirit of the Lord is, there is freedom" (2 Cor. 3:17b).

1 I don't think we will ever be able to imitate that.

JESUS AS A KASHMIRI MUSLIM?

Kashmir. Ungovernable Kashmir. This beautiful land-locked "Switzerland of Asia" is now tragically divided with Pakistan occupying one-third and India the other two-thirds. This bitterly contested division is the result of the unhappy stalemate that resulted after the last of three great wars fought by India and Pakistan over the mountains, valleys and lakes of Kashmir.

Today the Indian army has to conscript soldiers to fight here and there are casualties every day. The enemy? Numerous guerrilla bands of native Kashmiri Muslims, illegal Pakistani *mujahuddin* (Muslim "holy war" fighters), and foreign Muslim mercenaries.

The issue? For the Muslim majority population, the mandate of Muhammad. No Muslim should live under non-Muslim rule. For India? An unthinkable precedent! If India lost Kashmir, then every minority group in India would want to secede—and there are hundreds of them!

What about the churches? How are they doing? In Srinagar, the pastor of one church was confronted by a guerrilla group at gunpoint and told he had twenty-four hours to leave. He left. Today, that church is boarded up.

The other church? In the late 1970's and early 1980's it was burned to the ground twice. Why? Simply because they baptized Muslims who left Islam to follow Jesus. This church has been rebuilt. Solid concrete. No windows. No furniture. There is nothing inside to burn.

Christians come every Sunday for worship: expatriates, Christian government officials from various parts of India and two or three native Kashmiris.

Is that all there is in this land of eight million souls? No, there are other stories of what God is doing among the Kashmiri Muslims. Those tales will be told in due time.

But return to this surviving church, this building without windows—what would you do with all of those blank walls? I discovered an answer when I preached there during the All Kashmiri Christian Workers' Conference.

God gave this congregation the gift of an artist—a Kashmiri artist—and many Kashmiri people are gifted artistically. For example, walking down the main street of Srinagar, I was astonished to see sidewalks lined with artwork: scenic paintings of the glorious Kashmiri countryside, portraits of Indian saints and even portraits of Christ.

Thanks to this Christian artist, the walls of St. John's Church were decorated with stories from the life of Jesus. The scenes were familiar but something was different. It was the clothing of Jesus and all those he was interacting with. They were dressed as Kashmiri Muslims. Jesus dressed as a Kashmiri Muslim? Whoa! That was different.

And then came the second thought: Why not? The apostle Paul wrote of our Lord (Philippians 2:6, 7a): "Who, being in very nature God, did not consider equality with God something to be grasped, but made Himself nothing, taking the very nature of a servant...."

Of Himself, Jesus said (Mark 10:45): "For even the

Son of Man did not come to be served, but to serve, and to give His life as a ransom for many."

A servant—to serve. And that's how he was portrayed on the walls of St. John's Church in Srinagar. Jesus, kneeling on the floor with a basin and towel, washing his Kashmiri disciple's feet.

What a contrast! Outside, the blood-drenched land of Muslim and Hindu seeking to impose their rule on one another. Inside, the picture of Christ incarnate as a Kashmiri, letting go of His own cultural identity to bring salvation to the Kashmiri people. No guns, no weapons of any kind. Only a towel and a wash basin. Jesus, dressed as a Kashmiri Muslim, washing the feet of his Kashmiri disciples.

That inspired artist captured the spirit of what Jesus was all about. His paintings etch into our memories the essence of Jesus' love for each of us—of whatever cultural background. What a great lesson for church and mission, captured there in art and also preserved forever in Jesus' own words, as He finished up that servant-like foot-washing service with his original disciples (John 13:15,17): "I have set you an example that you should do as I have done for you....Now that you know these things, you will be blessed if you do them."

ARE YOU A PROPHET?

Security is always an issue in Muslim work. Believe it or not, Muslims or their friends visit churches to pick up prayer letters that tell of mission work in Muslim lands. I have friends who are serving in Muslim countries where they have been confronted by the secret police, holding copies of their prayer letters. This, of course, endangers any ex-Muslim who has become a Christian in that country whose name may have been unwisely mentioned in those letters.

On a certain occasion, the Women's Missionary Society of a church invited me to show slides of the work in Central Asia, including photos of Muslims who had recently come to the Lord. I wrote to them and said I would be glad to do this with one proviso: they must not advertise my coming in the local newspaper. That church was located in a university town where hundreds of Muslim students were enrolled. I did not want unwelcome Muslim guests at my presentation.

Unfortunately, like most of us, these ladies must have been ruled by their presuppositions. In this case, it must have gone something like this: "No Muslim would read the church section of a public newspaper. Therefore, there would be no harm in advertising Dr. McCurry's visit." So the public was invited to see my slides of Muslims coming to Christ in Central Asia.

Not knowing this, and believing that my request had

been heeded, I arrived at the church parking lot on a January night, got out my projector and carousel with beautiful color slides of new work in Uzbekistan, Tajikistan and Kazakhstan, and proceeded to enter the church. From that back parking lot, the entrance took me on to the rear of a stage. Fortunately, the curtain was drawn. As I parted the curtain to go down the steps to the social hall, I saw that every table was filled with young Muslim men from the university. No one had noticed me yet. I quickly shrank back behind the curtain.

What would you have done next? I went back to my car and locked the projector and slide carousel safely in the trunk. As I returned to the church, I said to the Lord, "Okay, Lord, it's Your turn. What do You suggest I do now?" This is what He said: "Give your testimony, all of it, including how I taught you to work with Muslims." I had forgotten that Muslims admire boldness—the Lord had not forgotten.

Upon entering the social hall, I immediately sat down at the first table, where the Muslim young men were devouring the cakes and tea or coffee. I learned their names and what country they were from. I did the same at every table. These fifty guys were from thirteen different Muslim countries. They were all part of the 500-strong Muslim Student Association at the local university.

After dessert, it was my turn to speak and I did exactly what the Lord suggested. At the end of the presentation, I was mobbed by the students with the usual barrage of attacks on our beliefs: "Your Bible is corrupt. God doesn't have a son. God could not take human form. No one can die for another," etc. I expected this and was well prepared for it. What I did not expect was this strange question: "Who are you? Do you think you are a prophet of God?"

Whoa! Where was that question coming from? Then I remembered. Muslims believe that God has not spoken to a single human being since Muhammad died on June 8, 632 A.D. In my testimony, I had used these words, "And then God said to me…" I reviewed again how the Lord spoke to me and added further words of explanation. That seemed to satisfy them.

The next night, in a town twenty miles away, I was to speak again. This time, ten of those fifty young men showed up. They were very quiet and respectful. At the end of the presentation, they came up to me and in a true spirit of inquiry, asked, "Sir, tell us how God speaks to people today." They really wanted to know. I believe they were hungry for God.

In careful detail, I explained how all of us have failed to live up to God's law for us. The Bible calls this sin. This sin separates us from God. We cannot save ourselves. Help has to come from the outside. God, in His love, chose to reveal Himself to us in the form of Jesus Christ.[1] I explained how, in order to save us, the Messiah,[2] who was also called the Lamb of God, became a sacrifice for sin for us. He satisfied the demands of the law by shedding His own blood in our place. He tasted death for us—for the result of sin is death—and then conquered death by rising from the dead. If we truly believed in Christ, He would save us from the consequence of our sins, reconcile us to God and come and live in us by His Spirit. I do not know how many of those ten truly believed. All I know is that they heard the message of the Good News of salvation in Christ and they received it with joy.

What this experience taught me was that the Islamic faith, with its strange teaching that God has not spoken to a single human being since Muhammad died, has created in the Muslim heart a great hunger for God.

Practically speaking, we are to give our testimonies. We are to share the details of how God became real to us. We are to openly provide the answer to that great question: "How can one know God?"

1 Jesus Christ means "Anointed Savior."
2 *Messiah* is translated as *Christ* in the Greek language.

A NIGHTMARE IN DAMASCUS

Some choices are really tough. One of mine was while in seminary. Under Dr. James Kelso, I studied Hebrew, watched the Old Testament come alive and discovered the amazing world of Biblical archeology.

Shortly before graduation, Dr. Kelso invited me to join him and his team on an archeological "dig" in the ancient city of Shecham. Just to remind you of its significance, this is the city where Jacob had his dream. It is one of the places where Jacob built an altar and dug a well.[1] It is where Jacob's sons pastured their flocks and where Joseph's bones were finally buried. It was where Solomon's son, Rehoboam, was crowned king, where the united kingdom divided and where Jeroboam set up his capital of the northern kingdom (Israel). Previous excavations at Shechem have confirmed many of the events of the Bible. Another dig would add to those wonders.

What an invitation! To accept would have meant abandoning my wife and our children for the summer, going into debt to finance their support while away, plus financing my own expenses. I could not do this. Nevertheless, this fascination with biblical archeology never left me. What a surprise I got in Pakistan years later when the Lord revived all of this interest in his unique way. Let's follow the trail.

After a brief two-year pastorate in Colorado Springs, Mary Jo and I with our children were sent as missionaries to

Pakistan. After fifteen years of work at many other tasks, I was invited to teach in our seminary in Gujranwala. My assignment? To teach Hebrew, Old Testament and archeology! All that early training was for this. What a joy it was to revive these subjects, jump in and begin teaching things that still fascinated me.

Much to my surprise, my dear wife, Mary Jo, registered for my class in biblical archeology. She turned out to be a good student. In fact, she won top grades—and no favoritism shown. We often talked about how much fun it would be to visit some of these archeological sites together. Then the Lord opened a door for this to happen.

The course that Mary Jo took was in the spring of 1974. Later that summer, the historic Lausanne Consultation on World Evangelization would be held in Lausanne, Switzerland. This year also happened to be our twenty-fifth wedding anniversary. Why not celebrate by going on an archeological tour in the Middle East after the consultation was over?

We decided to rendezvous in Beirut, Lebanon. I would stop there on the way home from Switzerland and she would come from Pakistan. Then we would tour Lebanon, Jordan and Syria. The highlights of that tour were Byblos, Tyre and Sidon in Lebanon; Petra, Amman and Mount Nebo in Jordan; and ancient Palmyra in the Syrian desert, a place made famous by Solomon and later by the Romans. After that, we would end our tour in Damascus.

While in Damascus, we found, of course, the street called "Straight" and the house where the apostle Paul was supposed to have stayed. We viewed the ancient wall from which Paul was let down in a basket to escape his murderous enemies. Additionally, with our interest in things Islamic, we took in the famous Ummayid Mosque which used to be a church.

Later that evening, after a wonderful dinner in an *authentic* Middle Eastern restaurant and a leisurely time discussing the wonders we had seen, we tumbled into bed, two very tired and happy trekkers.

In the wee hours of the morning, I was awakened with a hideous nightmare. Every inch of ground was saturated with blood and it was crying out, "How long?"

Up to that point in time, our trip had been an academic one. We delighted in viewing these ancient ruins that testified to the historicity of the Bible. It never occurred to us to ask what caused the ruins. Wars, of course. Bloodshed, massacres, pillaging, raping and the leveling of cities—the extermination of their inhabitants.

We were sleeping in Damascus, one of the bloodiest spots on earth. Every power in the region had its turn through history in conquering this city: Babylonians, Assyrians, Medes, Persians, Greeks, Romans, and finally, the Muslims. Damascus, a city drenched in blood. What a shock to be made aware of the human bloodshed that attended the creation of these ruins. What started out as an innocent and enjoyable archeological tour ended with a bloody nightmare.

It brought home to us the great realities of Jesus' words in Revelation 12:17. "The dragon...went off to make war...against...those who hold to the testimony of Jesus." In that book we also read of the martyrs crying, "How long?" Jesus' answer was so sobering: "Until the full number of their fellow-believers to be killed was completed."

Perhaps one day some of us will be among those privileged to shed our blood for the One who shed His blood for us. If so, Jesus' words[2] about His faithful servants are so uplifting: "They overcame him by the blood of the Lamb and the word of their testimony; they did not love their lives so much as to shrink from death."

1 "Jacob's well." Read John 4.
2 Rev.12:11

THE IMAGE OF GOD

It was a secret meeting. My books had all been black-listed in Malaysia. When I went through immigration in Kuala Lumpur, "Alert Red" stuff came up on the computer screen. I was an enemy of Islam because I taught Christians how to evangelize Muslims. The Muslim lady glared at me from across the counter, but granted me a tourist visa anyway. On that visit I was a marked man.

Being under surveillance was nothing new. You develop a sixth sense about it. My greatest fear is not about being detained; it is the fear of getting our local Christian brothers and sisters in trouble. We can be deported. They can be harassed endlessly or, worse, put in jail.

After dark I was driven through twisting and tortuous, nonsensical routes to shake off anyone who might be following us. We eventually got to the meeting place.

There were fifty-one people there: thirty-five Chinese believers, fourteen Indians, and one Malay convert from Islam, plus the missionary. I was drawn to the Malay convert, of course. He wasn't supposed to be there. It is against the law in Malaysia for a Muslim to leave Islam.[1]

After my lecture, I went straight to him. "Brother, how did you get here? How did you come to Christ?" He laughed and, with a twinkle in his eye said, "By reading Genesis 1." I had never heard of anyone coming to Christ by reading the first chapter of Genesis. So I said, "You will have to explain that to me." He told me the following story:[2]

"On my job, I worked beside a Christian named Oscar. We argued religion all the time. I tried to convert him to Islam and he tried to convert me to Christ. One day, in utter exasperation, he thrust a Bible at me and said, 'Here, Rafiq, read this.' He gave no suggestions on where to start. That night I started at the beginning. When I got to the following words I was stunned: "God said, 'Let Us make man in Our image, in Our likeness...' So God created man in His own image. In the image of God He created him; male and female He created them" (Genesis 1:26, 27).

Rafiq said, "There is nothing in all of Islam that even remotely suggests this. According to Muhammad, God is high, far away, transcendent and unknowable. He is not like us. He is totally different. Man is simply his servant. And women are men's property."

Rafiq continued his story: "I picked up the telephone and called Oscar. 'Oscar, it says here in the Bible that we were made in God's image. What does this mean?' Oscar said offhandedly, 'I don't know. Let's find out.'"

With the help of a concordance and a reference Bible they made the following discoveries:

- "The Son... is the exact representation of His [God's] being" (Heb. 1:3a).
- "Anyone who has seen Me [Jesus] has seen the Father" (John 14:9b).
- "He [Christ] is the image of the invisible God" (Col. 1:15).
- "In Christ all the fullness of the Deity lives in bodily form" (Col. 2:9).

- "For those God foreknew He also predestined to be conformed to the likeness [image] of His Son" (Rom. 8:29).
- "...I [Paul] am again in the pains of childbirth until Christ is formed in you" (Gal. 4:19).

Then Rafiq said, "One day it all came together for me. I saw that man originally was made in God's image. Then he destroyed that divine image in himself by sinning in his great rebellion against God. In due time, God sent His Son who was an incorruptible man made in the perfect image of God. When we believe in Christ (His death on the cross, burial and resurrection) and receive Him, we are born again. We become a new creation. God begins the work of remaking us in His own image again. Through His divine promises, we partake of His divine nature."

I was dumbstruck. In all of my previous years in Muslim work, it had never occurred to me that Muslims don't really know who they are. They don't know what they are supposed to be. Islam has led them astray. They have been taught that they are not like God and God is not like us. They have been taught to submit (Islamicize) without asking questions.

What a powerful new idea this was for me. Genesis 1 is a place to start. We can help Muslims find their true identity in Christ through the theme of "the Image of God."

1 And for a Christian to try to convert Muslims.
2 The names have been changed to protect the two men.

IF THIS MAN IS A PHARAOH...

The West African Muslim country of Guinea went through some rough times under a Communist dictator name Seko Toure. The economy was destroyed. Freedom was taken away. The oppression of the people was exceptionally cruel.

Under this man's rule, all missionaries were kicked out of his country, with the exception of workers from the Christian & Missionary Alliance. Seko Toure, as a young boy, had gone to a mission school of C&MA with the children of the missionaries. One of them was Paul Ellenberger. It was because they were classmates as children that Paul and others of C&MA were the only missionaries allowed to stay in Guinea.

It was through Paul's special influence with people in the government that Gerry Swank of SIM Mission and I got visas to enter Guinea. Our tour of Conakry, the capital, revealed a scene of economic collapse, the result of bad decisions on the part of the dictator-president.

As depressing as this was, there was something even more horrifying. At nighttime, if you happened to walk by the city jail, you could hear the screams of the political prisoners who were being tortured.

On the very day we were visiting Conakry, this capital city was decked out with all kinds of flags and banners. It was the anniversary celebration of the day Toure had come to power. We heard there was going to be a parade of marching bands, including those of school children, in the stadium.

The three of us, Paul, Gerry and I, went to view the celebrations. At first, I was fascinated by the school children. Freshly scrubbed, wearing starched white uniforms with colorful sashes, they looked so attractive, marching so smartly in the sun. But my sense of admiration didn't last long.

As we sat there cooking in that tropical heat, disturbing thoughts intruded themselves into my mind. This wasn't fair. These precious school children were helpless pawns in the cruel hands of a ruthless dictator. They were forced to march in this blistering sun to pay honor to an evil man who had staged all of this in praise of himself.

I thought of King Nebuchadnezzar's words: "Is not this the great Babylon I have built as the royal residence, by my mighty power and for the glory of my majesty?" Then God's words came: "Your royal authority has been taken from you...[You] will live with the wild animals...until you acknowledge that the Most High is sovereign over the kingdoms of men and gives them to anyone He wishes" (Daniel 4:29-32).

The Bible "case study" that came more forcefully to mind, though, was that of Pharaoh. Here was a man who had ample time to repent. Step by step, he saw the mighty acts of God. At each step he had the opportunity to change his mind and give glory to God. And the Word of God says that each time "Pharaoh's heart became hard." Towards the end of those "power encounters," the Scripture says, "The Lord hardened Pharaoh's heart." This went on until Egypt was destroyed and Pharaoh's army perished in the sea (Exodus 7-14).

Pharaoh's story had often caused me to think about people's hearts. They are either like clay or like butter. When you bring God's testing fire close to butter, it melts. That's a picture of repentance. But when you put clay into the fire of a brick kiln, it grows harder and harder until it becomes a brick. The fire reveals what is in the human heart. And according to its essential nature, the heart either softens or hardens.

Would it be right to talk to God about this cruel Marxist-Muslim dictator?

Seco Toure knew these Bible accounts of God's dealing with people. He had gone to school with "mish kids." Apparently, he had not taken these lessons to heart. Perhaps, like so many today, he thought those were just fables from long ago. As a Marxist, he had scoffed at the idea of God having a hand in the affairs of men today.

These were the thoughts going through my mind as I watched these beautiful young children, innocent and unsuspecting, marching to the praise of an evil man. All the while as I watched, echoing in my mind was the sound of screaming men being tortured simply because they wanted to live in a free country. When I could stand it no more, I said to my companions, "Can we go somewhere to pray?" We found a shady place under a great beobab tree and there we prayed.

It went something like this: "Oh God, You who know men's hearts—You know whether this man is a Pharaoh whose heart will grow harder and harder, or whether he will soften and open up this country again to your people. Oh God, if You know that one day he will repent and let Your people come back, then spare him. But if You know that his heart will just grow harder and harder in your testing fires, then, Lord, please remove him and bring to power a more kindly ruler who will open up Guinea to Your Word and Your workers again."

Having prayed that prayer, we then returned to Paul Ellenberger's home on the coast and made preparations for the long trip up country to the Telakora Bible Institute in the town of Kissidougou. (But that's another tale.)

After our ministry in that country was complete, Gerry and I returned to the States. We continued to pray for that hapless land, God's people there and all the unreached Muslim people groups.

In less than a year we heard that Seko Toure had died. A new ruler came to power. He permitted missionaries to come back into that 83% Muslim country where evangelical Christians are only 0.6% of the population. What were the results of those prayers? Today there are about 190 missionaries from about 24 agencies working in all of the major Muslim people groups in Guinea, a country of 10 million people.

WHAT HAPPENED IN THE CHAPEL IN KISSIDOUGOU

"Men ought always to pray and not to faint" (Luke 18:1 KJV). Guinea was a land under a Marxist-Muslim dictator. The country was in economic shambles. The Russians had looted the land of its bauxite and other precious resources and gave only bad ideology in return. All the missionaries had been kicked out—all but two. Christians, only 0.6% of the population, were fearful and apprehensive.

Through the courageous efforts of one of those remaining missionaries, Paul Ellenberger of the C&MA, Gerry Swank of the SIM Mission and I got entry visas. We hoped we would get exit permits when it was time to leave.

Guinea, there on the west coast of Africa, was a land of forty people groups with an eighty-three percent Muslim population. Our assignment was to gather the surviving pastors, live with them for a week, and try to impart hope and faith and the courage to believe that God could use them, against all odds, in bringing Muslims to Christ. Our destination was 325 miles inland—the Telekora Bible Institute where we would rendezvous in a "safe" place with the gathering pastors.

The long trip up-country to the Bible school was an unforgettable journey. With our experienced missionary driver, Paul Ellenberger, as our tour guide, we drove through some of the most beautiful countryside in all of tropical West

Africa.

Starting out from Conakry, the capital, on the Atlantic coast, with the beautiful mountains of the Kakoulima Range in the background, we made our way inland. As we climbed through the hills, we began to notice many sparkling streams and spectacular waterfalls. This is the land of many headwaters for the rest of West Africa. Our spiritual prayer was that the Guinean Christians would become the source of great rivers of living water—salvation for West Africa.

Along the way were exotic African birds and butterflies, plus an abundance of wildlife: monkeys, gazelles, random hippos in the rivers and elephants. As beautiful as this was, there was something far more beautiful in God's eyes—the people—these forty different ethnolinguistic tribes of His lost children.

Thanks to endless potholes and horrible road washouts on this road that had not been maintained for years, Paul had the leisure time to give us a running commentary on all these unreached Muslim people groups along the way. So we began to learn their names. The Susu, Maninka, Yalunka, Konyanke, Kuranka, Bandi, Bambara, Wassalunke, Kpelle, Toma, Fula and Kissi. And, of course, there were many other smaller groups (twenty-eight of them) whose names I could not retain.

A remarkable feature of our journey was that we passed through only four towns: Kindia, Mamou, Dabola and Faranah. Each was the center of a major people group. The rest of the countryside was either wild or dotted with small villages.

It was at Faranah that we turned south, hugging the border of Sierra Leone and still in the area where the headwaters began. We stopped to see the place where the famous

Niger River began. As we bathed our feet in this tiny beginning of a mighty river, again we prayed that the believers of Guinea would become a source of living water for all the peoples of West Africa.

Many hours later, we arrived in the town of Kissidougou. Red dirt roads, huge beobab trees, villages of thatched roofs and picturesque market scenes greeted our eyes. At the edge of town, we entered what was like an oasis of orderly green lawns, neat cottages, well-tended orchards and gardens, a gorgeous white chapel and other buildings connected with the Telekoro Bible School.

As so often happens in tribal settings, there is a sense of rivalry and even animosity between the tribes. Even worse, there is a great sense of fear among the animistic tribes toward the Muslim ones. The memories of the atrocities committed by Muslims against those they sought to conquer or convert live on.

Over the next few days, we did Bible studies that dealt with the elements of fear and forgiveness. Jesus' examples in word and deed were used to show how He taught His disciples to overcome the barriers of racism. All of this teaching was leading to a simple goal: to get our Christian friends inside of Guinea, as a first step, to pray for their Muslim neighbors.

To help facilitate this, Gerry and I drew a large map of Guinea and attached it to the chapel wall. On it we outlined the major Muslim people-groups. After more teaching, this time on the value of intercessory prayer, we all gathered at the map. Taking one people-group at a time, we all placed our hands on that area and began to pray. We asked God to awaken the Muslims there and raise up Christian workers to begin the formation and discipling of churches in that area.

Three years later in the States, while teaching a class of mission candidates at Wheaton University, I discovered that one of the couples was going to Guinea to work with the Maninka people. That same week, one of our related churches called and said they were sending a missionary couple to work with the Susu in Conakry. I remembered our prayers at the Telekora Bible Institute. At last count (1993), we learned that there are now about 190 missionaries with 24 different mission agencies working in every major Muslim people group in the country!

Does prayer really make a difference? You bet! God answered the prayers of those Guinean pastors. What about you? What are you asking God for? What can you learn from our Guinean brothers?

"Men ought always to pray and not to faint."

SAADI KAMAARA

The greatest problem Jesus had with His disciples was *racism*. The most dramatic illustration of this is seen by His disciples' reactions to contrasting events in Nazareth and a village in Samaria.

Let's look at them. The first occurs at the synagogue in Jesus' hometown of Nazareth. Jesus has just read the great prophecy in Isaiah 61:1, 2, and explained that those words were fulfilled on that day in Him. The audience was impressed with the gracious words that came from His lips.

A few seconds later, to the same audience, Jesus referred to two miracles done by the prophets Elijah and Elisha, respectively, to show that no prophet is ever honored in his hometown. The first miracle was about how the prophet multiplied a *Canaanite* widow's food supply at a time when Jewish widows were starving. The second had to do with curing the *Syrian* general Naaman of his leprosy at a time when no Jewish lepers were cured.

Suddenly, the mood of the Jewish audience turned ugly. The people took Jesus to the brow of a hill to hurl Him to His death (Luke 4:24-30).

What did Jesus' disciples do in His defense? The answer is "nothing." Jesus escaped the people's wrath by His own devices with no help from His disciples. He simply turned and walked untouched through the hostile mob.

But on another occasion in Samaria, under far less provocative circumstances, the disciples' reaction was totally irrational. Or shall we say, "typically racist"?

Luke 9:54 says that in passing through a Samaritan village, Jesus had asked for lodging for the night. The Samaritans did not welcome Him. John and James, two of the inner core of Jesus' disciples, asked Jesus for permission to call fire down from heaven and burn up the village. Interesting.

They did no such thing in Nazareth when their Master's life was in real danger. But in a village of hated Samaritans, they wanted to destroy their "enemies" for their lack of hospitality.

The explanation for these two starkly contrasting attitudes is not hard to find. Why total passivity in Nazareth on the one hand and murderous intent toward the Samaritans on the other? The only answer is racism.

Jesus rebuked His disciples on that occasion in Samaria. Later, He healed ten lepers: one was a Samaritan—the only one to come back and thank Him. He called attention to that. On another occasion, He led His disciples to Jacob's Well, where He had that memorable experience with the woman who led her whole Samaritan village to believe in Jesus as the Savior of the world.

Perhaps the story that has become the most famous of all Jesus' parables is that of the "good Samaritan," the man who showed mercy when no one else would (Luke 10:25-37).

What about us? Are the Muslims of our day like the Samaritans of old? Are we like the Jews? I think so. How would Jesus shame us into loving our "enemies" if He were here today? He would find a story or an experience that would illustrate His point and tell it as a tale that would teach us.

Our tale takes place in the West African country of Guinea. We had been driving all day from the interior toward the coast. At sunset we stopped for a break and to take some food before driving on into the night.

And so it was that we pulled off the road into a clearing at the edge of a village. As we were unpacking our food, a Malinka lady walked by covered from head to foot in her traditional African dress. She noticed us, walked a few paces and then stopped. Taking the huge bundle off of her head, she pulled something out, tucked it in her copious sleeve and came and greeted us in the Malinka language.

These were long exchanges of greetings, all the while bowing toward us in respect. Paul Ellenberger, our guide, replied in a similar fashion. At the end, she reached into her sleeve, pulled out a giant tuber of manioc, handed it to Paul, and then with more elaborate expressions in the Malinka language, accompanied by more bows, she withdrew, tied up her bundle, put it back on her head and walked into the village.

Overcome with intense curiosity, I plied Paul with questions. The gist of what happened was that this Malinka lady had offered to cook our evening meal and to give us her house for the evening. I was overwhelmed. I said to Paul, "She knew you, didn't she?" He replied, "No, I have never stopped here before." Then I suggested that she was a Christian. Again, he said, "No, she was a Muslim."

I was even more amazed. A Muslim lady in an African village would offer to cook our evening meal and give her house to three perfect strangers who happened to stop at the edge of her village at nightfall. Incredible!

I asked Paul if he had caught her name. He said it

was Saadi Kamaara. I said to no one in particular, "She is the good Samaritan of our day. Saadi Kamaara is the 'good Muslim.' And I am going to tell her story to Christians everywhere. Jesus would."

You see, we, like Jesus' early disciples, also have prejudices that plague us in our work. Jesus would have shamed us with this story—to teach us that Muslims may love us more than we love them. When I am tempted to have negative thoughts about Muslims, I remember Saadi Kamaara, "the good Muslim."

WE'RE NOT AFRAID ANY MORE

The name "Uthman dan Fodio" (1754-1817) is synonymous with *jihad*, the Arabic word for "holy war." Even though he has been dead for nearly two centuries, his name still strikes terror in the heart of non-Muslim peoples in West African countries.

Here was a Muslim man who was disgusted at the way other Muslim clerics compromised with pagan practices. Also, as a cleric himself, he suffered horribly at the hands of brutal pagan rulers. Inflamed by the fiery preaching of his Islamic teachers, he burned with a "holy" zeal for the expansion of the regime of divine (Islamic) law.

The news of successful *jihads* in other parts of sub-Saharan Africa spurred him on to begin his own *jihad*. He regarded himself as the chosen instrument for the execution of the decrees of the divine will, as spelled out in Islamic law.

He exhibited a courage and steadfastness that inspired true Muslims to gather around him. His followers swore to be loyal to him in his *jihad* against all unbelievers, whether pagan or nominal Muslims. He commissioned chosen followers to carry his special flag throughout West Africa in their holy wars. His spirit lives on to this day in his disciples.

The above material is background information to keep in mind as I describe a ministry trip to Ouagadougou, the capitol of Burkina Faso, formerly called Upper Volta.

Through mutual friends, I received an invitation to teach at a pastors' conference in the capital city. This place was really different. There were very few paved roads. What was more normal was this lovely shade of brick red dirt. Fortunately, it was not the rainy season.

The venue for our meetings was a newly constructed concrete building with a corrugated tin roof, no electricity, no running water. The temperature outside was well above 100 degrees Fahrenheit. Every day for a week we fried in that "cooker." I could never keep a piece of clothing dry for more than thirty seconds the whole time I was there.

The participants were, with one exception, all pastors from various pagan tribal backgrounds. They had come in from near and far for this conference. Racially, these brothers were all descendants of tribes that had resisted or escaped the ferocious *jihads* that had been inspired by dan Fodio. Stories of atrocities committed by these Muslim *mujahaddin* ("fighters of *jihad*") fed the decidedly anti-Muslim attitude of these Christian pastors.

The one exception to all of this was the pastor who was from a Muslim background. His situation was a bit awkward. The ninety-nine other pastors talked and acted as though he didn't exist. There was no effort on their part to learn his point of view or see in what way he could help them reach their Muslim neighbors. He had been pressed into their mold and was a pastor to their kind of people. This brother turned out to be my hidden ally in all that I was trying to do.

It was strange that I, an outsider, was asked to come in and teach and train about winning Muslims to Christ. Most of the time, in such gatherings, the audience presupposes that you are going to teach them sure-fire techniques for magically converting Muslims to Christ. Little did they realize that we were going to work in the area of attitude change first.

Showing them[1] their own racism was the first step: letting them gain insight into just how prejudiced they/we are. I usually do this by sharing the way the Lord dealt with me in my days in Pakistan. In a sense, in the light of my experiences, they began to see themselves. They began to realize that this obstacle of racism and fear was what kept them from reaching out to their Muslim neighbors.

Eventually, we discussed Jesus' teaching on loving your enemies, blessing those who curse you and praying for those who despitefully use you and persecute you.

It was after these lessons that we began to teach new ways to approach Muslims. Part of this had to do with responding to Muslim needs. But the other part had to do with showing them the Islamic material that lends itself so beautifully to a presentation of Christ.

At the end of such a week, one or two of the elderly "statesmen" among them summarized what they thought they had learned. It was very satisfying to me, the teacher, to hear them repeat the things I had wanted them to learn. During this time of sharing, it was the pastor from the Muslim background who shone as he mentioned so many things that confirmed what I had been teaching.

What touched me most was the testimony of the oldest pastor there. This was the sentence that leaped out at me: "Before you came," he said, "we were afraid of Muslims. Now we are not afraid of them anymore." I wanted to shout "Hallelujah!" Mission accomplished. We are not afraid of Muslims anymore. Are you?

1 And this goes for *any* audience.

TEACHING IN THE MOSQUE

Avtov lived in the village of Lagodekhi. This is on the eastern border of Georgia—a trans-Caucasus country wedged in between Azerbaijan on the east, Armenia and Turkey on the south, Russia on the north and the Black Sea on the west.

Because of its strategic location between the Persian and Turkish empires to the south and the Russian empire to the north, this land has been one of the bloodiest battle-grounds of history between "Christian" Russians and Muslim Turks and Persians. Recently, with encouragement from Turkey, the Muslim enclaves of Abkhazia and Adzharia on the coast of the Black Sea began a war of secession.

With this kind of historical background, it is no won-der that there is a lot of bad feeling between Christians and Muslims in this newly independent country. This is what makes Avtov's story all the more remarkable.

You see, Avtov loved Muslims. This made him dif-ferent from all of his Christian family, friends and even the members of the church of which he is the pastor. After I preached in his church, he and his wife invited me to their home for a typical Sunday meal. There were heaps of every kind of good food. It was when we got to the cakes and cof-fee that he told me his remarkable story.

"After my conversion as a young man, I was filled with the love of God for all people. Because we lived in a Muslim village, I naturally felt love for all of my Muslim neighbors. I talked with them a lot about God."

"One day, a group of my Muslim friends said to me: 'Avatov, since you love God so much, why don't you come to the mosque with us and see how we worship God?' I agreed.

"We took our shoes off at the door. My Muslim friends washed their feet, face and hands, and then we went in and sat on the floor. When the *amir* called them to prayer, they lined up facing Mecca and recited their prayers in Arabic. When they were finished, we sat around and talked. They asked me if I had ever read the Quran. When I said no, they gave me a Russian translation of it and asked me to read it and tell them what I thought. At home, I began to read the Quran. The first thing that struck me was how many Biblical characters were mentioned in the Quran—twenty-five of them—going from Adam to Jesus. In fact, Jesus was mentioned frequently. I noticed the similarities and the discrepancies.

"Since I knew that they had the typical misunderstanding that the Bible had been corrupted, I wondered what I could do to get them interested in the original biblical accounts. Then God gave me an idea. I decided to study one biblical character at a time, memorize the story, then go back to the mosque and tell the story in my own words. I went to the mosque with my Quran, knelt on the carpet, and opened the Quran to the story of Adam, and asked, 'Would you like to hear the story from the ancient books?' They said they would, so I told the biblical story in my own words. They were very interested. Then I told them I didn't have time to stay but I could come back next Friday and tell another story.

"In this way, I began to work my way through the biblical characters. One day one of them asked if they could see these ancient books for themselves—the ones mentioned in the Quran—the Law of Moses, the Psalms of David and the Good News of Jesus. I gave them copies in the Russian language. They were amazed. They asked to borrow them."

Then Avtov said to me, "Brother Don, some of them came to believe in Jesus. I am so happy. But I can't go to the mosque anymore because some Muslims became angry when their friends believed in Jesus as Lord and Savior. So now I go all over the countryside, and even across the border into Azerbaijan, visiting their sick, praying for them, and leaving the real Word of God with them after showing them the connection to the Quran. Now more are coming to Jesus."

I was totally amazed. The Holy Spirit taught this precious brother what to do. My role in this situation was not to teach but to affirm Avtov in the presence of his wife and children, family and friends and ultimately in the church. Avtov began by telling stories in the mosque, of men mentioned in the Bible and Quran. I believe he modeled for all of them a way to relate to their Muslim neighbors.

A SCENE FROM THE MOSQUE AT REGENT'S PARK

Mosques have a fascination all their own. It is where the Muslims go to pray with their fellow Muslims at appointed times and even to meditate and memorize their scriptures when the mosque is relatively empty.

Ron George[1] and I decided to go "fishing" in that great showplace mosque at Regent's Park, London. To our amazement, when we arrived, there were only two men seated, quite apart from one another, on the floor of this cavernous hall.

It was decided that Ron would sit with the Arab-looking man and I would sit with the Caribbean-looking man.

I asked the man if I could sit down beside him. He welcomed me. We exchanged greetings. He told me his name was Suleiman and that he was from the island of Trinidad. When I asked if he had been born a Muslim, he replied, no, he had been born into a Baptist family.

Now I was curious so I asked, "How in the world did you become a Muslim?" This was his story. To escape the poverty of his environment, he migrated to England and entered the country illegally. There he fell into a life of drugs and crime. He was finally apprehended and put in jail. In jail, his Muslim cell-mate won him over to Islam.

"Suleiman," I asked, "what are you doing here in the

mosque now, all by yourself?" He told me that he was trying to memorize the Quran in Arabic.

I asked if I might see his Quran. Leafing through it, I found the passage that reads, "Behold, the angel said: 'O Mary! God gives you glad tidings of a Word from Him: His name will be *Christ Jesus, the Son of Mary*, held in honor in this world and the hereafter and of [the company of] those nearest to God'" (Quran 3:45) (emphasis added).

Then I handed the Quran back to Suleiman and asked him if he could read that verse in Arabic. With difficulty he did. The reason for choosing this passage is rooted in the violent history that attended the great debate among Muslim theologians of the thirteenth century. It was all about the question: Is the Word of God created or uncreated? Those who claimed the Word of God was created were massacred by those who claimed it was uncreated. Since the time of Baidawi (died 1291), one of the greatest Muslim commentators on the Quran, all Muslims have embraced the idea that the Word of God is uncreated.

With this kind of background knowledge, I asked Suleiman if he thought the Word of God was created or uncreated. Without a moment's hesitation, he blurted out, "Uncreated." Then I asked, "Does that mean that Jesus, who is called the Word of God[2] is uncreated, that is, eternal?" He snapped his head around and stared at me and said, "Who are you?" I replied, "It doesn't matter who I am; all that matters is what that book says."

That was the beginning of two hours of leafing through the Quran and asking Suleiman question after question about Jesus, such as: "What does it mean 'He is nearest to God?'" "Why did He have this power to give sight to those born blind and to cure leprosy and to raise the dead?" "Why does the Quran say He is coming back to the earth as a sign of God's judgment on all people?" "Why is He called 'All Righteous,' [or sinless] when everyone else is described as sinful?" "Why is He called 'a Holy Son' and 'a Sign for All People'?"

As time wore on, Suleiman became more and more confused. You see, a Muslim is not supposed to have questions. A Muslim is taught to submit[3] to what is, without asking questions. In a cultic fashion, Islamic teaching is drummed into the submitter. For Suleiman, who still had residual memories of his Baptist upbringing, these questions began to remind him of his early Christian teaching and to destabilize his sense of equilibrium—in other words, he began to wonder who Jesus really is. In the end, he could not avoid the conclusion that Jesus was much more than Islam allowed.

As time would have it, he had to go back to work, but before he left, he said in his rich Caribbean accent, "Man, you just knocked me out. Just like Muhammad Ali knocked people out; you knocked me out." I replied, "No, it wasn't me; it is God knocking at the door of your heart. Jesus is who He claimed to be: the Way, the Truth, the Life, the Savior of the world and the Lord of all."

I may never know the result of this interview, but this I know: The Quran has in it, its own undoing. It says too much about Jesus. And those verses about Him are your stepping stones to lead your Muslim friend back to the real Jesus, the living Lord Himself.

1 Founder of People International.

2 *Kalimatullah* in Arabic.

3 Muslim means "one who has submitted."

NOOR

This was to be my first preaching trip into Egypt. I was invited by the leaders of the Khalas-un-Nafooz Society (The Society for the Salvation of Souls). The trip would take me from one end of Egypt to the other. All previous guest speakers had been good men seeking to revive the churches. My ministry would be different in that I would be speaking to Christians about evangelizing Muslims. This was all agreed on before I arrived. Still it was a shock for them when I began.

Our meetings began in a beachfront Beth-al-Khalas (House of Salvation) in a suburb of Alexandria. A refreshing sea breeze was blowing through the open windows. Although it wasn't necessary for this small gathering of sixty pastors and lay leaders, a loudspeaker had been hooked up to amplify my messages.

As soon as the audience heard me speak so boldly about winning Muslims to Christ there in Egypt, pandemonium broke out. The meeting was abruptly stopped. I was told I could not do that. I reminded the leaders that this had been agreed upon before I came. The highly agitated core of leaders put their heads together to figure out what to do. I was the honored guest. They had agreed to the subject matter. But when I actually began—they panicked.

I had never seen men so ruled by fear. Before the

meeting could resume, the microphone was turned off. Then the windows were shut and the shutters banged closed. No one had ever spoken so openly about evangelizing Muslims before. I had no idea that Islam had so thoroughly intimidated the Christian community of Egypt. This proved to be a ground-breaking experience for us all.

At the other end of Egypt, in the city of Assiut, a real stronghold of the Muslim Brotherhood, the state of mind of the Christians bordered on hysteria. They asked for our passports.[1] Then they closed all the windows, bolted the doors and said that we could not go out in the streets.

We would not give in to fear. My son and I literally had to remove men's hands from our arms and force our way out the door just to walk along the Nile as free men. On the way, we met two young Muslims who were carrying a large photo of Ayatollah Khomeini. We stopped and talked. Later, John even got involved in a "pick-up" sandlot soccer game and immediately became very popular with these Muslim youths. We returned to the apartment jubilant, exulting in our conquest of fear. Our hosts were visibly relieved when they saw us back safe and sound.

It was only when we got back to Cairo that God introduced us to a truly fearless Christian. We shall call her "Noor," meaning "spiritual light." Mutual friends had arranged for us to meet in Shoubra, the mostly densely populated area of Cairo. The late afternoon sunlight was filtering through the dusty windowpane. We sat there in its warm glow as Noor, radiant with God's love, told her story.

"My father taught law at the prestigious Al-Azhar University. One day, spotting an Arabic Bible on a newsstand, he pounced on it, paid for it, brought it home and told us he was finally going to prove that Christianity was wrong.

"He was fascinated with the rich and full details of the biblical accounts, details that were missing in the Quran. It wasn't until he got to the New Testament that the shock waves began. With his fine lawyer's mind, he began seeing prophecy after prophecy come alive in the life of Jesus. At first he was surprised, then angry—angry because no one had ever told him these beautiful truths, angry at Muhammad for not being true to the details about Jesus Christ.

"Then my father quit going to the mosque. He said that he had, through these long weeks of study, discovered that Jesus really was the Son of God, the Savior of the world. Word of this spread quickly through the family and then the neighborhood. It wasn't long before the police came. When my father told them yes, he had been born a Muslim and, yes, he believed Jesus was the Son of God, they took him off to jail.

"I found his study notes on his desk—a Bible, too. I began to read what my father had written. Then I began to read the Bible. Soon, I too believed. I decided to manifest my new faith in Jesus by discarding my head veil.[2] The first day, my fellow lady teachers asked why. I told them I had become a Christian. It wasn't long before the police came for me."

What Noor said next shocked me. She said, "Don, it was wonderful! I didn't know other Muslim women had become Christian. I met some in jail. And Jesus was there with us. We learned to pray and sing together. We even led other women prisoners to the Lord. We grew in our faith there in prison.

"The police tried to frighten us. They even used our relatives to tell us what horrible things were going to happen if we did not recant and become Muslims again. Our relatives could see that we were not afraid. We told them what we had discovered in the Bible: 'Perfect love casts out fear.'"

Then Noor looked me straight in the eye and said, "Brother Don, the enemy of the Gospel in Egypt is not Islam; it is fear." Then she said, "Tonight you are going to preach in this church.[3] I want you to tell all the Christians that their real enemy is not Islam; it is fear."

And that is what I did. The ripple effect of that (taped) message is still going on. I learned it from my Cairene sister, Noor; beautiful, radiant, fearless Noor. In the Muslim world, our real enemy is not Islam; it is fear.

1 My son was with me.
2 I never would have counseled her to do this.
3 The mother church of the "Salvation of Souls Society."

YOU ARE MY SON'S SPIRITUAL FATHER

The Saudi Arabian government approached the government of Pakistan for help in re-training their pre-medical students in English. Up to that point in time, Saudi Arabia did not have its own medical school. These bright young men had done all of their studies in Arabic. Naturally they could not be admitted to English-language medical schools in the West.

Pakistan referred them to Karachi University. It had a modern language-learning laboratory. But there had been much political in-fighting in the university and the lab was in a state of disrepair. Karachi University refused to touch it. They referred the Saudis to Punjab University in Lahore, the city where I worked. Their staff also felt unprepared for such a challenge and said they couldn't do it.

The Registrar of Punjab University was a Christian. He informed the officials that Forman Christian College, where I was teaching at the time, had an excellent English department.

The next thing I knew, Dr. Anwar Berket, the principal of our college, asked me to negotiate a contract with the Saudi Arabian government for re-training twenty Saudi pre-medical students. Then Dr. Berket asked me to direct the program. I thank God that my mission had allowed me to get a mid-career master's degree in English Education at Temple

University while on furlough.

At Forman we formed a team of six professors: one each in chemistry, physics and biology, and three in English.

These special students were also assigned to my dormitory. They would constitute twenty of my ninety-six Muslim residents in Velte Hall. Most of them were excellent soccer players. Velte Hall had the best team in the college.

There were many other things that we did together, including bus trips, picnics and tours of historic places. I also mediated in settling their fights with the Pakistan students in the dormitory. All of these things contributed to a warm and affectionate bonding between us.

As a result of a very successful program, I was invited by my students to visit them in Saudi Arabia during the coming summer vacation. That turned out to be do-able, as our mission had arranged for me to attend a conference on Islam in Beirut with Dr. Kenneth Cragg. Visiting them was something I could do on the way.

That led to one of the most memorable experiences I have ever had. Each night was party night. One night it was a cookout with a sheep baked in an underground fire pit. Another time we feasted sitting on Persian rugs under palm trees at an oasis with Arabic music playing in the background. Still other times we dined in sumptuous homes.

Every night there was always one question. I think they had agreed ahead of time on their list of questions. Here are some of them:

- "Sir, you are an intelligent and well-educated man. How could you possibly believe one human being could die for the sins of everyone who ever lived?"
- "Sir, you think very logically. How can you believe one

God is three Gods?"

- "Sir, how could God possibly become a man and still be God?"

- "Sir, how could you believe that God would allow a good prophet like *Isa Massih* (Jesus Christ) to be executed as a criminal?"

- "Sir, if salvation came by simply believing in what you say about Jesus Christ, then we could sin as much as we wanted, right?"

These are wonderful questions. And because I was their friend and their respected teacher, I could take my time in answering them without interruption or argument. All of these answers were duly reported to their fathers, I'm sure.

That is what made what happened on the last night so startling. The father of Fayyaz, the leader of the students, took me by the shoulders as we were saying goodbye and said, "Mr. McCurry, as you and my son return to Pakistan, there is one thing I want you to know. I consider you my son's spiritual father." I gasped and said, "Mr. Abdullah, you know I am a Christian missionary." He said, "I know, I know. But you are my son's spiritual father."

Unfortunately, Fayyaz and I got separated after this. I never knew how Fayyaz felt about what his father had said. But this I do know. All of the time, energy, and love poured out on these guys were worth it. Perhaps I will never know this side of eternity what kind of fruit came of this effort. But I do know that God took the occasion to sow the Gospel message among some of the highest families of Saudi Arabia. Heavenly Father, I thank You again for the privilege of such a ministry.

TELL US ABOUT THE FUTURE OF THE JEWS

This tale took place in Riyadh, the capital of Saudi Arabia. I was there as the guest of my students, the ones I had been teaching English in beloved Pakistan.

By way of background information, twenty Saudi Arabian pre-medical students had been assigned to my care. Not only did I have them in my dormitory as residents, but I was also in charge of a special program to re-train them in all of their pre-medical subjects in English.

The leader of this band of Saudis was an intelligent young man named Fayyaz. He was married to a beautiful young Saudi woman named Sosen. Fayyaz asked my wife, Mary Jo, to teach his wife English. Sosen was not one of the pre-med students and would not have been allowed to sit with the men anyway.

It so happened that my daughter, Mary Beth, had taken a leave of absence from her studies at Gordon College to come to Pakistan and teach music at Murree Christian School (MCS) high in the beautiful Hindu Kush Mountains. In the winter months, MCS is closed because of heavy snows. So Mary Beth was with us in Lahore.

Together Mary Jo and Mary Beth accepted the job of tutoring Sosen. Fayyaz was extremely grateful for this loving, voluntary service. That may have contributed to my being given an invitation to visit Saudi Arabia.

One day, while in Riyadh visiting my students, Sosen's father, Mr. Sultan, called on the telephone and invited me to tea to meet some of his friends. It sounded like such an innocent invitation.

After being chauffeured to a very important looking building that turned out to be the Home Defense Guard headquarters—Mr. Sultan was the number-two man at the time—I was ushered straight through the building to an interior garden.

What awaited me there was a circle of very important-looking officials and a Pakistani military translator. If we failed to communicate in English, we could always switch to Urdu. And of course, there was Mr. Sultan along with several smartly dressed attendants serving tea.

I barely got the first tiny cup of tea down when Mr. Abdullah came right to the point. He said, "Mr. McCurry, we have invited you here for one reason. We want you to tell us what the Bible says about the future of the Jews."

That took my breath away. Two thoughts crossed my mind in rapid order. The first was, "This is my last hour." The second: "This is my golden hour." I decided on the latter. There were several factors in my favor. I was their honored guest. They would not kill me. I knew also that I was among Middle-Easterners. For them, time meant nothing. I could take as long as I wanted to answer.

So, starting with the call of Abraham, I went through the whole Bible on the subject of redemptive history, hitting only the high points, of course. This included a full explanation of the work of Jesus Christ. When I got to the subject of end times, Romans 11:25, to be exact, I explained that, first, the "full number of the Gentiles" would have to be brought into the kingdom—and that included this group—and after that "all Israel will be saved." With that I concluded.

Mr. Sultan then made three comments: "Mr. Mc-Curry, you are the first American we have ever met who believes God is the Living God of history today. Secondly, we don't agree with your conclusion about the Jews. We believe God is bringing them back to Palestine so we can massacre them. They are all atheists and God hates them. And lastly, we like you. We want you to go get your wife and children and come and live among us."

What mixed reactions I had: There was anger that no other American, among all the military, industrialist and government visitors, had ever borne witness to Christ. There was revulsion at their attitude of hatred toward the Jews. And there was utter confusion in my mind, wondering whether this was a sincere offer.

In the end, I said that commitments in Pakistan had to be kept and I was not free to accept their generous offer. But I have always wondered, "What if...?"

TAKE IT BY THE TAIL

One of the strangest tales in the Bible concerns Moses' staff. This story is in Exodus, chapters 3 and 4. It begins with God appearing to Moses and saying, "I have indeed seen the misery of my people in Egypt. I have heard them crying out...."

God, of course, was setting Moses up for a very difficult assignment: freeing a million Israelite slaves and their families from the hands of the most powerful nation on the face of the earth.

Moses, like most of us, told the Lord that he was not the man for the job. God said, "I will be with you." Evidently Moses did not know God well enough to understand just what that meant. So Moses went through a long series of excuses and "what if's"—in the presence of God!

Then the Lord said to him, "What is that in your hand?" Moses replied, "A staff." The Lord said, "Throw it on the ground." It became a snake. Moses ran from it and the Lord said, "Reach out your hand and take it by the tail."

Anyone who has ever worked with snakes knows that you always catch snakes behind the head, not by the tail. The Lord is not bound by our wisdom. Moses reached out and took hold of the snake by the tail and it turned back into a staff in his hand. The Lord explained the purpose of this sign was so that the Egyptians would believe that the Lord had appeared to him.

You may want to read the rest of the biblical account to satisfy your curiosity as to how all this worked out. In the end, Moses was God's instrument for delivering the Israelite slaves from their oppressors.

Today in Egypt, if you were a silent listener to the sermons of some Egyptian pastors, you would find that many of them like to teach and preach by allegorizing the Scripture. That leads to a question. If you had to speak to a hundred or so of those pastors, knowing they like to allegorize, how would you use the above encounter between God and Moses, especially this reference to Moses' staff?

That was the dilemma I was in at one of the recent AWEMA[1] conferences on the island of Cyprus. Most of the one hundred-plus attendees were from Egypt. And I was asked to speak without prior notice. As I prayed, the Lord suggested I use the story of Moses' staff in an allegorical fashion. This was something new for me.

To appreciate what follows, you need to know there is a great feeling of antipathy between Christians and Muslims in Egypt. Since Christians think the Muslim holy book, the Quran, is the root of all the evil that befalls them, they hate this book. In fact, they are absolute geniuses at tearing it apart, showing all of its errors and follies and, in a figure of speech, throwing it on the rubbish heap. It would never occur to them that the Quran could actually point Muslims to the Bible.

This was the setting for my interesting challenge, namely, how I was to get Egyptian Christians to consider a constructive use of the Quran, using Moses' staff in some allegorical fashion. How would you have done it? Here's what

I did.

I started with the same question the Lord used with Moses: "What is that in your hand?" In modern-day Egypt, the most common thing found in a Muslim hand is the Quran. For the Christian, then, this book is readily available. I suggested they look at it as Moses' staff. "Pick it up. Hold it in your hand," I said. "When you throw it down [reject it] it really does look like it is the invention of the devil—a snake." I continued, "Don't pick it up the normal way [by the head]. Don't read it at face value. Don't let it bite you. Pick it up another way [by the tail]. Come at the Quran in some new way."

In picking it up "by the tail," I suggested that it could become a powerful staff in their hands. "Instead of rejecting it," I said, "Use it to your advantage." This was a new thought for most of the audience, even an unthinkable thought for some.

I went on to point out the many borrowings, allusions and, in one case, a direct quote from the Bible that is found in the Quran. In fact, many Bible characters are mentioned in the Quran and scores of other useful points of reference. "These can be used as starting points to lead your Muslim friend to the true Scriptures," I added.

Muhammad's use of "Jesus material" in the Quran touched only the tip of the story. Thus, it neglected the rich detail found in the full Gospel accounts. For example, the Quran mentions the virgin birth in sparse detail, whereas Luke's Gospel tells us of the activities of angels singing in the heavens, shepherds coming to worship, the song of Zechariah, the blessings of Simeon and Anna and, most powerfully of all, Mary's response to God in that great song called "the Magnificat."

With a few other illustrations, I showed how easy it is to use the analogy of the "staff of Moses" in this allegory, the Quran in your hand, to lead Muslims to the Scriptures.

It so happened that the most famous of all Egyptian preacher-theologian-pastors was in the audience. Afterwards he said, "You have given us a new way of looking at the Quran. Formerly, we used to set about destroying it. Now I see it can be a tool for evangelism, by getting Muslims into the Bible."

1 Arab World Evangelical Ministry Association.

HALLELUJAH HOUSE

When persecution comes, then what? When it keeps coming over hundreds of years, what does it do to your corporate mindset? When it keeps coming from the same source, your Muslim neighbor, your Muslim government, police, educators, lawyers, what does that do to your attitude toward Muslims? Toward Islam? Are these two different questions? Or is it just one question, that is, making no distinction between Muslims and their religion?

So far, in the West we do not have that question, at least not on our own soil. It is a question of our brothers and sisters who live in the East: countries like Afghanistan, Egypt, Jordan, Iran, Pakistan, India, Bangladesh, Indonesia and many more.[1]

Horror stories abound: Christian schoolgirls being beheaded in Indonesia; whole Christian families forcibly converted to Islam, including compulsory circumcision of men and boys in the Christian islands of Indonesia; young Christian boys being abducted and sold into slavery in Pakistan; Christian men being killed and their wives and children taken as slaves in Sudan; Christian shopkeepers killed and their stores looted by Muslims in Egypt; Christian leaders in Iran who disappear, their mutilated bodies found later in fields or forests.

If these were just isolated incidents in modern times,

we might look for contemporary reasons for such aberrations—if they are aberrations. But when this happens consistently over the centuries, then what? What would we do if we were forced to live under Muslim rule where the mindset of the Muslims is decidedly anti-Christian?[2] This is the dilemma of our Christian brothers and sisters who have lived under Islam for well over thirteen hundred years in the Middle East.

In reading Paul Fregosi's book, *Jihad in the West*, we learn that in the hundreds of years of their ascendancy, the Ottoman Turks regularly went to war against the West on both land and sea and routinely sold captured Christians in the slave markets of the Muslim world.[3]

Today, all of this is beginning to touch us as a nation. Because Muslims think all politics is religion, they charge us with the same. Whatever America does, it does as a *crusading nation*. So we have these bewildering episodes that shock us beyond belief: the attacks on our embassy in Iran (1979) and in Beirut (1983); the sabotage of a PanAm flight over Scotland (1988); the first attack on the World Trade Center (1993); the attack on our embassies in Kenya and Tanzania (1998) and on our navy ship in Aden (2000); the second attack on the World Trade Center and on the Pentagon (2001). And more could be said about events in Spain, Italy, France, Great Britain, Canada and now right here on our own doorstep in the USA.

Where does Jesus' teaching fit in all of this? Can we really love our enemies, bless those who curse us, do good to those who persecute us, pray for those who despitefully use (abuse) us and overcome evil with good?

Well, there are good responses and unacceptable ones. Let me recount one that happened in Egypt that took me by surprise. I was the guest of a wonderful Christian Egyptian couple who called their apartment "Hallelujah House." They spared nothing in hospitality. While in their living room, scenes came on the TV of hundreds of Muslim pilgrims being trampled to death while on their pilgrimage to Mecca.[4] My host cried out, "Hundreds have just been killed in Mecca! Hallelujah! We wish thousands had died! We hate Muslims!" Whoa! Not good! This is not Jesus' way. Sad to say, I am afraid there are many Americans, even in our churches, who might have said the same.

No, our "hallelujahs" will be when Muslims come to Jesus. Our hallmark as Christians is love. "Love is not easily angered...love does not rejoice in evil...*love never fails.*" We overcome evil with good. The true "Hallelujah House" will be filled with love, prayers and blessings. Let's face the Muslim challenge Jesus' way: "Love your enemies."

1 There are fifty-five countries that call themselves Muslim, even where they are not in the majority.
2 And even more anti-Jewish.
3 Miguel Cervantes, who wrote the classic novel of *Don Quixote*, was one of them.
4 It happens almost every year.

WITH GROANINGS TOO DEEP TO BE UTTERED

Mary Jo and I had set ourselves to pray through *Operation World*. This is a 621-page day-by-day guide for praying through the whole world in one year. Every major country of the world is listed, including the ethnolinguistic people-groups in each country.

It's a tough discipline. What should have taken us a year actually took us, due to unforeseen interruptions, about a year and a half. We recommend this intercessory prayer life for everyone.

One morning, we were praying for the country of Algeria. This North African country on the coast of the Mediterranean Sea has a population of over thirty-five million. The largest cluster of minority peoples is the Berbers. It is the Berbers that concern us in this tale, specifically, the largest people group among them called Kabyles.

In the early centuries of Christianity, these people were Christian. In fact, St. Augustine (354-430 A.D.), the Bishop of Hippo, was a Berber. Then came the Islamic invasions. By 670 A.D., the Muslims had totally destroyed Christian rule in North Africa. But interestingly enough, crosses are still made and sold as objects of art by these people.

It was while we were praying for the Kabyle Berbers that I had one of the most unusual experiences in prayer I have ever had. I began to sob gutwrenching sobs and groanings while interceding for these people. That could only come from the Holy Spirit, who travails in intercession for us with groanings that are too deep to be uttered (Rom. 8:26).

When this travail in prayer was over, I turned to Mary Jo and said, "I have never prayed like that in my life." Evidently God wanted to do something among His lost children in the Atlas Mountains for a long time. He found a vessel He could use for intercessory prayer.

What did this intercession mean to God? I thought of how God "lost Jerusalem." Those were His people. That was His city. There was the temple in which He was supposed to reside. And it was all doomed. Its days were over. Jesus prophesied the destruction of the temple and the city. Yet when He came up over the brow of the hill and looked down on Jerusalem for the last time, before His crucifixion, He broke down and wept.

The Kabyle Berbers—what do they mean to the Lord? Why would His Spirit cause someone to pray for them with such weeping? Was He thinking of His lost children of long ago and the generations of their descendants who died, never knowing the Lord? I don't know. But I will tell you what I do know.

Six months after that gutwrenching prayer time, I was invited to London by a group called the "Servants Fellowship" to give two presentations on discipling ex-Muslims. Many new Christians were there of Muslim backgrounds from all over North Africa.

Many of these young believers were invited to give their testimonies. No one was more surprised than I to see two young men being presented who were Kabyle Berbers from the Atlas Mountains of Algeria. I was transfixed by their testimonies. Both of them said that six months earlier they had visions of Christ that led them to find Christians who gave them Bibles. They then spoke of how they came to genuine faith in Christ through their studies of the Scriptures.

As I sat there listening, the tears started streaming down my face. I remember saying, "Oh, that's what that agonizing time of intercession for the Kabyle Berbers was all about six months ago." To this day I cannot express the joy the Lord allowed me to experience in seeing with my own eyes the fruit of that prayer.

Recently, while in Spain, I met the chairman of the North African Coalition, a consortium of over a hundred ministries working in North Africa. When I asked about the Kabyles, he shared the most astonishing comments.

There are now, conservatively speaking, about ten thousand believers. No missionary is helping them. They have told the missionaries to stay away. Missionaries drag the secret police in behind them. These believers said, "We will come to you when we want training or resources. Don't come to us. Let the work grow."

Again, I am awe-struck at the mighty works of God. I am further overwhelmed by the fact that God would allow me to be a very small part of that glorious work through the ministry of intercessory prayer. I am sure that my prayer was only one among thousands that were being offered up for those dear people.

What a lesson for all of us. God allowed me to experience in prayer "groanings that are too deep to be uttered." Then He let me see the results of that prayer effort. He didn't have to do that but I believe, from time to time, God does it to encourage us to keep coming to Him in intercession for the lost.

MAKUMBA DRUMS

It was the first night any of us had slept in this newly acquired ex-Masonic Lodge. Our friends from the Brazilian Operation Mobilization team had just purchased this property for their training base. Beautifully situated in the former imperial city of Petropolis, this property was perched high on the mountains overlooking the faraway lights of Rio de Janeiro.

Before coming to Brazil, we did quite a bit of background reading on its spiritual condition. We were immensely pleased to read that there was a growing percentage (twenty-five percent) of evangelicals there. From them, we knew the Lord would draw many workers as missionaries to the Muslim world. That is why the leader of OM Brazil at that time, Decio Carvalho,[1] had invited us to come and teach.

The background material on Brazil in Operation World also mentioned that there were three major spiritistic sects in that country which claimed the loyalty of one-third of the population. We wondered what that was all about. We were soon to find out.

Our windows were wide open on that hot summer night. Sleep came late due to the disturbing, mantric beat of the drums from the slums across the valley. Only later did we learn what was actually going on.

Around two o'clock in the morning, my wife was shaking me awake. "Don, Don, what is the matter? Are you choking?" As soon as I came to my senses, I completed the sentence that I was struggling to articulate in my nightmare: "In the name of Jesus Christ I command you to leave." She said, "Honey, what is going on?"

In the nightmare, this is what I saw. I was approaching a "mini-castle" located at the top of a hill. Along the steep, paved driveway leading up to the entrance, servants were stationed at intervals, servants with painted white faces and grotesque expressions etched in black on those faces—like evil mimes.

Gaining entrance to the castle, I was ushered through a hall to a circular room completely encased in heavy drapes. On knee-high pedestals around the edges of this sunken room were little lewd statues of women in various stages of undress. I turned to my wife who was with me (in the dream) and was saying, "This place is evil," when out from the drapes an evil witch emerged and was walking menacingly toward me. It was then, in the nightmare, that I was struggling to say, "in the name of Je...In the name of Jes..." The words were stuck in my throat, for I was trying to speak out loud while still in the dream. That was when my wife, in bed beside me, was shaking me awake.

Thank God I was fully conscious now and able to burst forth with these words, "In the name of Jesus Christ, I command you to leave." As soon as these words were out of my mouth, I got up and walked to the open window. They were still drumming. It was then I remembered that members of the Makumba cult use drums to accompany their evil incantations of curses against those they hate. I lifted my hands in the directions of the drumbeats and said something like, "In the name of Jesus Christ, I resist your curses. I belong to Jesus who has broken your master's power and gives us authority over you evil spirits. In Jesus' name, I command you to desist and be still." The drumming stopped. All was peace and quiet.

The first thing in the morning, I shared this with the leaders of the training program. At the moment, they thought this was interesting but then let the whole thing pass. Later, one of them came to me and said, "Don, I think you had better share this with the whole group."

As soon as I shared this with the class, a group of women who had been in the room next to ours spoke up and said, "We, too, had similar nightmares. And some of us saw these evil creatures go from our room to yours."

At this, a horrible realization came over the whole group. We had moved into a Masonic lodge, never imagining that evil spirits could be lingering around after their hosts had left. Those more experienced than I in such matters then organized an exorcising committee. This group went through every room, every space on the property, commanding any lingering spirits to leave in the name of the Lord Jesus Christ. There were no more nightmares.

But that wasn't all. As a group, they walked over to the slum and asked which house the Makumba spiritists lived in. They then stood in front of that house and prayed strong prayers binding the evil spirits there and forbidding any further activity from them. It wasn't long before the inhabitants of that house moved away.

When new people moved into the house, evangelistic teams from our group visited them. They explained what had happened and asked to be allowed to come in and pray for the cleansing of their whole house. Permission was granted. The team was invited to stay for coffee and cake. It wasn't long before all the members of that household came to Christ. That former Makumba spiritist house soon became a house-church for the whole community.

This all happened during our stay in Petropolis. So many thoughts raced through our minds. This is what they are going to see in some parts of the Muslim world. This is part of their training. Praise God, "Greater is He who is in us than he who is in the world."

For some readers, this may be a disturbing story. If so, I have some questions for you. Has secular humanism, taught from kindergarten through to the universities, corrupted your understanding of Scripture? Did Jesus deal with demons? Did He cast them out? Did He give this power and author-ity to His disciples? Did He command them to teach suc-ceeding generations to do the same and keep on doing so down through the ages? Was Jesus' trial in the wilderness with a real Satan? Does the Bible teach that Satan still walks around like a roaring lion seeking those he can devour? Do these believers in Brazil have a spiritual insight that you don't have?

---

1 He later became a missionary to Turkey.

THE CUTTING OF THE GRAPES

Catanduva is an interesting city deep in the hinterlands of the Province of Sao Paulo, Brazil. It is also in the heart of vineyard country. The name "Catanduva" actually means "the cutting of the grapes" or "harvesting of the grapes."

Decio Carvalho, the leader of Operation Mobilization for Brazil, and I had been invited by the young people of this city to speak at a missions conference for those who wanted to go to the Muslim world.

The morning after our arrival, since all our meetings were to be night meetings, I decided to make the long walk into town to see what kind of a place Catanduva was.

Growing up in Washington, D.C., I learned all kinds of street games. But here in Catanduva, I came upon one of them that was new to me. I walked by slowly, taking it in—fascinated by it—not even paying attention to where I was walking.

Point one: in Catanduva most of the men were of short stature. Point two: they grow lovely shade trees over the sidewalks in this blisteringly hot, tropical city. And they trim the trees according to the height of the people—meaning about five and a half feet between the sidewalk and the tree branches.

You guessed it. While watching the children's game, I walked into a gnarled stump of a branch that cut my head. Blood began trickling out. I used my handkerchief as a compress and kept walking. I had come too far to turn back. At the end of the block my head was still bleeding, so I stood in the shade of a tree until it stopped.

In the meantime, two little wizened old men came up to me, holding in their hands a cutoff branch of a tree. This is what they said. "Señor, we saw what happened. We are very sorry. We have punished the branch that struck you in the head. We have cut it off. Here it is." Interesting logic. You punish the offending object by cutting it off.

I finally made it to town, went into a washroom, cleansed the blood out of my hair, and headed for the town center. It was typically Roman Catholic, with a huge cathedral dominating all other buildings. Opposite the front entrance there was a public park covering an entire city block. Nothing out of the ordinary here. Then I began to walk around the park block to investigate the shops. And *voila!* What a surprise!

Unknowingly, I was in the very heart of an occultist, cristo-pagan culture. Shop after shop of fetishes, charms, magic potions, palmists, astrologers, numerologists and séance parlors. Whoa! And then, out of nowhere, streakers with painted bodies were racing naked in the streets. I felt like I was back in the darkest of Old Testament times, when God's people had apostatized.

Eventually, I made my way to the highest part of town: a cemetery. There, dominating it was a huge stone statue, supposedly representing Jesus with arms outstretched, towering over the city. The local people told me this was their pride and joy. Nothing could ever harm them because "Jesus" (this block of stone) was protecting them.

That night I spoke on "Folk Islam and Power Encounter" to the assembled young people. I pointed out the similarities between what I had seen downtown and what I had seen in Muslim cities. We talked about what to do. Many of these young people had never thought about this before. It was just part of the scene. But that night, the Spirit of God stirred them to do something.

The next morning, they formed an impromptu parade with homemade banners proclaiming the Gospel of Christ and warning the people against all such godless practices. They marched around that park, singing to the Lord and then stopped at each corner to preach. Some people listened, others mocked. After the meeting that night, the young people stayed on to pray: to pray against the spirits that ruled that town and to pray for the people to leave their occultist ways and turn to the Lord.[1] We all went home about midnight.

Later, in the wee hours of the morning, a violent, raging rain and thunderstorm came up. I was asleep in my bed when great dazzling bolts of lightening lit up the city, accompanied by this enormous clap of thunder that literally made my bed bounce on the floor.

When dawn came and the storm had passed, the city was abuzz with the startling news. God, with His lightning, had decapitated the totem of "Jesus" there in the cemetery! Their false sense of protection was gone. They learned that the real God doesn't live in stone blocks to protect an apostate people. He judged their false "god." Again, I felt like I was back in Bible times when God openly displayed His power in answer to the cries of His people.

Catanduva—the cutting of the grapes. The two little men cutting off the offending branch of a tree that inflicted a wound on the Lord's servant. And now this display of the cutting off of the head of "Jesus"—the offensive statue that people trusted to save them rather than turning in repentance and faith to the one true God.

What do you make of all of this? Here in our country, we are not accustomed to such simple faith, a faith that believes God would actually do something to teach us to turn from our wicked ways. Do we have something to learn from our more believing brothers and sisters in these faraway lands?

1 This was good training for the Muslim world.

THE ELEPHANT OF A THOUSAND MIRRORS

Mary Jo and I were privileged to be the paying guests in the home of a single mother in Costa Rica. She happened to teach history at the University of Costa Rica. It was only natural that during summer vacation time she would want to visit an exotic country that came up in her course on world history. The summer before we came to live with her, she and her son chose to visit India.

After her return home, her son, who had been such a healthy little five-year-old, was now a chronically sick six-year-old. The doctors tried everything under the sun to find out what was wrong but all of their diagnostic techniques had not yielded a clue.

It was now a year later and the mom was getting more and more depressed. This was her one and only child. She asked us to pray for her boy. We did but in the prayer we also asked the Lord to show us the cause of this chronic illness. Nothing happened until...

One day, it suddenly dawned on me that every time we entered Bejani's[1] living room, our eyes were drawn repeatedly to the shiny elephant on her central mantelpiece. It sparkled with a patina of uncountable tiny mirrors. It seemed to draw every eye to itself.

Having been to India several times and being somewhat aware of the pantheon of gods they worship there, I began to suspect something. And so I asked, "Bejani, tell me about that elephant on the mantelpiece." "Oh, I bought it in India," she replied. Then I asked her if she could remember the shop where she bought it. Without a moment's hesitation, she responded, "How could I ever forget it? The whole shop was filled with every size and shape and color of elephants that you could imagine. And on either side of the front entranceway, there were two gigantic carvings of elephants at least eight feet high. And there was one over the doorway too."

"Ganesh, Ganesh," I cried out, "You have brought an idol representing the Hindu elephant god, Ganesh, into your home!"

If you had been in my shoes, what would you have done next? Better yet, what does the Bible have to say about such things? Plenty! Let's have a look:

Deut. 4:16, 17, "Do not...make for yourselves an idol...like any animal."

Deut. 7:5, "Burn their idols in the fire."

Deut. 7:26, "Do not bring a detestable thing [an idol] into your house, or you, like it, will be set apart for destruction."

Deut. 13:17, "None of these [idols]...shall be found in your hands."

Interesting verses, aren't they? The problem for a secular humanist is this: He or she doesn't believe these fascinating art forms are anything more than the *harmless* creations of human hands. Unfortunately, secular humanists don't believe there is a spiritual world either, with a real God, angels, Satan and demons. Much less do they believe these human artifacts, even though dedicated to pagan gods, can be invested with evil power. Experiences teach us otherwise.

Three times I have been asked to help people who have been chronically ill. In one case, it had to do with African demon-god masks. In another, it had to do with a South American Indian pipe used by a witch doctor. And in the third case, it had to do with Chinese vases guaranteed to bring one health and wealth. These are other "tales" waiting to be told. For the present, let us return to the account of the "elephant of a thousand mirrors."

Because this discussion has to do with things in the unseen world, there is no way to prove the existence of such phenomena as the connection between bringing an idol of a pagan god into your home and human sickness. In such cases, you have to let the results speak for themselves.

To be sure, there are assumptions involved in dealing with this kind of situation. In this case, the assumption was that this elephant plastered with tiny bits of mirrors had been devoted to the Hindu elephant god, Ganesh. In other words, a spirit or spirits had been invited to attach itself to this idol, thus imbuing it with some kind of "power." Since the Living God, our real God, has forbidden this kind of activity, that power is not from Him: it is from the enemy, in other words, a harmful power.

After explaining these things to Bejani, I asked if she was willing to destroy this thing and, because she was a believer, to command any spirit or spirits attached to this thing to depart in the name of the Lord Jesus Christ and not come back. She agreed and immediately took it outside and smashed it to smithereens and commanded any spirits attached to it to "depart in Jesus' name" and not come back. The needful was done.

And her son? He became well from that moment on.

And so ends the tale of "The Elephant of a Thousand Mirrors."

1 Not her real name.

ANTIGUA—AND WHAT HAPPENED THERE

Although its ancient name was "the Nobles of St. James of Guatemala," later it was changed to Antigua. Founded in 1524 in the midst of the ruins of the Mayan Empire, it became the capital of Guatemala and the third most important city in the Latino New World after Mexico City and Lima, Peru.

Antigua, located on the Panchoy Plateau, in the shadows of three awe-inspiring volcanoes, developed into a metropolis of masterpieces of baroque architecture: cathedrals, churches, monasteries, convents, a university, beautiful plazas and, of course, the necessary administrative buildings. In all of its magnificence, it represented the glory of colonial Spain.

Disaster struck in 1773. Of the nineteen architectural masterpieces, ten were destroyed by the earthquake never to be rebuilt. So extensive was the destruction of Antigua that it was abandoned as the capital and a new capital city was built twenty-five miles to the east in what is now called Guatemala City.

Antigua survived, but its glory was gone. Walking the cobblestone streets, my overriding impression was of a place where time had stopped. Gradually, it evolved into a great cultural center, filled with museums of artifacts, both colonial and Mayan. In 1942 the Pan American Institute of History declared it a "Monument of the Americas."

In truth, it is a monument to two civilizations, the Mayan and that of Colonial Spain. With the monuments come the cemeteries. Standing in the midst of Mayan burial sites, one is struck by the darkness of the spirit world of those past generations. Is it fair to ask, "Where have all the evil spirits gone that used to empower those ancient rites?" The answer may be disturbing.

Remember Jesus' words? "When an evil spirit comes out of a man, it goes through arid places seeking rest and does not find it. Then it says, 'I will return to the house I left.' When...it finds the house unoccupied,.... it takes with it...other spirits...and they go and live there" (Matt. 12:43-45).

What strikes one in visiting Antigua today is the large amount of occultist paraphernalia in the numerous shops, the talk of witches, covens, and the swarms of New-Agers living there, seeking to get in touch with their "spirit guides." Under such circumstances, even the churches, if not careful, are prone to evil spirit infestations, especially when the leaders themselves open the doors to it through foolish practices. Let me describe our visit to one of them.

It happened this way: Evangelical leaders in Guatemala City had invited me to come and speak on the subject of Latin missions to the Muslim world. Wonderful! That's what I'm all about. So that's what I did.

After the seminars, a friend offered to take me to visit Antigua, that now famous touristy "Monument of the Americas." Once in Antigua, he took me to a cathedral-like church that was still in use. In fact, for some strange reason, he felt drawn to this particular one. I think he wanted to show me the horrible things going on there. I am afraid he felt overwhelmed by what we were about to see. He had felt utter despair in the face of such rampant enemy power.

What a spiritual shock I got as we entered. The beautiful vaulted arches were obscured by hundreds of yards of swirling white muslin draped from the beams. I felt like I was in a Halloween spook house. Creepy. Off to the side, he showed me the tomb of a Brother Peter, where people went to pray for healing. My whole being revolted.

I took my friend by the hand and said, "We are going to pray." We lifted up our hands against the tomb and prayed for God to remove it and to give all glory to Christ, the true Healer. We lifted up our hands against the white gauze swaying overhead and asked God to cause the leaders to remove it. Finally, we went up to the pulpit, put our hands on it and prayed, "Oh, God, may only your Word be preached from this pulpit."

We both felt the surge of Holy Spirit power as we prayed this way. This was a new experience for my friend. Suddenly, he became joyous and began praising the Lord. He was absolutely revived by this infusion of power.

The following year, I was again invited to minister in Guatemala. After completing my teaching, I returned to that cathedral in Antigua to see what God had done.

The tomb was gone! The spooky cobwebs of gauze were gone! And the priest was gone! In the intervening year he had truly gotten saved and created such a ruckus that he was forced to leave the priesthood. *Not to be silenced, he had opened up a storefront church in the downtown central square of Antigua. Wow! Wow!! Wow!!!*

Afterwards, God brought these passages to mind: "*Zeal for your house consumes me, and the insults of those who insult You fall on me*" (Psalm 69:9). And "*all things whatsoever you shall ask in prayer in my name, believing, you shall receive*" (Matt. 21:22; Mark 11:24; John 16:24) (emphasis added).

Glory be to God! His Spirit stirred us up to pray. He heard our prayers! One tired servant was revived and the enemy was driven out! Hallelujah! Lead me, Lord, teach me more.

EMBRACING WITH
TEARS AND LOVE

Being asked to lead a seminar on Ministering to Muslim Women is a crazy thing to ask a male missionary teacher to do for Guatemalan Christian women. But that's what happened to me in Guatemala City, Guatemala.

CEMCA, the coalition of mission societies and mission churches, along with Misiones Nueva Esperanza, rented the gorgeous, newly built Korean church for the event.

The eyestopper at the spacious entrance to the church was to be greeted by a group of Guatemalan sisters dressed as Muslim women of many cultures. More was to come. The registrar, the ushers and all women leaders were dressed as Muslim women—twenty-one in all. Among the colorful *saris, shalwar-gamees, dopattas, galabias* and *burqas* were three women dressed in black from head to toe—a grim reminder that all is not colorful in *el mundo islamico* (the Islamic world).

At this point in the worship service, the leader invited all of these ushers onto the stage where they formed a large semi-circle behind the pulpit. In worship, the only thing missing was music in the languages and styles of Morocco, Turkey, Uzbekistan, Pakistan, India, Indonesia, Iran and Saudi Arabia.[1]

On the wide pulpit, a cloth painting of the great Badshahi (King's) Mosque of Lahore, Pakistan, was hung. Let me describe it to you. It was a masterpiece of eighteenth century Moghul architecture. One hundred thousand men could fit inside the open courtyard with the crenellated walls on the two sides and the rear wall. The narrow front chambers were covered with massive onion-shaped domes that came to points on their tops. At each corner of this vast structure were magnificent, tall minarets. The crowning touch of beauty was the beautiful marble pool of water with an ever-running fountain of water in the center.

When it was my turn to speak, after calling attention to the details mentioned above, I described my visit to the Badshahi Mosque and how impressive it was to observe the rows upon rows of thousands of barefoot Muslim men repeating their formal prayers in Arabic on a Friday afternoon.

Then I asked the audience, "Where are the women in this picture?" There were none. The role of women in the mosque is miniscule. Indeed, women are told not to come to the mosque, but to pray at home. It is a man's world!

This led to teaching on the sense of powerlessness and meaninglessness that characterizes the lives of so many Muslim women. Shut out from the mosque, women turn to the occult to get in touch with spirits and spirit powers. The most dramatic of all these practices is the ancient *Zar* ceremony.

It is conducted in the home of a female occultism leader. After food and social chitchat, the musicians arrive. The ladies undo their long hair and form a circle for a swaying kind of dance. The woman in the middle of the circle dances most vigorously with hair swishing as she bends over from the waist and twirls around in tune with the rhythmic intonations of the musicians and the encircling women.

The purpose of all of this is to induce a *Zar* spirit

(demon) to come and enter the woman in the middle. This happens when, after sufficient time, the woman, exhausted physically and emotionally, collapses on the floor. The madam in charge puts a veil over the fallen lady's face—to keep others from seeing the demonic expressions that come.

After describing this, I taught from Matthew 24:14. I pointed out that all human suffering would go on until the church has completed its mission. This Gospel of the Kingdom must be preached to all ethnic groups, Muslims included, before the end (of human suffering) will come. A spirit of deep conviction came over the audience.

When I finished, the worship leader led in appropriate songs and then invited women from the audience to come forward if they wanted to dedicate themselves to praying for, or volunteering to go to, these oppressed women in the Muslim world.

More than a hundred women came forward. Most were weeping. All spontaneously knelt in the front of the church or in the aisles. The worship leader led in a prayer of consecration and then, in an inspired moment, invited all of these Christian women who had come forward to come up on the stage. In a symbolic act of commitment, they embraced the costumed "Muslim" women and told them how much they loved them and how much God loved them. Tears rolled down my cheeks and Mary Jo's, too.

This was beyond role-playing. Something deep and spiritually powerful happened there that day. This dramatic enactment of Christian love for Muslim women was a powerful way of making a statement: "We will go forth into the Muslim world and share the love of Christ with our unfortunate sisters and bring them into the true family of God. And those who were only our sisters in terms of shared humanity will become our true sisters in faith, through new birth into the Kingdom of God."

Where are you in this real-life drama of bringing Muslims to Christ, both men and women? It starts in kneeling with broken hearts before the Lord, doesn't it? It's because we finally see how great the darkness is in lands where the Gospel is never preached.

I thank God for these precious Guatemalan sisters who did not hold back. In a loving gesture, by embracing these "Muslim" women with tears, they affirmed their commitment to pray and, if God calls, to go and share God's Word with them. And what about you? Will you hold back? Or will you allow God to touch your heart as He did these women? They offered themselves and embraced these "lost" sisters with tears.

---

1 Hopefully, that will come later—after some of these women become missionaries in the Muslim world.

MY GOD IS MUHAMMAD!

Sosen[1] was born a Muslim in Tangier, Morocco. She was fortunate to get a college education. Soon after graduation, she found work in Spain. Through contacts with Christians, and then reading the Bible, she became a believer in Christ.

Suleiman[2] grew up in the same neighborhood as Sosen. In fact, he hoped to marry her some day. He was outraged when he heard she had become a Christian.

Questions raced through his mind: "How could she betray her people and her God?" "How did the Christians get her?" Suleiman had to find out. He had to bring her back to Islam. Islam's honor demanded this. God's word[3] mandated this.

Through friends, he discovered that Sosen was staying with a Christian family in Spain. He proceeded to Spain at once, phoned the Christian family where she was staying, and asked permission to visit her. He assured them he was coming as a friend and only wanted a chance to persuade her to become a Muslim again. They agreed to receive him. I was invited to be there when he came.

Never before had I met such an arrogant, disrespectful, scoffing Muslim.[4] He exhibited utter contempt for Christians who, in his opinion, were all blasphemers and going to hell. He showed the same contempt for the Bible and all major biblical teaching about Jesus and salvation. His strategy was to so disparage Christianity that Sosen would leave it.

It was his attitude, as much as the false accusations, that stirred up a holy zeal within me. He had come in his high-handed, mocking way to set Sosen's mind "straight" and take her back to Morocco to be his wife. And so began one of the most intense encounters with a Muslim I have ever had. I felt compelled to not only defend the truth, but also to help this young believer learn how to stand against these vicious attacks.

Suleiman first stated the Bible was corrupt and claimed the Quran was God's perfect and final revelation to man. I defended the authenticity of the Bible and showed some errors in the Quran. He proposed the idea that we Christians worship three gods. I opened the Scriptures to show that God is *One* from Genesis to Revelation. He claimed that God could not become a man, for then He would no longer be God. I pointed out that God *chose* to fully reveal Himself in Jesus Christ because He loved us and wanted us to know Him. Suleman denied that Jesus died on the cross, saying it only looked that way. Answering this one took a long time. He claimed no one could die for anyone else, everyone must answer for his own sins. Another long explanation followed in which I showed how wisely God dealt with the sin question and the problem of how to save man at the same time. I explained that the death of Jesus on the cross was the place where God's justice and mercy met to accomplish this. He was unmoved.

Then Suleiman switched to his defense of Muhammad. He vehemently stated that Muhammad was the last and greatest prophet and that Jesus was no more than a prophet for His time. From the Quran, I showed him the superiority of Jesus over Muhammad. Suleman was furious. Finally, he blurted out, "Okay, Mr. McCurry, there is one thing I want you to know. In the last analysis, my God is Muhammad!"

At this point, I said, "Suleiman, according to the teaching of orthodox Islam, which you have been strenuously defending for the last two hours, you have just blasphemed. In fact, you have committed the one sin that is unpardonable in Islam. You have ascribed deity to Muhammad. Your life is over. You are doomed to hell. There is nothing you can do to change your fate. There is no reason for you to go on living."

All the color drained out of Suleiman's face. His mouth went shut and he was unable to speak the rest of the evening. I wish I had had the presence of mind, at that point, to say that in the eyes of the real God, the door to forgiveness was still open. The next morning, the family had the opportunity to share the hope of forgiveness that we have in Christ. However, I am sorry to say, Suleiman has not yet opened the door of his heart.

Later, thinking about what had happened that night, the realization hit me that what Suleiman had said really was the logical conclusion of Islamic teaching. For the orthodox Muslim, God is unknowable, high and far away. But human beings long to worship a God they can know. Where can a Muslim turn, except to Muhammad?

Thanks to Suleiman's final outburst, I saw firsthand the tragic dilemma of the God-hungry Muslim. His religion gives him nothing else to hang onto but Muhammad. This experience helped me to see that Islam, then, is nothing more than the *Cult of Muhammad*.

Oh God! Help us to undo this great deception. Give

us the courage to go to Muslims with the truth. Prepare us to patiently deal with the errors they have been taught from childhood. Empower us to bring them out of that deep darkness into Your marvelous light. Use us to show our Muslim friends that Jesus, who loves them and died for them, is the One they have longed for all along.

1 Not her real name.
2 Not his real name.
3 He thought the Quran was God's Word.
4 There are many polite, humble and respectful Muslims.

PAYBACK TIME!

Mission work can be a story of heartache. My first shock came in Sialkot, Pakistan, where Mary Jo and I were studying the Urdu language with a very wonderful young college graduate. We really took a liking to him. It was obvious that he was very talented and destined to be an outstanding leader. We could see him as the spearhead of a great work among the ninety-seven percent Muslim population in Pakistan.

After two weeks of studying with him, he bowled us over with the announcement that he was leaving for America. My sense of outrage was instantaneous. "How could you do this," I protested. "All of the scholarships that you benefited from were designed to make you a leader in Pakistan! And now you are going to run away to America!"

This was only the beginning of such shocks. What started out as a trickle, soon became a stream and then a river of talented Christian men flowing out of Pakistan into the countries of Western civilization: America, Britain, Germany, France, Australia, Canada and so on. They were doctors, engineers, businessmen, teachers and even pastors. An Urdu proverb fit this phenomenon so well: "*Qatra, qatra, deriya bun jata*" ("Drop by drop, it becomes a river").

Our goal as missionaries was to win Muslims to Christ—or so I thought. Had I missed something? Did I misunderstand God? Why was this massive exodus of talented Pakistani Christian young men happening?

All of this reached a climax when I was a professor at Forman Christian College in Lahore. It involved an outstanding Pakistani Christian leader. He had recently been appointed to our faculty. While waiting for his wife to join him, we invited him to live with us.

One day, out of the clear blue sky, he said, "Don, I am leaving for America in two weeks." My sense of outrage was just as intense as years before when our first language teacher said the same thing. This young professor was the advisor to the whole InterVarsity Christian Fellowship movement of Pakistan. And he was walking out on it!

When I protested that he couldn't do this, he floored me with a question: "Were your ancestors any better than I am?" I was speechless. My ancestors came to America for the same reasons he held: freedom from religious persecution, better employment opportunities, more money, a better future for his children. What could I say?

But there was a difference between my ancestors and me. We were called to be missionaries in Pakistan and we saw everything through "spiritual eyes." How do we further the Kingdom of God? How do we multiply the churches? We measured everything by those questions. For talented, young Christian leaders to abandon Pakistan was unthinkable. But nothing could stop this flood of émigrés.

The years rolled by. After eighteen years in Pakistan, we found ourselves back in the States. Since we were no longer on the field, we were in no position to judge. Gradually, the sense of outrage and bitterness subsided—kind of.

Then came this big surprise. One day an old Pakistani friend phoned me from California. Many years before, he had been in one of the college summer camps that we held high in the beautiful Hindu-Kush Mountains. He remembered me well and even recited some of the memorable events of that time. His name is Dr. Manzur Gill, researcher for Intel in Silicon Valley, working on next-generation software programs. Impressive.

But what was more impressive was the subject of our conversation. He was grateful for everything the missionaries had done for him. He had been lifted out of a hopeless life of poverty and illiteracy and put in a position to go for advanced education. The rest of his story is of hard work and the grace of God in getting him where he is today.

He went on to say, "Now it is payback time. I want to do something to show how grateful I am for the missionaries who made my success possible." Then he began to unfold a vision he had of rebuilding the Christian school systems that the Muslim government of Pakistan had so assiduously destroyed. The vision focused on his alma mater, the CTI (Christian Training Institute) high school in Sialkot.

To implement his vision, Manzur began a diligent search for anyone who had either taught at CTI or who had attended it. Right now I am holding in my hand an email from Manzur that lists 141 names on his mailing list. Most live in the States.

He set up a steering committee. Many were invited to gather back in Pakistan to inaugurate this work. Local Christian leaders who had not emigrated were formed into a supervisory committee. Work was begun: Walls are being rebuilt, scholarships given, the latest in computers have been purchased, buildings are being rebuilt and enrollments are growing. In short, new life has come into a despairing Christian community in Pakistan.

God is using Manzur to prick the consciences of so many talented Pakistani Christians who have "made it" in the West. He is calling them to look back in gratitude and do for others what had been done for them. He is calling them to look to the future in revitalizing the Christian community in Pakistan.

To my knowledge, Dr. Manzur Gill is the first outstanding product of our missionary enterprise in Pakistan to look back in gratitude and to express that gratitude in concrete action. And he has done it by rallying Pakistani graduates of CTI with the cry, "It is payback time."